THE STATES AND THE NATION SERIES, of which this volume is a part, is designed to assist the American people in a serious look at the ideals they have espoused and the experiences they have undergone in the history of the nation. The content of every volume represents the scholarship, experience, and opinions of its author. The costs of writing and editing were met mainly by grants from the National Endowment for the Humanities, a federal agency. The project was administered by the American Association for State and Local History, a nonprofit learned society, working with an Editorial Board of distinguished editors, authors, and historians, whose names are listed below.

North Carolina

A Bicentennial History

William S. Powell

W. W. Norton & Company, Inc.
New York

American Association for State and Local History
Nashville

Copyright © 1977
American Association for State and Local History
Nashville, Tennessee

Published and distributed by
W. W. Norton & Company, Inc.
500 Fifth Avenue
New York, New York 10036

Library of Congress Cataloguing-in-Publication Data

Powell, William Stevens, 1919–
    North Carolina: a Bicentennial history.

    (The States and the Nation series)
    Bibliography: p.
    Includes index.
    1. North Carolina—History. I. Series.
F254.P59   975.6   77–22440
ISBN 0–393–05638–4

Printed in the United States of America
2 3 4 5 6 7 8 9 0

For
Virginia
John
Charles
Ellen
Tar Heels born and
Tar Heels bred

Contents

Illustrations

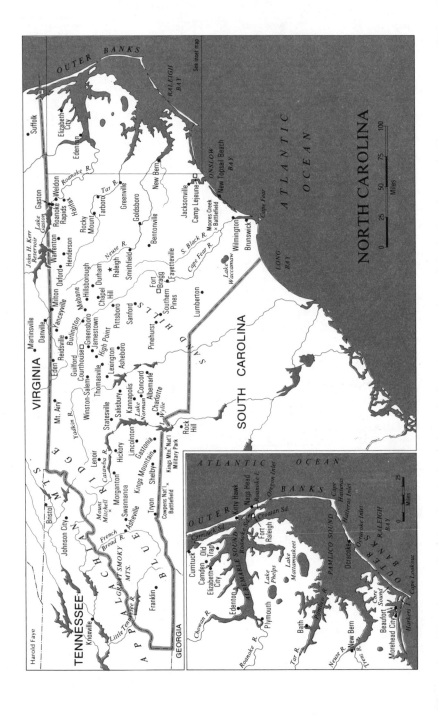

NORTH CAROLINA

ATLANTIC OCEAN

OUTER BANKS

RALEIGH BAY

LONG BAY

ONSLOW BAY

Cape Fear

100
75
50
25
0
Miles

VIRGINIA

TENNESSEE

GEORGIA

SOUTH CAROLINA

Suffolk
Elizabeth City
Edenton
Roanoke R.
Lake Gaston
John H. Kerr Reservoir
Gaston
Weldon
Warrenton
Roanoke Rapids
Halifax
Tar R.
Tarboro
Greenville
New Bern
Henderson
Oxford
Rocky Mount
Goldsboro
Milton
Yanceyville
Hillsborough
Neuse R.
Bentonville
Durham
Raleigh
Smithfield
S. Black R.
Martinsville
Danville
Eden
Reidsville
Mebane
Chapel Hill
Fayetteville
Cape Fear R.
Wilmington
Brunswick
New Topsail Beach
Camp Lejeune
Jacksonville
Moores Creek × Battlefield
Lake Waccamaw
Lumberton
Southern Pines
Fort Bragg
Pinehurst
Sanford
Pittsboro
Asheboro
Lexington
High Point
Jamestown
Greensboro
Guilford Courthouse
Burlington
Thomasville
Mt. Airy
Bristol
Johnson City
Winston-Salem
Statesville
Salisbury
Kannapolis
Concord
Albemarle
Charlotte
Lake Norman
Lake Wylie
Rock Hill
Lenoir
Hickory
Lincolnton
Gastonia
Kings Mountain
Shelby
Tryon
Morganton
Swannanoa
Asheville
Mount Mitchell ×
Catawba R.
Yadkin R.
Knoxville
Franklin
Little Tennessee R.
French Broad R.
Cowpens Nat'l × Battlefield
Kings Mtn. Nat'l Military Park

GREAT SMOKY MTS.
APPALACHIAN MTS.
BLUE RIDGE
SAND HILLS

See inset map

Harold Faye

(Inset map)

ATLANTIC OCEAN

OUTER BANKS

PAMLICO SOUND

RALEIGH BAY

Currituck Sd.
Kitty Hawk
Nags Head
Roanoke I.
Oregon Inlet
Fort Raleigh
Croatan Sd.
Cape Hatteras
Hatteras Inlet
Ocracoke Inlet
Ocracoke
Core Sound
Harkers I.
Cape Lookout

Currituck
Camden
Old Trap
Elizabeth City
Edenton
Chowan R.
Roanoke R.
Plymouth
ALBEMARLE SOUND
Roanoke Sd.
Lake Phelps
Bath
Lake Mattamuskeet
Pamlico R.
Tar R.
Neuse R.
New Bern
Trent R.
Beaufort
Morehead City

25
0
Miles

Invitation to the Reader

IN 1807, former President John Adams argued that a complete history of the American Revolution could not be written until the history of change in each state was known, because the principles of the Revolution were as various as the states that went through it. Two hundred years after the Declaration of Independence, the American nation has spread over a continent and beyond. The states have grown in number from thirteen to fifty. And democratic principles have been interpreted differently in every one of them.

We therefore invite you to consider that the history of your state may have more to do with the bicentennial review of the American Revolution than does the story of Bunker Hill or Valley Forge. The Revolution has continued as Americans extended liberty and democracy over a vast territory. John Adams was right: the states are part of that story, and the story is incomplete without an account of their diversity.

The Declaration of Independence stressed life, liberty, and the pursuit of happiness; accordingly, it shattered the notion of holding new territories in the subordinate status of colonies. The Northwest Ordinance of 1787 set forth a procedure for new states to enter the Union on an equal footing with the old. The Federal Constitution shortly confirmed this novel means of building a nation out of equal states. The step-by-step process through which territories have achieved self-government and national representation is among the most important of the Founding Fathers' legacies.

The method of state-making reconciled the ancient conflict between liberty and empire, resulting in what Thomas Jefferson called an empire for liberty. The system has worked and re-

mains unaltered, despite enormous changes that have taken
place in the nation. The country's extent and variety now sur-
pass anything the patriots of '76 could likely have imagined.
The United States has changed from an agrarian republic into a
highly industrial and urban democracy, from a fledgling nation
into a major world power. As Oliver Wendell Holmes remarked
in 1920, the creators of the nation could not have seen completely how it and its constitution and its states would develop.
Any meaningful review in the bicentennial era must consider
what the country has become, as well as what it was.

The new nation of equal states took as its motto *E Pluribus
Unum*—"out of many, one." But just as many peoples have
become Americans without complete loss of ethnic and cultural
identities, so have the states retained differences of character.
Some have been superficial, expressed in stereotyped images—
big, boastful Texas, "sophisticated" New York, "hillbilly"
Arkansas. Other differences have been more real, sometimes instructively, sometimes amusingly; democracy has embraced
Huey Long's Louisiana, bilingual New Mexico, unicameral Ne-
braska, and a Texas that once taxed fortunetellers and spawned
politicians called "Woodpecker Republicans" and "Skunk
Democrats." Some differences have been profound, as when
South Carolina secessionists led other states out of the Union in
opposition to abolitionists in Massachusetts and Ohio. The result was a bitter Civil War.

The Revolution's first shots may have sounded in Lexington
and Concord; but fights over what democracy should mean and
who should have independence have erupted from Pennsylvania's Gettysburg to the "Bleeding Kansas" of John Brown,
from the Alamo in Texas to the Indian battles at Montana's
Little Bighorn. Utah Mormons have known the strain of isolation; Hawaiians at Pearl Harbor, the terror of attack; Georgians
during Sherman's march, the sadness of defeat and devastation.
Each state's experience differs instructively; each adds understanding to the whole.

The purpose of this series of books is to make that kind of understanding accessible, in a way that will last in value far

beyond the bicentennial fireworks. The series offers a volume on every state, plus the District of Columbia—fifty-one, in all. Each book contains, besides the text, a view of the state through eyes other than the author's—a "photographer's essay," in which a skilled photographer presents his own personal perceptions of the state's contemporary flavor.

We have asked authors not for comprehensive chronicles, nor for research monographs or new data for scholars. Bibliographies and footnotes are minimal. We have asked each author for a summing up—interpretive, sensitive, thoughtful, individual, even personal—of what seems significant about his or her state's history. What distinguishes it? What has mattered about it, to its own people and to the rest of the nation? What has it come to now?

To interpret the states in all their variety, we have sought a variety of backgrounds in authors themselves and have encouraged variety in the approaches they take. They have in common only these things: historical knowledge, writing skill, and strong personal feelings about a particular state. Each has wide latitude for the use of the short space. And if each succeeds, it will be by offering you, in your capacity as a *citizen* of a state *and* of a nation, stimulating insights to test against your own.

James Morton Smith
General Editor

Preface

ORTH CAROLINA frequently puzzles the unini-
tiated who try to understand the attitudes and actions of its people; sometimes the state puzzles its own natives as well. Even
generalizing about the state's basic physical character is difficult. Within its long span from the Atlantic Ocean to the crest
of the Appalachian Mountains, level coastal plains blend into
the piedmont's rolling hills, which in turn rise into the highest
peaks east of the Mississippi River. Such enormously varied terrain makes possible a variety of activities for natives and newcomers, with attractive resorts at seaside, year-round golf and
tennis havens in the interior, and ski slopes for winter sportsmen
in the west.

Noted for its agriculture, the state ranks among the nation's
leaders in the production of tobacco, sweet potatoes, soybeans,
and peanuts. Yet its industries also are nationally—even internationally—known. The world's largest towel factories lie within
its bounds. Fabrics from the Burlington Industries complex are
sold in nearly every country on the globe. Carpeting, cotton
textiles, and furniture of high quality are manufactured in impressive quantities. Throughout the state farms and industry
exist—often side by side as industries have moved to rural settings.

Although the state still is clearly rural, it has developed urban areas of importance. Charlotte, regarded in some ways as a rival of Atlanta, is the financial and distribution center for a large area of the Southeast. Greensboro and Durham are headquarters for important life insurance companies—including Durham's North Carolina Mutual Life Insurance Company, which prides itself on being "the world's largest Negro business."

The nation's first lunch counter sit-in occurred in Greensboro, and much of North Carolina went through a period of racial tension and unrest. But in general the state's people have come to accept the new order, and the younger generation seems to view the daily association of races as natural. Today black teachers, secretaries, clerks, bankers, engineers, television newsmen and announcers, lawyers, and representatives of other business and professional groups work harmoniously with their white counterparts. There is still some resistance to such change, of course, but the change that came in less than two decades was striking.

It is difficult also to make a positive statement about conditions, past or present, in North Carolina, because inevitably an exception can be cited. Responses to questions on education, politics, race, religion, energy conservation, the equal-rights amendment, and a host of other current topics suggest the diversity of opinion that exists in the state. In the case of the equal-rights amendment, for example, Albert Coates, distinguished founder of the Institute of Government in Chapel Hill, and William B. Aycock, former chancellor of the University of North Carolina and now a member of the law school faculty, have given hearty support. On the other hand, the beloved and honored Senator Sam Ervin, now retired, speaks just as openly in opposition. So does Chief Justice Susie M. Sharp of the North Carolina Supreme Court, the first woman elected to that position in any state. After many days of public hearings, the North Carolina General Assembly in 1977 declined for the second time to approve the amendment.

A confusing inconsistency in the people may be seen in the fact that North Carolinians regularly vote against "liquor by the drink" whenever the question is raised, yet gross sales at state-owned alcoholic beverage control stores in 1975–1976 amounted to $206,769,825. It has often been said that "North Carolinians will vote dry as long as they can stagger to the polls." The problem of alcoholism, not surprisingly, is a source of concern to the state. In 1974–1975 state mental-health facilities treated 26,447 persons for alcoholism. Similarly the inhabitants of Charlotte find great satisfaction in the city's large number of churches, but at the same time they are embarrassed by its unusually high crime rate.

In 1976 North Carolinians took a strong, and successful, stand for the preservation of New River Valley, a magnificently wild and beautiful gorge in the northwestern part of the state that was about to be flooded by a hydroelectric company. Others organized and fought with tenacity to preserve Jockey's Ridge, the highest point of land along the Atlantic coast, when it was threatened by commercial development. On the other hand, North Carolinians have stood idly by while river valleys, farms, and woodland have been flooded by dams that seemed unnecessary, and while large, unspoiled areas of forest or savannah land were cleared and put to the plow by commercial agricultural interests often financed by investors from abroad.

Sometimes North Carolinians whose families have been Tar Heels for generations are unable to characterize themselves. For most, the state's motto, *Esse Quam Videri* (To Be Rather Than To Seem), is appropriate. But patient newcomers can eventually discover identifiable characteristics and idiosyncrasies of the state's people.

Many natives feel an exceptionally strong loyalty to their place of origin, placing home county and state well ahead of the nation in their affection and attachment. This may be, in part, because they have not traveled far beyond the bounds of their native county. Most North Carolinians also have a strong attachment to church and to political party. For example, frequently the only reason for being a Presbyterian or a Democrat is that the family has "always" been of those persuasions. And although a person may have little more than a passing acquaintance with the facts of the "Lost Colony," Tryon Palace, or the

old state capitol, he is likely to demonstrate pride in them simply because to him they represent North Carolina. Likewise he
may profess a surprising allegiance to one of the state's colleges
even though he did not attend it—the institution belongs to
North Carolina, and for that reason alone he values it. This is
not a new trait of character in the state. It was recognized as
long ago as 1840 when William Gaston wrote the words for a
song, "The Old North State," eventually adopted as the state
song:

> Carolina! Carolina! Heaven's blessings attend her,
> While we live we will cherish, protect and defend her,
> Tho' the scorner may sneer at, and witlings defame her,
> Yet our hearts swell with gladness whenever we name her.
>   Hurrah! Hurrah! The Old North State for ever,
>   Hurrah! Hurrah! The good Old North State.

There is a strong feeling of kinship among citizens of the
state, and at least two factors contribute to this. First, large
numbers of North Carolinians are descended from families that
have lived in the state for generations, and, second, North Carolina has always had the nation's lowest percentage of foreign-
born. North Carolinians, when introduced to one another, almost invariably exchange animated questions as they seek to
discover relatives in common or at least mutual friends and ac-
quaintances. Chance meetings of North Carolinians in faraway
places invariably bring forth a similar exchange.

Certain families in the state appear always to have lived in
specific places. Most North Carolinians with any appreciable
understanding of the state know that the Averys came from
Burke County and the Polks from Mecklenburg; the Blounts are
from Washington, and the Collinses from Edenton. If someone
named Gurganus is mentioned, there is no doubt that he is connected with Martin County or that the Zollicoffers are from
Henderson. These names and many more were all associated
with those places at the time of the 1790 census or even earlier,
and they are still to be found there nearly two centuries later.

Place names can be confusing to a newcomer and can be the

undoing of one who seeks to conceal his out-of-state origin. A native Tar Heel would not pause for a moment over such names as Pactolus, Oconaluftee, or Chalybeate, and he unfailingly gives the proper local pronunciation to Bertie, Duplin, Rowan, and to a host of other names that are not what they appear to be. A new North Carolinian, who, although a native of Brooklyn, would like more than almost anything else to be taken for a native North Carolinian, might do so successfully until he was obliged to seek directions to a place having a local pronunciation.

There is a variety of speech patterns in the state. Easterners can usually be distinguished from westerners; a distinctive accent may even be a clue to a specific county. Residents of Hyde County, for instance, have in many cases retained their Old English accent. To a lesser degree the same has happened in other eastern counties. Duplin and Sampson counties, located in the interior coastal plain, were settled by both Scotch-Irish and Highland Scots in the eighteenth century, and many people there still have a unique accent that has survived in this isolated section of the state. In the mountains, where for generations people lived in almost total isolation from the rest of the state, many words and expressions, as well as unusual accents, are clearly related to the language of Elizabethan England.

Though some North Carolinians might be considered "provincial," the fact remains that most of them are content with their way of life. Until the 1940s few traveled far from home, most placed only reluctant trust in strangers, and like virtually all Southerners they had no wish to be told by anyone what they should or should not do.

World War II, the Korean conflict, and the war in Vietnam took many young people away from home for the first time and placed them in cultures that were totally alien to them. Returning with new ideas, an altered outlook on life, new ambitions, and often with new or changed values, many of them began to exert influence in their home communities. Their desire for additional education triggered an expansion of higher education in the state. With specialized skills many of them became more mobile and sought opportunities farther from home. Fewer young people remained on farms, while the towns and cities grew. Nevertheless, rural life remained attractive to some. The comfort and feeling of security found in familiar surroundings held enough people on the farms and in small towns to enable the state's provincial character to survive.

Industrial development in the 1950s and the 1960s brought countless thousands of new people into North Carolina. Many moved in when established industries from other states opened new plants in North Carolina. This brought a strong infusion of new life into many communities. Ideas, attitudes, and standards totally new to many Tar Heels came with these people. The result was that the areas touched by this movement of industry changed quickly and dramatically.

The story of North Carolina clearly has many facets. Within her bounds lies the site of England's first American exploration and settlement in the days of Queen Elizabeth I. The state was next to the last of the thirteen original colonies to join the Union because of her citizens' distrust of a strong central government. Yet by 1861 she was reluctant to pass an ordinance of secession and resisted until May 20, before joining the Confederate States of America. North Carolinians are proud of their state university, the first state university in America; they are justly proud, too, of their public school system (even though it was for white children only) established prior to 1860. Some aspects of life in the state—the standard of living, the quality of schools and medical service, the public transportation system—have occupied low ranks in the national scale in the past. Efforts are being made by state leaders to improve these aspects of life in North Carolina. The pages that follow will introduce some of the people and events, some of the grounds for both pride and regret, from which North Carolina's character is derived.

North Carolina

1

The Land—Discovered
and Rejected

ENGLISHMEN, lacking detailed information about
the part of North America to which they sent colonists in the
seventeenth century, marked off administrative units in a very
arbitrary manner. Natural boundaries were seldom observed,
and geographical features that might have served to unify the
people of a colony were disregarded. The area in which North
Carolina and South Carolina grew might more logically have
been made into three colonies. A long colony below Virginia,
extending perhaps a hundred miles inland through what is now
the two Carolinas, would have contained a colony with unified
commercial and agricultural ambitions. Behind it a second colony laid out in the piedmont region of rolling hills and swift
streams, now the industrialized center of the two states, would
have had its own related interests. A third colony might have
been anticipated in the west where the high mountains of the
Appalachian chain rendered that area almost inaccessible for a
long time. It eventually became the home of people who for
many generations clung to old-fashioned ways, attitudes, and
sentiments that were usually at variance with those of their eastern neighbors.

The future could not be anticipated, of course, and the unify-

3

ing features of these three different sections were not identified for a long time for the simple reason that much of the back-country remained unexplored. Settlement was by gradual waves or infiltration as people pushed farther and farther west or moved in from the north and south. By the time regional influences became apparent, the original single Carolina had already been divided into two colonies. Each of the Carolinas then had a portion of coastal plain, piedmont, and mountain territory. Conflicts between these internal sections broke out from time to time, and geography came to be one of the chief factors affecting the course of North Carolina's development.

North Carolina is a long state extending from the Atlantic Ocean to the crest of the Appalachian Mountains. Under its original charter of 1663 its western limit was the South Seas, as the Pacific Ocean was then called in England, but in time the Mississippi River was accepted as a more logical and defensible boundary. The state, although considerably reduced in size today, is still a large state extending over five hundred miles from the Atlantic Ocean to its western limit in the mountains. Virginia, its northern neighbor, was the source of most of its people in the seventeenth and early eighteenth centuries, and for a long time Virginia dominated North Carolina politically, economically, and socially. Tennessee to the west was created out of land that North Carolina reluctantly ceded to the federal government in 1789. Attempts by frontiersmen in 1784 to establish a separate state there, the State of Franklin, failed after five years. North Carolinians have often looked down upon their western neighbors as not quite their equals even though distantly related by both blood and geography. This is a weakened version of Virginia's attitude toward Carolinians. Most of North Carolina's southern boundary is shared with South Carolina, a region also sometimes held in contempt by North Carolinians, especially in the late twentieth century. The haughty, aristocratic superiority often assumed by Low Country South Carolinians seldom impresses anybody in North Carolina. The old saying that ''North Carolina is a vale of humility between two mountains of conceit'' may have had some validity at one time, but that is no longer true. The remainder of the southern boundary, the far western portion, is shared with Georgia, a fact that many North Carolinians often forget. Georgians from time to time have protested the accuracy of this line. In 1803 the Georgia legislature created Walton County partially in territory claimed by North Carolina. The militia from the two states fought several skirmishes in what became known as the Walton War, but the question was resolved when both sides agreed to accept the 35th parallel as a boundary. As recently as 1971 a delegation of Georgians in business suits and carrying briefcases returned to North Carolina to protest the location of the boundary. They claimed that both North Carolina and Tennessee held territory which rightfully belonged to Georgia. After spending several days examining nineteenth-century records in the state archives in Raleigh, the intruders closed their briefcases and quietly departed.

South Carolina on one occasion had more cause to complain than Georgia did. In the 1730s commissioners from the two colonies were appointed to establish a boundary line. Because there was no marked line, sheriffs from one colony tried to collect taxes in the other, militia officers forced men from the other colony into their ranks, and land records of both were hopelessly confused. By mutual agreement the line should be not closer than thirty miles to the Cape Fear River in North Carolina and would follow a straight northwest direction until it reached the 35th parallel. The parallel would then mark the boundary as far west as necessary. The line running northwest thirty miles from the Cape Fear was begun in 1735, and the surveyors stopped when they thought they had reached the 35th parallel. They were not very accurate, however, as it was later discovered that they had stopped some fifteen miles short of the 35th parallel. Nevertheless, in 1764 when the time came to mark more of the line, surveyors took up where the previous ones had left off, still thinking they were on the 35th parallel. They marked the line to the edge of the Catawba Indian settlement. It had already been agreed that the line should go around these Indians to leave all of them in South Carolina. This accounts for the peculiar jagged line between the states south of Charlotte. In running the line around the Catawbas in 1772 the surveyors again missed the elusive parallel. This time, however, they were about as far north of the line as the others had been south of it. A few years later when South Carolina discovered that an error of some kind had been made, she threatened to go to war against North Carolina until someone pointed out that each state had gained about as much as it lost, and the controversy died. As a matter of fact, however, South Carolina gained more territory, and it may have been this discovery which prompted her to withdraw the war threat quickly and quietly. The next segment of the line as a matter of practicality was simply declared to follow the crest of the mountains down to the true 35th parallel. From that point, which is now the junction of North Carolina, South Carolina, and Georgia, the line was run in 1821 in a westerly direction on the long-sought parallel.

Had the Carolina boundary been run earlier, the two states might have been spared another subject of dispute—the precise birthplace of Andrew Jackson in 1767. He was certainly born near the future line in the Waxhaws section, and both states claim him. Since he studied law in Salisbury and was licensed and practiced law in Greensboro, North Carolina lays strong claim to him. President James K. Polk was born in Mecklenburg County in 1795 after the line had been marked—and far enough north of it that South Carolina has no claim on him. Since both men later moved to Tennessee, however, that state also claims both.

North Carolina consists of the three distinct regions. The coastal plain in the eastern section is part of a vast plain, once an old sea bottom, that stretches from New York harbor south and west to the Gulf of Mexico. The plain is just a few miles wide in the north but several hundred miles in the far south. In North Carolina it varies from one hundred to one hundred fifty miles of level, dark loam land with swampy areas, called "pocosins" locally, and with a number of natural lakes. The state's shoreline is formed by the Outer Banks, a strip of narrow, sandy islands extending along most of the coast. Behind these long islands are five large, shallow sounds. Rivers flowing from the interior often deposit silt in these sounds necessitating almost constant dredging to keep channels open for shipping. There are several inlets through the chain of Outer Banks permitting ships to pass, but these too must be kept open by frequent dredging. At the same time the Banks must be protected from erosion; occasionally newly cut inlets must be closed. Protecting and preserving the coastline has sometimes been very costly to the state.

Several qualities of the coastal plain proved quite valuable to the state. The fertile soil certainly benefited farmers and planters who settled there. In some places landowners discovered that they had acquired an unexpected bonus. As the ancient sea receded, marine life took refuge in pockets of water that remained. When these eventually dried up, skeletons were left to form marl beds. This marl, when spread across the fields, was an excellent source of lime. Another coastal plain feature is the Sandhill section, an area of low hills in which the winter temperature is usually warmer than in other nearby places. Longleaf pines, evergreen shrubs, and luxuriant winter grasses add to the illusion that the Sandhills are almost subtropical. In this part of the state the winter resorts of Pinehurst and Southern Pines have been developed, and their golf courses are among the most popular in the country. The Golf Hall of Fame in Pinehurst is to that sport what Cooperstown, N.Y., is to baseball.

Behind the coastal plain lies the great middle portion of North Carolina known as the piedmont. It is an area about two hundred miles wide composed of rolling hills of red clay. The soil is generally rocky and sometimes marked by enormous boulders. At Mount Airy in the western piedmont there are granite quarries, from which stone has come for many of the buildings in the national Capital. Other quarries are also worked. The countryside around Salisbury, for example, is marked by cranes, often higher than the trees, used to raise blocks of granite from open-face mines. The piedmont rises in easy stages to the foothills of the mountains.

The mountain region of western North Carolina is a part of

the great Appalachian system extending from New Hampshire into northern Alabama. On the east these mountains are known as the Blue Ridge because a blue haze seems perpetually to hang over them. Beyond are the Great Smoky Mountains, the crest of which forms the dividing line between North Carolina and Tennessee. The Appalachians here reach their greatest height and attain their largest mass. There are nearly fifty peaks over six thousand feet in elevation, while nearly 175 are over five thousand feet. Mt. Mitchell at 6,684 feet is the highest point east of the Mississippi River. This is extremely rugged country, marked by the main ridge running northeast and south-west but by lesser spurs shooting off to the east and west from them.

Physical geography has played an important role in determin-ing the history of North Carolina. In spite of its coastal position the area did not develop a significant maritime commerce as its neighbors did. Except for the Cape Fear River in the southeast no important river flows directly into the Atlantic from the state. The Outer Banks successfully discourage the entry of all except the smallest ocean-going vessels into the sounds and rivers be-hind them. This caused North Carolina, with no deep-water ports, to be bypassed by the earlier settlers reaching America from overseas. Vessels went to more hospitable colonies, leav-ing North Carolina a colony with large regions of unsettled and largely unknown wilderness. Even today there are eastern places so swampy and western places so steep, rugged, and impenetra-ble that no human is known to have passed through them. When colonists did make their way to North Carolina, most of them came from other colonies. They usually were children or grand-children of immigrants who had already lived a long time else-where. One royal governor considered North Carolina to be an inviting frontier beckoning the discontented, the ambitious, or the crowded young people up and down the Atlantic seaboard to come and start a new life. These Carolina settlers sometimes had stronger attachments to other colonies than they did to Great Britain or to some country in Europe, but as often as not they had no strong feelings of devotion or loyalty to any place at all.

They may be counted Americans more than Pennsylvanians, the colony from which many of them came, or North Carolinians.

The nature of the land these people found had a great deal to do with differences that soon became apparent in the colony. The loose, fertile, sandy loam of the eastern section—savannah land or pine forests—was both productive and easy to clear. Men who could cultivate it were tempted to acquire a large amount. Land was inexpensive, taxes not burdensome, the climate mild, and labor available either from one's own children, from indentured servants, or from slaves, so a plantation system developed in much of the coastal plain.

Piedmont land was red and coarse, often covered with tough oaks and hickories, which were much more difficult to remove than pines. It was a place far removed from ready markets. The people who took up land here were not often tempted to acquire more than could be tilled by one man and his sons. The piedmont, therefore, evolved into a land of small, independent farmers. The swift streams nevertheless invited some to construct gristmills and, at a later time, textile mills as well.

The forbidding mountains, ancient home of the Cherokee Indians, were simply bypassed until near the end of the eighteenth century. A few people, like Daniel Boone, Richard Henderson, and James Robertson, blazed trails through the mountain passes and led settlers to the distant grasslands that became Tennessee and Kentucky. They were the exception, however, and seem to have had no thought of taking up any of the mountain land.

Eastern North Carolina was the first part of what is now the United States to be visited by Europeans, and what they reported having seen there influenced their understanding of the New World for many years. Giovanni de Verrazzano's description of the Outer Banks north of Cape Hatteras in 1524 was the basis of the belief that the South Sea lay only a short distance beyond the shores of the Atlantic. He could see, behind the narrow strip of sand, a vast body of water that he mistook for the Pacific Ocean. His brother, Girolamo, drew a map showing a large but indefinite mass of land in the south, connected here by a narrow isthmus to another large body in the north. This thin strip of land separated the two great oceans, and it was believed that Marco Polo's world of the Orient lay not far beyond.

Both imagination and a lack of understanding played tricks on these explorers. They knew that they were near the 34th parallel, which girdled the globe through or near the fertile valleys of the Tigris and Euphrates, through the spice-producing lands of the Middle East, and down the length of the Mediterranean Sea. Products of great value that came from both sides of that magic line in the East would undoubtedly be equally as marvelous in the West. This newly discovered land, they concluded, would surely be of great worth to whatever country possessed it.

Francis I of France, who had sent Verrazzano on this expedition, was involved with problems at home of such magnitude that he could not pursue Verrazzano's dream. Forty years passed before attempts were made by some French Protestants to settle at a place they named Charlesfort—now Parris Island, S.C. All attempts failed, but while one of the leaders, Jean Ribaut, was in London in 1563 seeking support for his colony, he published a book, *The True and Last Discovery of Florida*. This book made it possible for Englishmen to read in their own language of some of the wonders of America. Walter Raleigh, a Devonshire youth about eleven years old, may have seen a copy of this little book, and it perhaps fired his interest in America. England's great role in overseas expansion, however, lay some years in the future.

Spain was truly the giant in New World activity, and land along the 34th parallel did not escape her scrutiny. In 1526, just two years after Verrazzano's pioneer voyage up the coast, a Spanish official from Hispaniola, Lucas Vasques de Ayllon, led an expedition from Santo Domingo to the River Jordan—now the Cape Fear River. In July, with about five hundred men and women, including some black slaves, and nearly ninety horses, he entered the mouth of the river. As they neared the shore, one of their ships was wrecked and valuable stores of supplies were lost. The colonists landed, nevertheless, and attempted to establish a settlement. A new ship was built to replace the lost one, while another vessel, smaller and more suitable for river exploration, was also constructed. These two were possibly the first ships built by Europeans in North America. Illness and mutiny soon broke out. Leaders of the colony grew frustrated, feeling that they had failed in their assignment. Ayllon set out to lead the group overland to the south where he thought a more hospitable site might be found. Yet fever and starvation continued their toll in the new location, and Ayllon himself died in October. The colonists, reduced to a mere one hundred fifty persons, returned in distress to Hispaniola. Their route of march down the coast from the Cape Fear was identified many years later by the bits of rusty armor and other equipment that marked the spots where the sick and dying had fallen by the wayside.

The most noted Spanish explorer in the region was Hernando de Soto, who set out from Havana in 1539, landed in Florida, and marched north in search of gold that Indians had told him was to be found in the mountains. By early 1540 he and his men reached the present southwestern corner of North Carolina. After staying for about a month, resting their horses and enjoying the Indian hospitality while they searched in vain for gold, they turned west. Shortly afterwards they crossed the Little Tennessee River (in present Macon County) and discovered that its water flowed in an entirely different direction from that of other rivers they had seen. This westward-flowing river was the first tributary of the Mississippi to be seen by Europeans, and they began to wonder whether the country was as small as their maps had led them to believe.

The Spanish were also anxious to establish mission stations along the coast to convert the natives to their religion. In 1566 a small colony under Pedro de Coronas set out for Chesapeake Bay for this purpose as well as to open trade there. His countrymen suspected that this bay extended into Canada and perhaps even connected with a route to the Orient. By having outposts near the mouth of the bay, they might control the entire route. The colony was composed of two Dominican priests, a captain in command of fifteen soldiers, and an Indian called Don Luis, who had been captured on an earlier visit to the Chesapeake. In August a sudden storm drove the little group ashore on the northern end of the Outer Banks. Without really knowing where they were, the men discovered Currituck Sound and spent several days exploring about twenty miles inland. Before leaving they set up a wooden cross on the beach and claimed the land they had discovered in the name of the king of Spain.

In the winter of the same year Spain made a final attempt to confirm the persistent reports of gold in the mountains. Captain Juan Pardo and Sergeant Hernando Boyano landed on the South Carolina coast and led an expedition toward the mountain. At the foot of the Blue Ridge they constructed a log fort, where Boyano and about twenty-five men spent the winter. Captain Pardo and a small contingent of men marched east to the coast, exploring as they went. During the winter messengers passed back and forth between the fort and the coast, and in the spring the captain rejoined the expedition. They all then marched through the southwestern corner of North Carolina as De Soto had done, but at various sites along the way they constructed small forts, leaving a few men to hold each of them. One account suggests that a man and his wife and children were among those left at one of the forts. In recent years, near the town of Franklin in Macon County, in caves dug into the side of mountains, bits of rope and rusted shovels have been found, which are believed to date from this time.

Spain concluded that this part of the world was of little value, and, except for having a theoretical claim to the region, she abandoned it. She made no further attempts to explore or settle it. It remained for England some years later to see in this part of the New World possibilities that Spain had not seen. A hospitable climate, fertile soil, friendly natives, and a willingness to carry on a trade for less exotic products than gold made possible the transplanting of English culture to much of North America. This was a move that had its earliest testing in North Carolina.

2

"The Goodliest Soile Under the Cope of Heaven" [1]

$\mathcal{E}$NGLAND'S interest in the New World was demonstrated in 1497–1498 when John Cabot, sailing under a charter from Henry VII, discovered North America. Although he probably did not sail south of New England and quite likely not even south of Nova Scotia and Labrador, it was this voyage which gave England the claim to North America that she perfected.

The first step toward implementing England's claim was taken in 1578, when Queen Elizabeth granted a charter to Sir Humphrey Gilbert to discover and settle lands "not actually possessed of any Christian prince or people." His efforts were centered in Newfoundland, and it was there that he attempted to plant a colony in 1583. After about a month he gave up hope of establishing a lasting settlement and the colony returned home. On the way Gilbert was drowned when a severe storm struck his fleet. [2]

Queen Elizabeth renewed Gilbert's charter in the name of his

1. Ralph Lane to Richard Hakluyt the Elder, September 3, 1585, quoted in David B. Quinn, ed., *The Roanoke Voyages,* 2 vols. (London: The Hakluyt Society, 1955), 1:207.

2. Mattie E. E. Parker, *North Carolina Charters and Constitutions, 1578–1689* (Raleigh: Carolina Charter Tercentenary Commission, 1963), pp. 3–5.

half-brother, Walter Raleigh, on New Year's Day, 1584, which was March 25 under the now outdated Julian calendar that England retained until 1752. Raleigh's charter, like Gilbert's, provided that any traveler to or settler in the colony "shall and may have and enjoy all the privileges of free denizens and persons native of England and within our allegiance, in such like ample manner and form as if they were born and personally resident within our said Realm of England, any law, custom, or usage to the contrary notwithstanding." [3] This was the basis for the oft-spoken claim that the American colonists had the same rights as native Englishmen. It was repeated in subsequent charters concerning Carolina. In North Carolina on a number of occasions in the colonial period people quoted this provision to their royal masters and insisted time and again that they were not to be treated by crown and Parliament any differently from people in England. Even as late as 1776 leaders of the colony publicly maintained that they wanted only their charter rights as Englishmen, not independence.

Raleigh set about in a most logical way to colonize his grant. He reasoned that financial support would be offered and that potential colonists would come forth when more was known of the prospects for a settlement. Just one month and two days after receiving his charter, Raleigh dispatched a reconnaissance expedition to America under Captains Philip Amadas and Arthur Barlowe, whom he employed at his own expense. A naturalized English subject, Portuguese-born Simon Fernandez, was engaged as pilot of the small fleet. Fernandez quite likely was with the de Coronas colony in 1566 and he knew a desirable place near the Currituck landing to begin the exploration. Sailing southwest through the West Indies, the ships encountered the Gulf Stream and soon were sailing up the Atlantic. They entered the sound through Ocracoke Inlet on July 4, 1584, landed on Roanoke Island, and quickly began exploring and collecting plants, rocks, soil samples, and other material to be examined and tested in England. When they weighed anchor in mid-

3. Parker, *North Carolina Charters and Constitutions,* p. 7.

September, they took back with them two willing and intelligent young Indian men, Manteo and Wanchese. This was an especially fortunate move as the Indians attracted a great deal of attention wherever they appeared in England and proved to be a valuable means of publicizing Raleigh's new plans for a colony. The reports made by Amadas and Barlowe were so full of promise for this "goodliest soile under the cope of heaven," as the region was soon being described, that Queen Elizabeth knighted Raleigh and named the new land Virginia in honor of herself, the Virgin Queen. From these reports Englishmen began to understand and to appreciate many qualities of the New World.

Financial support came rather quickly. A share in such an expedition as Raleigh proposed appeared to be a good investment. The queen furnished a ship and so did the secretary of state. Many individuals subscribed money, and by April 1585 a colony of 108 men sailed from Plymouth, Devonshire, for Roanoke Island. Queen Elizabeth recalled her servant Lieutenant Ralph Lane from Ireland and put him under Raleigh's command although she continued his pay herself. John White, a gifted artist, and Thomas Harriot, a professor at Oxford who was a noted mathematician and scientist and one of the most versatile men of the age, also sailed. Harriot had already learned some of the natives' language from Manteo and Wanchese, and undoubtedly they had also learned some English.

By the middle of August this colony, England's first mainland American colony, arrived at Roanoke Island and began the construction of Fort Raleigh. The men were organized along military lines under Lane's command. Cottages were constructed nearby and a suitable base created for a variety of expeditions that set out in different directions. Some went north to the Chesapeake Bay and others into the backcountry a hundred miles or more. People in England were as anxious to know everything about the New World as we have been in recent times to know about the moon, Mars, and Venus. The written reports, the watercolor drawings of John White, and the collected specimens in some cases satisfied their curiosity, but many people wanted to know more. Indians proved to be good sources of information for the colonists, as many of the Englishmen were good students of Indian culture. From the natives Lane's men learned to make dugout canoes. They also learned to plant crops in rows and hills, as well as to keep weeds out of their gardens. This was a particularly important lesson for them. In England, where land had been tilled for generations, a field would be plowed and the seed broadcast over it. In America, however, the warm climate and the presence of weed seed would not permit this. Such a field would quickly be covered with vigorous weeds of many kinds. They also adopted the Indians' name for unfamiliar things, hence *moccasin, canoe, hickory, persimmon, opossum, raccoon, tomahawk, hurricane, hominy,* and a host of other Indian words began to enter the English language.

Supplies anticipated by Ralph Lane's colony were late in coming, and on June 1, 1586, when Sir Francis Drake visited Roanoke Island on the way back to England after an expedition against the Spanish in the West Indies, Lane decided to return home. To make room for the colonists Drake put ashore and apparently abandoned some black slaves who had been captured from the Spanish. A severe storm arose, and Drake felt obliged to leave quickly. Some of the collected specimens and perhaps even some of White's paintings were thrown overboard to lighten the boats as they passed from shore to ship. Lane also abandoned three of his men who had not returned from an expedition. Apparently it was only a few days after Lane and Drake left when Sir Richard Grenville arrived with the long-expected supplies. If Lane had remained but this brief time longer, his colony might well have been England's first permanent American colony.

Grenville, when he departed soon afterwards, left fifteen men with enough supplies for two years. He could easily have spared additional men thereby more certainly ensuring the permanence of the beachhead. Why he did not is merely one of many puzzles associated with these earliest English ventures in America.

Raleigh's personal fortune was dwindling, and if he expected to plant an English colony in America, he had to act quickly. By the spring of 1587 he had succeeded in enlisting the aid of nineteen merchants and thirteen gentlemen of London. He abandoned the idea of a military organization and instead created a civil government for his new colony, with a governor and a dozen assistants. He gave these men a charter and incorporated them as the "Governor and Assistants of the Citie of Raleigh in Virginia." The new colony consisted of one hundred twenty people, including seventeen women and nine children. John White was named governor, and he and the other leaders were instructed to sail by way of the West Indies to get some plants that might grow in Virginia and to round up some livestock abandoned there by the Spanish. The colony was then to stop at Roanoke Island for the men left by Lane and Grenville, to drop off Manteo, who had gone to England with Lane, and then to go to the Chesapeake Bay to settle at a place recommended by Ralph Lane. A colony at that location would have the advantage of a deep-water port that could be used by English ships as a base for attacking Spanish settlements in the New World as well as Spanish ships in the Atlantic.

The colony reached Cape Hatteras on the Outer Banks on July 22, and an advance party went ahead to Fort Raleigh, which was found to be damaged. The houses were deserted and covered with vines. The men left by Grenville had disappeared, but some human bones suggested that they had been killed. Pilot Fernandez refused to take the colony any farther, and White was unable to prevail over him. Fernandez seemed anxious to put to sea, perhaps to try to capture Spanish treasure ships for himself. The colony had no other choice than to disembark at Roanoke Island. Men began cleaning up the old houses and building new ones. They had brought over some brick and two thousand roofing tiles, perhaps intended for their most important buildings—a chapel and a house for the governor, which would also serve as a capitol for the colony. As soon as the people were moderately comfortable, the friendly Manteo was baptized and created Lord of Roanoke as Raleigh had directed. This was the first Protestant baptismal service in the New World and the first time an American was elevated to the peerage. Through these ceremonies Raleigh recognized

Manteo as leader of the Indians of Virginia, and it was to him that the colonists were expected to turn for guidance in their relations with the natives.

On August 18 Eleanor Dare, daughter of Governor White, gave birth to a daughter, who was christened Virginia on August 24 because she was the first child of English parents to be born in Virginia. Her father was Ananias Dare, one of the assistants in the government. A few days later a child was also born to Dyonis and Margery Harvie, but Governor White recorded nothing further in his journal about this child.

One colonist who strayed too far away from the fort while searching for crabs along the shore was attacked by Indians who broke his skull with a wooden sword. Beyond that there was no suggestion of trouble with the natives. Indeed, the attacking Indian was from the mainland, not a local Indian. Still, all was not well with the colony. It arrived too late to plant crops, and the previous season had been such a poor one that the Indians had no food they could share. Officials of the colony persuaded a reluctant Governor White to return with the fleet to hasten the shipment of supplies. They agreed to care for his personal possessions; and if they carried out their intention of moving to a more suitable place, the name would be carved on a tree near the fort. A cross above the name would let him know when he returned that they had left in distress.

After a very rough voyage White arrived home late in 1587 to find all of England busily preparing to defend the country against the powerful Spanish Armada that was set for an invasion. The queen commanded that no ship could sail if it might be of any possible use in defending England. Nevertheless, by April 1588 White managed to find two small ships that could be spared. Loaded with supplies and with some additional colonists, the ships sailed for Roanoke. The captains, however, were less concerned about the welfare of England's pioneer American colony than with their own profits. Once in the Atlantic, the English crews turned to piracy, but instead of capturing treasure ships themselves, they were boarded by French pirates who took all the supplies intended to relieve Roanoke. There was nothing to do but return to port. It was not until 1590 that White was again able to sail. When he arrived at Fort Raleigh a few days before his granddaughter's third birthday, he found the place overgrown with melon vines and the houses abandoned. Nearly everything that could be moved was gone, but he found a half-buried chest of his own containing rusted armor and ruined pictures and maps. The word CROATOAN without the feared cross above it was carved on a tree. Before he could go out to Croatoan, now called Hatteras, on the Outer Banks where Manteo lived, a violent storm came up, and he was forced to leave in haste. Because of the damage to his ships he could not continue the search, and his colony became the "Lost Colony" of Roanoke. No trace of the colonists was ever found although Chief Powhatan later told Virginia colonists that most of the people from Roanoke had been slaughtered as they made their way toward Chesapeake Bay. They were caught quite by chance, Powhatan explained to Captain John Smith at Jamestown, between two warring bands of Indians—one from the southwest that was invading the region and the other composed of local Indians trying to defend themselves. This seems to have occurred just a short while before the English colony arrived at Jamestown. As evidence of his account, Powhatan showed Smith some copper pots that he picked up after the battle ended.[4]

Raleigh had invested a fortune in his efforts to plant an English colony in America, and many other people had also contributed generously to the scheme. Many lives had been lost, but all of this was a part of the price that England had to pay for America. Gerald Johnson called these first colonists "the expendables,"[5] yet their contributions were significant. They enabled England to try several forms of colonial government and to develop and test theories of colonization.

Queen Elizabeth died in 1603, and men interested in English

4. David B. Quinn, *England and the Discovery of America, 1481–1620* (New York: Alfred A. Knopf, 1974), pp. 454–456, 467–468.

5. Gerald Johnson, *Our English Heritage* (Philadelphia: J. B. Lippincott Company, 1949), p. 9.

expansion overseas waited a few years to determine the attitude of the new monarch, James I. By 1606 it seemed safe to raise the question, so a group of men who hoped to take up where Raleigh had left off approached the king about securing a charter to form a company for this purpose. James was not willing to see the wealth of his subjects drained away by worthless projects, so he sought the advice of some of the men who had had experience with the Roanoke ventures. Although these very men had lost money in the undertakings, they remained enthusiastic and assured James that America was a hospitable land, that Englishmen could flourish there, and that colonies in America were certainly desirable. Another attempt, they believed, would be successful, and the investors as well as the crown and the country might expect to benefit. With such confidence based directly on the attempts to settle at Roanoke, James promptly approved a charter for the Virginia Company. The following year Jamestown was established on the Chesapeake Bay, where Raleigh had intended to plant his 1587 colony, and this proved to be England's first permanent American colony. Its success had much to do with determining that this part of America would be English by heritage and not Spanish or French.

After a few years of struggling the Jamestown colony began to flourish, and plantations were established in the countryside. Population increased, and still more Englishmen began to look with interest at the wilderness of America. In London in 1629 the attorney general, Sir Robert Heath, appealed to the new king, Charles I, for a grant of land to explore, settle, and exploit. With little delay Heath became the sole proprietor of the southern half of North America, a region which his charter called Carolana, a name based on the Latin form of Charles. The charter contained a number of interesting provisions. For one thing, the proprietor was directed to keep on hand in Carolana for the king's use whenever he should visit the colony, a 20-ounce gold crown bearing the inscription DEUS CORONET OPUS SUUM—God Crowns His Work—suggesting perhaps that both Carolana and King Charles were God's crowning achieve-

ments. The charter also reflected the new idea that men might
be protected by law from the abuse of authority by government.
The theory was new, not very broad, and largely untried, but in
America it was to grow. In 1629 the theory referred to property
rights and protective procedures in courts. Freedom of speech,
press, religion, and assembly were to follow in due course.
Nevertheless, "the idea that individuals had rights which their
government was bound by law to respect was incorporated in all
the charters concerned with North Carolina." [6] As a result of
Heath's grant, there was a new interest in the region. Some colonists for Carolana reached Virginia but failed to secure transportation to the south. The governor of Virginia, anticipating
settlement in the region, sent two military expeditions to explore
it and to confer with the Indians.

North Carolina has been called "a state without a birthday" [7]
because there is no record of the time of its first permanent settlement. Nevertheless, by the early 1650s an overflow of colonists from Virginia had pushed beyond the line that one day
would separate the states of North Carolina and Virginia. A
map made in London in 1657 by Nicholas Comberford locates
"Batts House" at the western end of Albemarle Sound in what
is now Bertie County. Nathaniel Batts had settled there by September 1653 and built a two-room house twenty feet square with
a large chimney. From this frontier outpost he engaged in trade
with the Indians. When he was visited by a Quaker missionary
in 1672, he was called Governor of Roan-oak, perhaps because
of his priority in settling there. For a time this area was called
Roanoke or Old Virginia to distinguish it from the newer
Virginia to the north. Settlers who followed Batts purchased
land from the Indians and for their own security recorded their
grants in Virginia. For many years the oldest such deed was
thought to be one of March 1, 1662, but later one dated August
4, 1661, was found, and still more recently one made on Sep-

6. Parker, *North Carolina Charters and Constitutions,* p. xix.

7. Herbert R. Paschal, "A State in Search of a Birthday," *The Rebel,* 3 (Spring
1960): 11–14.

tember 24, 1660, has turned up. North Carolina history is truly growing at both ends.

In October 1662 the council in Virginia decided that the time had come to recognize the presence of colonists to the south, so Samuel Stephens was made "commander of the southern plantation" and authorized to appoint a sheriff. Sheriffs, of course, collected taxes and kept order, so the frontier community's government dates from this time.

Word of the growing settlement beyond the bounds of Virginia reached London at a propitious time. It so happened that King Charles II was indebted to many prominent men for assistance in regaining his throne after the Civil War and the Protectorate of the Cromwells. His Majesty was approached on behalf of eight such loyal and generous men who were seeking a grant of New World land which they might settle, Christianize, and make profitable for both the crown and themselves.

Charles's debt to these men was great, and he was in no position to refuse the request. In 1663 he named them the Lords Proprietors of Carolina, as it now was spelled, and gave them a tract of land that extended from the southern shore of Albemarle Sound to what is now the Georgia-Florida state line. On the west the vaguely known South Seas was the limit. Nevertheless, even with such a vast tract of land, when the Proprietors learned that their grant did not include the Southern Plantation on the northern side of the sound, they approached the king again. In 1665 they obtained a new grant that began at what is now the North Carolina–Virginia line and extended south into what was clearly Spanish territory, almost to St. Augustine. England was alerting Spain that she intended to control North America and that she didn't think Spain could (or would) do anything about it. The Proprietors' territory was virtually the same as that granted to Sir Robert Heath in 1629 as Carolana, and their grant included many of the other provisions of his charter as well. The section granting colonists the rights of Englishman was repeated, and additionally they were guaranteed rights of trade and freedom from taxation except "by and with the consent of the free people or the greater part of them." And an entirely new subject was touched upon. Churches in Carolina, the charter directed, were to be "dedicated and consecrated according to the ecclesiastical laws" of England. Nevertheless the Proprietors were given authority to grant "indulgences and dispensations" to those "who really in their Judgements, and for Conscience sake" could not conform to the ritual and beliefs of the Church of England. In accord with this provision, the Proprietors permitted all religious groups to follow their own forms of worship in Carolina. They forgot King James's dictum, "No bishop, no king," and the church's failure to provide bishops for America weakened the ties between colonies and mother country.[8]

On the other hand, the Proprietors themselves were given specific rights. They had "full power and authority" to do many things, among them: to create and fill offices, to establish courts of justice, to commute punishments and pardon offenses, to collect duties, fees, and taxes, to grant land, to confer titles of nobility, to raise an army and commission officers, and to wage war. Their charter contained the "bishop of Durham clause" under which they were expected to help protect England from foreign enemies who might appear within their domain just as the bishop of Durham, on the Scottish frontier, had been expected to do in olden times.[9]

No provision was made for resolving differences that might arise between the Lords Proprietors and the people, and this proved to be the undoing of the Proprietors in the northern part of Carolina. Many people who were already living there in 1663 had acquired their land from the Indians, and they were quick to resent the intrusion of outsiders, as they regarded the Proprietors.

The governor of Virginia, Sir William Berkeley, one of the Proprietors, began issuing land grants, and soon instructions

---

8. William S. Powell, *The Carolina Charter of 1663* (Raleigh: State Department of Archives and History, 1954), pp. 23–37. H. L. Mencken, ed., *A New Dictionary of Quotations on Historical Principles* (New York: Alfred A. Knopf, 1942), p. 107.

9. Parker, *North Carolina Charters and Constitutions,* p. xix.

were sent from London creating three counties in Carolina, each named for a Proprietor. Albemarle, named for George Monck, Duke of Albemarle and noted general of England's Civil War, was to be in the northern part. Clarendon, honoring Edward Hyde, Earl of Clarendon, lord high chancellor, was to be in the middle region. Craven, honoring William, Lord Craven, a close personal friend of the royal family, was in the south. Albemarle was already settled; Clarendon flourished briefly along the Cape Fear River when some New Englanders established Charles Town there in 1662 but abandoned it in 1663. The following year some Barbadians arrived and stayed until 1667. Craven, established along the Ashley and Cooper rivers in 1670, evolved into South Carolina.

In 1665 the Proprietors directed that Albemarle and the other counties, when they were established, should have a governor whom they would appoint, an elected legislature, and courts. An annual land tax of one-half penny per acre was levied, but its collection was postponed for several years as a means of encouraging settlement. This tax was called a "quitrent" because the payment of it "quit" the colonists of further obligation to the Proprietors as feudal masters. For about five years under this plan the assembly was the major agency in the government, setting the pattern that would prevail in North Carolina as colony, province, and state. When the Proprietors promulgated their elaborate Fundamental Constitutions in 1669, they said they did so to "avoid erecting a numerous Democracy." [10] The time had come, they reasoned, to exercise some of their feudal power, but they had the good judgment to realize that they could not suddenly reverse the course of events. The provisions for a hierarchy of noblemen, bearing such titles as landgrave and cacique and entitled to seats in Parliament, and lesser freemen with rank above the leetmen, who would be bound to the land, and slaves, would have to be implemented slowly if at all. The same was true of other features which might have worked in England or on the Continent a generation or so earlier, but Carolinians had

10. Parker, *North Carolina Charters and Constitutions,* p. 128.

already experienced a freedom equal to and perhaps greater than that enjoyed by their counterparts in England. They fought tenaciously to keep it, and by 1700 the Proprietors admitted defeat and abandoned all pretense of following any of the provisions of the Fundamental Constitutions.

It was during this period that the pattern of government developed in the County of Albemarle. A governor and council appointed from London came to be the chief units of the executive branch, while an assembly of delegates elected by the freeholders composed the chief unit of the legislative branch. Nevertheless, the governor and council sat with the assembly during the remainder of the seventeenth and a part of the eighteenth century. Gradually the council came to be considered an upper house, and the division into a bicameral legislature evolved. The governor's actions were determined by his instructions from the Proprietors and the instructions were cumulative from one governor to the next. It was through him that directives from London were passed to the colony, and he was expected to keep the Proprietors informed of conditions there. Sometimes a Proprietor would designate a councilman as his personal representative, and these individuals were called proprietary deputies. At other times the governor would name councilmen. With the advice and consent of the council he could issue writs for the election of delegates to the assembly. He could appoint certain administrative and judicial officers. His salary, strange to say, was set by the assembly and paid from funds received through quitrents, which the assembly was responsible for collecting. When the governor displeased the assembly, his salary was withheld, and this was often done. One colonial governor was never paid, and another one went unpaid for the last eighteen years of his life. Finally, during the royal period, the situation became so intolerable that crown officials ordered revenue from the West Indies used to pay the salary of the governor of North Carolina.

The makings existed for the formation of two political factions, and they were not long in taking shape. One was composed of the governor and the council and all who owed their appointment or position to the Proprietors. They supported those to whom they were indebted for the good life they enjoyed. As a group they maintained that the best interests of the colony would be served by a government just as independent of the people as possible. They composed the prerogative, or government, party with the governor at its head. Lacking anything like modern political party organization, it was more accurately a faction. Opposing it was the popular party, which was convinced that the will of the people should be dominant in the government. Its members understood quite clearly that the people's will found clearest expression through their representatives in the assembly—the "house of commons" as it soon came to be called. This was an early division in North Carolina, and it persisted until the American Revolution. The speaker of the assembly was the highest officer in the colony in whose selection the people had any voice, and he was the recognized leader of their cause. When the governor was absent, his place most often was filled by the president of the council, and North Carolina governors developed a habit of departing often and staying away for long periods of time. Some, of course, also died in office. This gave the colony a long list of chief executives of varying ability.

The Proprietors were never able to control the government in the County of Albemarle. The local faction was superior in number, in political maneuverability, and in the force of its threats to newcomers. Sooner or later, in every encounter, it triumphed. After the colony on the Ashley and Cooper rivers began to flourish following its establishment in 1670, the Proprietors became less interested in the unmanageable northern colony. Charles Town had good harbor facilities, a better climate, and other natural advantages, but it also had something else equally as important. All of its people settled there with the full knowledge that they would be living under a government directed from London. There was no resident opposition that had to be overcome. South Carolina, therefore, was more to the Proprietors' liking for many reasons.

There were persistent rumors in Albemarle that Sir William Berkeley, the Proprietor who lived in Virginia, might convince the other Proprietors to divide Carolina into eight parts and give him the Albemarle region. Berkeley was strict and demanding, and the people feared the consequences of such action. The possibility drew them together. Virginians, living in a royal colony, looked down upon the proprietary stepchildren of Albemarle with contempt. They claimed that the region was little more than a refuge for thieves, pirates, fleeing criminals, and runaway servants. To protect their own planters, the House of Burgesses in Jamestown placed restrictions on the shipment of tobacco from Albemarle through Virginia ports.

Tobacco farmers in Albemarle were hard pressed since their own ports could be used only by small ships. They were obliged, therefore, to resort to smuggling. Coastal traders from New England using shallow-draft vessels opened a profitable, although illegal, trade, and Carolina tobacco began appearing in Scotland, Ireland, Holland, France, and Spain without first passing through England as required by the British navigation acts. The Proprietors became concerned about what might happen to their charter if they permitted acts of Parliament to be ignored, so they sent customs collectors to gather the proper fees. They also directed their governor to see that all pertinent laws were enforced. These officers proved to be arbitrary in the extreme; it seemed to many residents of Albemarle that they demanded excessive fees from some people while favoring others. New England traders were successfully driven away and the whole colony seemed to face a very bleak future. Late in 1677 a group of old settlers drew up and signed a Remonstrance outlining their grievances and justifying what they were about to do. Under the leadership of John Culpeper and George Durant, a body of "rebels" seized the acting governor and threw him in jail because of a long list of acts that they judged to be illegal. At a public meeting to which everyone was invited, the rebels elected an assembly that met promptly and provided for the proper collection of taxes and fees. New taxes were levied to reimburse the Proprietors for losses they had unfortunately suffered in recent years, and a fair and honest government was installed. For two years this government conducted affairs in an open and businesslike manner. When the Proprietors learned of the arbitrary and illegal acts of their appointed officers, they apologized to the people of Albemarle.

Culpeper's Rebellion, as this event came to be called, is regarded as one of the first popular uprisings against a corrupt government in America.

In an attempt to provide the best government possible, the Proprietors decided to send one of their own body to Albemarle. They selected Seth Sothel, who had recently purchased the share originally granted to Edward Hyde. On the high seas Sothel was captured by pirates, so for the next five years local men, who had long lived there, served capably as acting governors. Sothel escaped, having suffered cruel treatment in the meantime as a prisoner in North Africa, and reached the colony in 1683. If he had been ideally suited for the position when appointed, he underwent a personality change while he was carrying bricks for his captors in the heat of Africa. In Carolina he proved to be one of the most arbitrary and corrupt governors in any of the English colonies. He completely disregarded instructions from the other Proprietors by illegally appointing officers, accepting bribes, jailing his opponents without trial, seizing estates that he was supposed to be settling, and in a variety of other ways offending many people.

In 1689 when Sothel's actions could no longer be tolerated, the assembly tried him and found him guilty of thirteen charges. Even though he was a Proprietor, he was banished from the colony for a year and declared to be forever ineligible to hold office. The Proprietors, upon learning of Sothel's behavior, once again apologized to the people.

The next proprietary governor, Philip Ludwell, was given a new title. The fact seems at last to have dawned upon the Lords Proprietors that there were two Carolinas, and Ludwell's commission referred to him as governor of the "Province of Carolina that Lyes North and East of Cape Feare." [11] He brought

11. William L. Saunders, ed., *The Colonial Records of North Carolina,* 10 vols. (Raleigh: P. M. Hale [and others], Printer to the State, 1886–1890), 1:360.

with him fresh instructions showing signs of genuine concern for the welfare of the people. These might have meant a significant turning point in the development of the colony, but unfortunately another rebellious Carolinian appeared. John Gibbs broke up a precinct court and took two magistrates prisoner; he boasted of the support of eighty men in his claim to the governorship. Since he held one of the colonial titles of nobility, he claimed to have been designated governor at Sothel's departure. He was apparently a man of some ability and standing. His daughter was the wife of Martin Bladen, a member of the Board of Trade in London, but his local support evaporated before Gibbs's Rebellion had run very much of a course. The Proprietors, nevertheless, were concerned and completely reversed their Carolina policy. In their estimation, the northern part of Carolina clearly was not qualified for any kind of independent status. Henceforth, that region would be under the close scrutiny of Charles Town. A deputy governor for the northern colony would be designated by the governor there. The idea was even proposed, but quickly abandoned, that there should be one "parliament" for the whole of Carolina.

For fourteen years this arrangement of a deputy governor operated, but the people of the area did not suffer. Their reputation was such that no self-respecting politician wanted to tangle with them. The governor in Charles Town had no choice but to appoint local men to office, and this suited almost everybody. During the period from 1691 until 1705 there were five longtime residents who occupied the governor's seat in turn, and each had a long term of experience in government behind him. They were all anxious to stabilize conditions and to expand the colony, so it was under their leadership that settlement at long last began to push out of the old area on the northern side of Albemarle Sound. A new county named Bath was formed in 1696 down on the Pamlico River, and in 1705 it attracted a colony of French Huguenots who had been dissatisfied in Virginia. In 1706 the town of Bath was incorporated there as the colony's first town. Four years later a second town was established still farther south. A Swiss land company promoted the settlement of some Swiss, German, and English colonists at the junction of the Neuse and Trent rivers where they laid out a town named New Bern. Care was taken in all of this expansion to purchase land not only from the Proprietors but also from the Indians. Nevertheless, the Indians grew more and more resentful over the loss of their hunting grounds and town sites. New Bern was built on top of the leveled site of the Indian town of Chattoka.

While expansion was taking place, several of the governors attempted to improve the colony in another respect. The establishment of the Anglican church, they believed, would benefit the people. Proper respect for form and order, the worship of God in decent surroundings, and the civilizing influence of the church, they concluded, would work wonders. Taxes were levied to support the church in the colony just as was done in England. The chief opposition to the Establishment was centered in the Quaker communities that had developed. Quaker missionaries appeared in Carolina as early as 1672 and quickly converted many unchurched people to that faith. With the Established Church, taxes were levied to support it and oaths were required of officeholders to support the church as well as the crown, as head of the church. Quaker practice forbade the swearing of an oath, so widespread opposition developed to the Anglican church. When Quakers complained to the governor in Charles Town, they succeeded in securing the removal of the northern governor whom they blamed for their predicament. In his stead a Charles Town merchant, Thomas Cary, was appointed. In Charles Town Cary had been a very moderate man, and it was expected that in his new position he could help both sides make necessary adjustments. Instead, he insisted that Quakers must swear an oath; and when they refused to do so, he declared their seats in the assembly vacated. Purged of Quakers, the assembly then passed even stronger acts in favor of the Anglican church and against Quakers. A Quaker mission to London returned with instructions from the Proprietors appointing another governor, but Cary refused to yield to him.

Another breach of the peace occurred in the colony when Cary's Rebellion erupted. The Cary party was victorious, holding office for about two years. The Proprietors sent over Edward Hyde, their choice for governor, who was perhaps a relative of the former Lord Proprietor of the same name. Proprietor Hyde was the grandfather of Queen Mary and of Queen Anne, and it was reported in the colony that Governor Hyde was related to the queen. Nevertheless, he was able to displace Cary only with the assistance of marines from Virginia. Hyde's commission in 1712 designated him as "governor, captain general, admiral, and commander-in-chief of that part of the province of Carolina that lyes North and East of Cape Fear called North Carolina." Henceforth, then, it is proper to speak of North Carolina.[12]

Warfare among the whites suggested to the unhappy Indians that a good time had arrived—perhaps the best and last opportunity ever—to rid their country of the invaders. Tuscarora Indians, who occupied much of the coastal plain, arose quickly and on September 22, 1711, began three days of slaughter that came very close to wiping out the whole colony. Men, women, and children fell indiscriminately beneath their bloody axes. The town of Bath and the old Albemarle area escaped only because a friendly Tuscarora chief in that part of the colony refused to join the fight.

North Carolina was in a deplorable situation. Not only had many people been killed, but livestock had also been slaughtered or driven off, houses and barns burned, and crops destroyed. The summer had been so dry that many crops had failed, trade had fallen off, the colony had little money or credit, and the Quakers refused to bear arms to help defend themselves. Governor Hyde in desperation called on Virginia for aid, and the legislature there voted token assistance. Governor Spotswood, however, refused to let his militia enter the colony unless North Carolina paid and equipped the troops and further agreed to surrender to Virginia the strip of land between the Albemarle Sound and the northern limits of Carolina set by the 1665 charter. Virginia never recognized that document and now tried to blackmail the helpless colony into relinquishing her

12. Saunders, *Colonial Records of North Carolina,* 1:750, 870.

most valuable territory. Governor Hyde refused to be taken advantage of, even in a moment of such great need. He turned instead to South Carolina, where the assembly promptly voted £4,000 and sent troops at once without asking for any assurance of support. Colonel John Barnwell with thirty whites and about five hundred friendly Indians marched through the wilderness and in due time defeated the Tuscaroras, who lost about eight hundred warriors killed or captured. Before long the papers of Philadelphia, New York, and Boston were advertising Indian slaves for sale from among these captives. The Tuscaroras who escaped soon left North Carolina and returned to New York where their ancestors had lived before moving to North Carolina a short while before the arrival of whites. When the Tuscaroras left, they took with them the name of their chief town, Chattoka, which appeared in their new home as Chautauqua.

Two years later North Carolina had an opportunity to repay her southern neighbor when troops went to help quell an Indian uprising between Charles Town and the Cape Fear River. In her helpfulness the colony also benefited herself. Not only was that part of North Carolina cleared of Indians but a fertile and valuable part of the province was also rediscovered. It had been unexplored since 1667 when Clarendon County was abandoned. Between 1717 and 1725 settlers in large numbers began to occupy land there. South Carolinians who viewed the land while marching against the Tuscaroras afterwards returned to take up some of it and become prosperous planters. Orton Plantation was established on the lower Cape Fear in 1728, and the house, built between 1735 and 1748, still stands.

The Tuscarora War served to unite factions in the colony with the Quakers even going so far as to furnish provisions for men under arms. It was because of this war that the colony issued its first paper money as the only ready way to pay official debts. Depreciation soon set in, and more paper money was issued. A precedent was established, and for the remainder of the colonial period this method was adopted to meet urgent needs for money. Depreciation always resulted, of course, making North Carolina money unacceptable outside the colony and all but worthless in it. The scarcity of a stable currency hindered the colony's commerce, and the presence of huge quantities of paper money to be redeemed plagued the young state after the Revolution.

The assembly in 1715 passed a series of very progressive acts designed to undergird the government and to bring about stability and prosperity. Among these acts was one that resulted in a road more than a hundred miles long from the Neuse River at New Bern to the Cape Fear River. Another act was intended to encourage sawmills and gristmills. Others called for the marking of channels in the sounds and rivers, the operation of pilot boats, the building of bridges and roads, and the maintenance of ferries. The powers and duties of local officers were defined and a schedule of their fees for services drawn up. Although the Anglican church was established, dissenters were protected in their right to worship as they pleased. To encourage the growth of towns as centers of trade and commerce, an act was passed giving all towns with as many as sixty families the right to a representative in the assembly. These borough towns, as they were called, continued to be represented until 1835.

In spite of the best efforts to set North Carolina on the road to prosperity and stability, it was geography, the cause of so much of her trouble, that interfered. About this time British officials cleaned out the nests of pirates that had flourished in the West Indies for many years. The nature of the coast of North Carolina made it an inviting place to these displaced robbers of the sea. The mouth of the Cape Fear River was ideal for careening their vessels, while the Outer Banks, the inlets through them, and the countless coves and creeks along the coast offered ideal refuge in which to sail when pursued or in which to hide while waiting for a likely victim to pass.

Although Blackbeard, Stede Bonnet, and over a hundred other pirates, a few of whom were women, were uninvited, they soon discovered that they were not totally unwelcome. Pirates, North Carolinians quickly discovered, brought in a good stock of wares and often in their haste to be away again offered them at a lower price than legitimate merchants. North Carolinians were not above seeking the best bargain they could find and winking at the source. It was even reported that one of the governors and perhaps even a colonial secretary worked very closely with a pirate. The discovery of pirate goods in a barn belonging to an official seemed to be good evidence, while a tunnel from the governor's house down to the dock was even more suspicious.

North Carolina was helpless to drive off these parasites, but with the willing assistance of her two neighbors her waters were soon cleared of them. The governor of South Carolina learned in the summer of 1718 that a pirate was operating off the Carolina coast and he sent an expedition under Colonel William Rhett in search of him. Rhett found his quarry lurking behind the sandbars at the mouth of the Cape Fear River and after a desperate five-hour battle the pirate was captured. It turned out to be Major Stede Bonnet, once a respectable British officer who reputedly had been driven to piracy by a nagging wife. Bonnet was taken to Charles Town, tried, convicted, hanged, and given a pirate's burial—under the water of the ocean at low tide.

A few weeks later the governor of Virginia secretly fitted out two sloops manned with crews from British men-of-war stationed in the James River and sent them out under the command of Lieutenant Robert Maynard of the Royal Navy in search of Blackbeard. They found the pirate near Ocracoke Inlet in the Outer Banks and on November 22, 1718, attacked. Blackbeard was killed and his crew overpowered. With the pirate's head swinging high in the rigging of his ship, Maynard sailed into Bath, where his officers faced several local residents with evidence that they had been partners in the pirate's deeds.

With removal of the Indian threat, the suppression of piracy, and a series of moderately good governors, a period of growth and improvement followed. New settlers began to arrive, and a number of new counties were created. A new town on Queen Anne's Creek was incorporated as Edenton in 1722, and it became the first designated center of government of the colony. Heretofore the government had been conducted in private homes wherever officials lived, and the assembly met in whatever accommodations were available.

Soon after the first settlers cleared their land along the Cape Fear, others began to arrive. This inviting region drew colonists from Albemarle and from South Carolina primarily, but some came from Barbados (a few in expectation of perfecting family claims to Carolina land dating back to the 1660s). Others came from the New England colonies, and from Pennsylvania, Maryland, and Europe. On the west bank of the river, about fourteen miles above the mouth, Maurice Moore in 1725 laid off a town which he named Brunswick in honor of the reigning family of Great Britain. Brunswick, like Bath, failed to take hold and before long it was losing out to its rival, Wilmington, sixteen miles farther up the river. These Cape Fear settlements at last gave the colony a deep-water port and access to the commerce of the world.

Queen Anne, granddaughter of Proprietor Edward Hyde, demonstrated considerable interest in Carolina during the years of her reign, 1702–1714. She assisted colonists with passage to Carolina, and she ordered that a proper line be surveyed and marked between Carolina and Virginia. Her royal colony of Virginia refused to obey, however. The matter of a marked boundary was often on the royal mind, and finally in 1727 King George II, on the verge of buying the shares of the Carolina Proprietors, ordered that the line be surveyed. This time Virginia responded. William Byrd, II, of that colony, led an expedition of surveyors from the two colonies which set out on March 5, 1728, from Currituck Inlet on the Outer Banks. They surveyed across island, sound, mainland, and swamp for over 160 miles. This was fifty miles beyond any settled area even in Virginia, and the North Carolinians could not imagine that anyone would ever look for a marked boundary beyond that point so they went home. The Virginians, however, ran the line for seventy-two miles more. The line was accurately located, and North Carolina retained all of the land that she had claimed since 1665, much to the disgust of the governor of Virginia.

Proprietary government in the northern part of Carolina had

been a failure. The eight absentee landlords and their successors, totaling forty-nine and including five women, never had a clear understanding of their possessions in America. They were both poorly informed and poorly advised. They attempted to implement a feudalistic government on a colony where democracy had already taken root. The governors they appointed were often inept or corrupt, sometimes both. King George II had been on the throne just two years when he realized how bad the situation was in North Carolina. On July 25, 1729, he acquired all of the rights of government in the colony as well as in the land rights of seven of the eight proprietary shares. The head of the Carteret family (soon to become Earl Granville) declined to sell, and the Granvilles continued to hold their New World possession until it was lost at the time of the American Revolution. As a result of the royal move North Carolina became a colony of the crown and joined her neighbors, Virginia and South Carolina (where royal control had been in effect since 1719), in a series of adventures that would have been regarded as unbelievable in 1729.

3

Poor Subjects of Britain

$\mathcal{A}$T the beginning of royal rule most people in North Carolina were of English descent, although there were some Lowland Scots and a few French Huguenots and Swiss. Gerald Johnson's "expendables" had all disappeared, and the land was held largely by those whom he called the "indispensables," the honest, reliable, hardworking class that gave North Carolina its character.[1] Many were descendants of the yeoman farmer class in England who reached North Carolina by way of Virginia. They or perhaps their parents had been indentured servants— sturdy, ambitious, industrious people who came to find a better life in America. In return for their passage they agreed to work for a period of time to repay whoever advanced the money. Having served the term of their indenture, they were at liberty to work for themselves, and in order to avoid any stigma that might have been attached to their recent status they left Virginia and settled in North Carolina. This simple fact explains why so many North Carolinians can trace their ancestors to a Virginia origin but not beyond that. These were people who generally owned no land, and did not leave wills or other legal records.

In North Carolina land was plentiful and settlers were welcomed, indeed sought out and invited. Land was valuable to the

1. Johnson, *Our English Heritage,* p. 44.

crown only when it was occupied, made productive, and subject to taxation. The coastal plain was not settled very far inland, while the whole backcountry lay fallow and open for a long time. Much of the interior region was a grassy plain of gently rolling hills burned over periodically by the Indians who considered it a common range for hunting by all tribes. Indians from as far away as Illinois and Ohio frequently passed through on long hunting and trading expeditions, and the Cherokees in the mountains often came down to hunt and trade.

With the opening of a port on the Cape Fear River it became easy for immigrants to move directly into the colony, and among the first to arrive were a few Scottish Highlanders about 1732. Within a year or two large numbers began arriving. They had learned from the advance guard of the welcome settlers received, the quality of the land, and the freedom to be enjoyed in North Carolina. After landing at Brunswick or Wilmington most of these people made their way up the river to a community that they named Cross Creek because of the strange phenomenon of two small creeks whose waters met, mingled, and crossed. A second community close by was named Campbellton, and after the Revolution the two were combined and named Fayetteville in honor of Lafayette.

Following the defeat of the Highlanders by the English at the Battle of Culloden in April 1746, Parliament dealt harshly with the Scots. Efforts were made to break up the clan system, and much Scottish land was taken out of cultivation and turned over to English army officers to raise sheep. With their means of livelihood gone, Scots fled their homeland in large numbers and made their way to North Carolina where a Scottish governor, Gabriel Johnston, offered them land at low prices, and he persuaded the legislature to exempt them from taxes for several years until they became established. Ships continued to bring over so many Scots that by the beginning of the American Revolution the Cape Fear River Valley of southeastern North Carolina was being called Little Scotland. Gaelic was spoken, the bagpipe was heard, and clan dress was retained. Before the end of the century a Fayetteville printer provided these people with sermons and tracts in Gaelic.

By 1754 the region was thickly enough settled that it seemed desirable to have a new county created there. The provincial assembly, controlled by men of English descent and sympathies, named the new county Cumberland for William, Duke of Cumberland. It was he who had commanded English troops at Culloden when they murdered the wounded on the field of battle. To give his name to this new county, filled by Scots, was a cruel thing for the assembly to do, but the local Scots had modest revenge. A popular flower that grew in their gardens, *Dianthus barbatus,* was called Sweet William by the English in the Duke's honor, but the Scots in North Carolina began calling it Stinking Billy.

The Highland Scots did not stray far from the Cape Fear Valley where they first settled and that part of the state is still known as "the land of the Macs." Scottish family names abound in every community. These Scots were thrifty people, of course, hard workers, and as devout Presbyterians they took great satisfaction in their heritage. Before leaving the Highlands, however, they had been required by their English masters to take an oath never again to oppose the British crown, and an oath to them was sacred. A man's honor in the eighteenth century was precious indeed, and an oath was not to be violated under any circumstances. At the time of the American Revolution, with rare exceptions, the Scots in North Carolina remained loyal to Great Britain. Whether this was because of the oath, because Parliament's bounty for the production of naval stores was too valuable to risk losing, or because memories of Culloden made them unwilling to risk a second defeat at the hands of the English is not clear.

While the Highlanders were moving up the Cape Fear River, two other streams of people were flowing into the province and spreading out over the hills of the piedmont. One was composed of Scotch-Irish and the other of Germans. In both cases they came down the Great Wagon Road from Philadelphia, and both were generally composed of second- or third-generation Americans whose parents or perhaps grandparents had lived in Pennsylvania, Maryland, New Jersey, or elsewhere. Good land was not often available in those colonies, and these venturesome, ambitious young people wanted to start life anew.

The Scotch-Irish were descendants of Scots sent to Northern Ireland by James I in an effort to displace the hostile Irish there with a more malleable people. They were so successful in their new surroundings that their woolen and linen industries became competitive with those of England. Because of this and because of overpopulation, they were encouraged to move to America. Queen Anne aided many of them by providing transportation as far as Philadelphia.

These people possessed the characteristics necessary to conquer the wilderness. They were independent and self-reliant, domestic by habit and with a strong love of home and family. They were austere and reserved, however, and often devoutly religious. As Presbyterians they encouraged their children to learn to read and write in order to be able to interpret the Scriptures for themselves. In operating their church government they gained experience in democracy. Theodore Roosevelt called the Scotch-Irish "the pioneers of our people in their march westward, the vanguard of the army of fighting settlers, who, with axe and rifle, won their way from the Alleghanies [sic] to the Rio Grande and the Pacific." [2] Three presidents of the United States, Andrew Jackson, James Knox Polk, and Andrew Johnson, were of North Carolina Scotch-Irish origin, and so was Daniel Boone, whose parents brought him to the North Carolina frontier as a child.

The Germans who moved into the province represented three branches of Protestantism: the Lutheran, German Reformed, and Moravian churches, Many of these people came to be called Pennsylvania Dutch by their English-speaking neighbors because they called themselves *Deutsch,* meaning German. Their

2. Theodore Roosevelt, *Winning of the West,* 6 vols. in 3 (New York: G. P. Putnam's Sons, 1889), 1:119.

immediate progenitors had left central Europe for England because of a series of wars, several extremely cold winters, which killed even trees and vineyards, and because of Roman Catholic oppression. Queen Anne provided transportation from England to Pennsylvania, but a few were among the earlier settlers of New Bern in 1710. In North Carolina these Germans left their mark in Rowan, Mecklenburg, Cabarrus, and adjacent piedmont counties. They often built stone houses and enormous barns. They spoke German, of course, and so did the few slaves they had, and there was a printer in Salisbury who published tracts and sermons for them in German. These people isolated themselves as much as possible because of the language barrier, but sometimes they had to transact business with county officers who had difficulty understanding them. Since their names seemed very strange to many of their neighbors, they changed them, sometimes merely by translating them: Schneider to Taylor, Zimmerman to Carpenter, for example. One elderly man named Klein was confused, however, when three of his sons translated the family name three ways: Small, Little, and Short, and two others followed the common custom of merely adopting English spelling when they became Kline and Cline. It was by the latter device that the Eckel family became Eagle, Durr became Dry, and Schaeffer became Shaver. The current telephone directories of Salisbury and nearby towns contain countless names of German origin.

Moravians began moving to the colony in 1752 to occupy a large tract of land that they purchased from Earl Granville. They developed a highly centralized church-business community with superior craftsmen, merchants, doctors, teachers, and other professional people who offered their services throughout the backcountry. Salem, now a part of the city of Winston-Salem, was one of their communities. Old Salem today consists of many eighteenth- and early-nineteenth-century buildings restored to their original uses and opened to the public as museums where early crafts are demonstrated.

As a planned community the Moravian towns and settlements were unique. A system of waterworks by which water was taken through wooden pipes to the buildings in Salem attracted considerable attention. Moravian merchants purchased regional produce which they took to markets in Cross Creek, Charles Town, Philadelphia, and elsewhere, and from those centers of trade they acquired stock for their shops. Salem was for a long time the leading center of commerce for the backcountry. Churchmen there were in frequent communication with leaders in Pennsylvania and in Germany, and many visitors to the colony called on the Moravians. Art and music were important to these people, and their presence provided a cultural oasis. Frontier farmers sometimes mounted their horses and rode from long distances to hear the Moravian church organ or to enjoy a band or an orchestra.

A number of individual Welsh families also came to North Carolina from Pennsylvania to settle in the lower Cape Fear Valley between the Highland Scots and the English at Wilmington. Between 1730 and 1734 some friends of Benjamin Franklin's from Philadelphia were among them, and the *Pennsylvania Gazette* in April and May 1731, printed a long account by one of them telling about their experiences in their new home.

Under the Proprietors North Carolina was settled almost exclusively by English people, yet the colonists were extremely unco-operative with their English masters. After 1729, during the royal period, available land in the east and nearly the whole of the backcountry filled up with people who were not English. Many, in fact, thoroughly disliked the English. Soon the stage was set for a series of disturbing events.

Farming was the primary occupation of most men, and North Carolina engaged in extensive trade with the New England colonies and the West Indies as well as with the British Isles. In the coastal plain something approaching the plantation system developed, while in the piedmont small farms were predominant on which the owner usually produced everything his family needed. In the east tobacco, corn, and sometimes rice were the common products, while a flourishing naval stores industry also developed there. Tar, pitch, and turpentine for the Royal Navy were shipped out of North Carolina in increasing quantities until the Revolution, and some even went out afterwards as last-minute attempts were made to pay off debts to British merchants. The tanned skins of wild and domesticated animals, and forest products in the form of shingles, planks, barrel staves and heads, as well as a few ships were also exported. Mills for grinding corn and wheat were set up on the swift streams of the piedmont by the Scotch-Irish and Germans, while sawmills in the Cape Fear Valley were operated by Highland Scots. In some parts of the colony Scottish merchants established factors who offered a stock of goods for sale or barter in exchange for tobacco. They also lent money to enable their customers to buy more land and slaves thereby producing more tobacco.

North Carolina during much of the eighteenth century was recognized as the "breadbasket" of the American colonies. Wheat was grown in the piedmont and ground into flour for shipment. Shallow-draft New England vessels, ideal for coastal trade, arrived every summer, soon after harvest, to transport the wheat and flour to market. In the fall they returned for corn and dried beans and peas. In the winter salt pork and beef, packed in wooden barrels, was sent out. Much of this produce was consumed in the northern colonies, but large portions of it went to the West Indies to support the slaves who worked on sugar plantations.

Some farmers were affected by a geography-related problem, which they continued to endure for many years. It was frequently difficult to transport produce to market. Many of the routes that were available led to South Carolina or to Virginia. The colony in many respects became merely an outpost of one of her neighbors. Roads were difficult to build through the sandy and marshy east, while the red and rocky clay of the piedmont was no better. Building bridges was also difficult because many rivers were wide, swift, and deep. Nevertheless, a drawbridge constructed about 1768 over the Northeast Cape Fear River above Wilmington was one of only two such bridges in colonial America. The other one was near Boston.

Accommodations for travelers in the colonial period in North Carolina, as elsewhere in the south, were inadequate. Many inns and taverns were improperly supervised, and travelers often complained of the quality of the food, the scarcity of beds, and the presence of bugs and insects. In this respect the south suffered seriously in comparison with the north, but in the south a hearty welcome awaited the weary traveler at almost any house where he chose to stop. Living in isolation from their neighbors, sometimes miles away, families welcomed strangers, offering bed and board in exchange for fresh news and good stories. Taverns, or ordinaries as they were also called, met a local need in most communities. Here men gathered in their spare time for drinking and games—card and dice games, of course, but also billiards, bowling, and horse racing. Lewis Shirley had a tavern and race track in Caswell County, just south of the Virginia line, in the late eighteenth century, and the season lasted several weeks. People came from great distances to enjoy the races and the food and drink of the tavern. Shirley later moved to Kentucky and bred fine horses in the Louisville area. He afterwards moved to Texas and is sometimes credited with introducing thoroughbred horses into the Lone Star State. Taverns were regarded very much as clubs by men in most communities, but to the women they usually represented something else. Early in the nineteenth century a name was sought for a new post office about to be opened in Camden County, and the women of the community persuaded the government to adopt their name for the local tavern where their husbands spent so much time. "Old Trap" they called it because it lured the husbands away from home and held them. Old Trap is still a post office.

North Carolina was isolated in another way. The colonial postal service ended in Virginia, leaving those beyond that point to do the best they could on their own initiative. Charles Town was a busy port, and letters could be dispatched easily enough, and after Georgia was established, the same was true of Savannah. But North Carolina was virtually cut off from the world. Various schemes were devised to meet the need for communication. Any provincial official who needed to send an official notice simply took it to the nearest farmer in the right direction and ordered him to take it to his nearest neighbor; that neighbor was instructed to pass it along in relay until it reached its destination. A heavy fine was levied on anyone who refused to accept such a missive and deliver it to his neighbor. There was regular passing between the Moravian settlements and Pennsylvania, the location of the church headquarters, of course, and for a "trinket" travelers usually could be persuaded to take a letter or a small package to some point where it could be posted. Men living in Wilmington, Halifax, Hillsborough, and other towns contributed to the support of a private rider who would go to Charles Town or to Williamsburg on a regular schedule, perhaps once or twice a month, to deliver and bring back letters and newspapers.

As time passed and communities became stable, social classes developed among the people, although class differences were never as clear in North Carolina as they were in the adjoining colonies. An upper level was composed of the better-educated people—the clergy and professional men, most of the officeholders, and large landowners. Some of these people affected titles after their names in the official records: gentleman, esquire, or planter. A few of them had received legal training at the English Inns of Court, and fewer still had attended the colleges of Oxford or Cambridge. Several were graduates of Eton and a little later some attended Harvard, Yale, Princeton, or William and Mary. There was a scattering of sons and daughters of the peerage, a baronet or two, and a few knights, together with an occasional family that used a coat-of-arms on its bookplate. It was the next class that left its mark on the state, however. This was the small farmer class, "husbandman" or "yeoman" as they sometimes described themselves. They were once delineated as "a strong, fearless, independent group, simple in tastes, crude in manners, provincial in outlook, democratic in social relations, tenacious of their rights, sensitive to encroachments on their personal liberties, and when interested in religion at all, earnest, narrow, and dogmatic." [3]

3. R. D. W. Connor, *History of North Carolina . . . Colonial and Revolutionary Periods, 1584–1783* (Chicago: Lewis Publishing Company, 1919), p. 182.

This characterization is confirmed in part by an observation recorded in 1775 by Janet Schaw, a Scottish lady who was visiting her brother near Wilmington. Many of the comments in her journal suggest that she may have been the nearest thing to an advocate of woman's liberation that the century produced. For one thing, she sometimes capitalized *Mother* but not *father*.

> The difference between the men and the women surprised me, but a sensible man, who has long resided here, in some degrees accounted for it. In the infancy of this province, said he, many families from Britain came over, and of these the wives and daughters were people of education. The mothers took the care of the girls, they were train'd up under them, and not only instructed in the family duties necessary to the sex, but in those accomplishments and genteel manners that are still so visible amongst them, and this descended from Mother to daughter. As the father found the labours of his boys necessary to him, he led them . . . to the woods, and taught the sturdy lad to glory in the stroke he could give with his Ax, in the trees he felled, and the deer he shot; to conjure the wolf, the bear and the Alligator; and to guard his habitation from Indian inroads was most justly his pride, and he had reason to boast of it. But a few generations this way lost every art or science, which their fathers might have brought out, and tho' necessity no longer prescribed these severe occupations, custom has established it as still necessary for the men to spend their time abroad in the fields; and to be a good marksman is the highest ambition of the youth, while to those enervated by age or infirmity drinking grog remained a last consolation.[4]

Next in rank were the "Christian servants," as the class of indentured people was sometimes called. In addition to the poor but ambitious people who came of their own volition, there were some others in this category. It was not unknown for orphans and other young people to be kidnaped in the cities of Great Britain and sent to America under indenture to a ship captain who would recover his investment from a planter in the colonies. Military prisoners, particularly Highland Scots, and those

4. [Janet Schaw], *Journal of a Lady Quality,* edited by Evangeline Walker Andrews (New Haven: Yale University Press, 1939), pp. 154–155.

convicted by civil courts for minor offenses were sometimes included, while occasionally a man had to leave England quickly because of a political indiscretion. One such political refugee who reached North Carolina was Joseph Gales, an outstanding newspaper editor in Philadelphia and Raleigh. Although he managed to pay his own fare across the Atlantic, he arrived almost penniless. His good training and experience and the fact that he had spoken out boldly in support of the downtrodden laborers in his native Sheffield enabled him to rise quickly into positions of prominence.

Blacks, both slave and free, had the lowest social status. There were some in the colony by 1701, but the number did not increase greatly until after 1740, when the white population also began to increase dramatically. In the eastern counties where tobacco and naval stores were produced, slaves were more numerous, but relatively few families in the backcountry owned any.

Not many years passed after North Carolina became a royal colony before the crown began to make it clear that a deep change had taken place. No longer would informality and indifference characterize instructions from London. Indeed, with the Board of Trade and other administrative agencies advising King George II, a definite colonial policy evolved, which sought to preserve and strengthen the political dependence of the colonies on the mother country and to bind both into an economically self-sufficient empire. Several things became clear to North Carolinians. The crown intended to make their governor, judges, and other officials more nearly independent of the assembly by placing them on fixed, permanent salaries. Before long the assembly's power was reduced by generous use of the royal prerogative in settling disputes. And the navigation acts, such as those that had brought on Culpeper's Rebellion in 1677, were amplified and strengthened.

North Carolina, however, was one of six colonies not represented at the Albany Congress of 1754, called at the direction of the British government to secure some united support in the war against France. The Albany Plan of Union, which grew out of this meeting, provided for a voluntary union of the colonies. The plan, submitted by Governor Arthur Dobbs to the assembly, was never seriously considered. North Carolinians showed no interest in Benjamin Franklin's scheme for an American government in which the colonies might co-operate for their mutual benefit.

The attempt to carry out the new British policy met with vigorous opposition in North Carolina. This was basically the result of differing views as to the authority of the crown, on one hand, and the privileges of the people on the other. Imperial interests required the subordination of local interests. The crown acted on the theory that its authority in colonial affairs rested in the royal prerogative and undertook to conduct government through instructions that it held to be binding on both the governor and the assembly. But this was clearly not in accord with the thinking of North Carolinians, and they resisted. At the local level the governor was the representative of the crown and upholder of the royal prerogative; the assembly, on the other hand, was the champion of the rights and privileges of the people. The challenge was clear, men on both sides recognized their duty, and the struggle which persisted until 1776 consumed the interest and energy of large numbers of people.

The course had been set many years earlier and it actually was little changed through the whole colonial period in spite of the crown's wishes. During the sixty-five-year proprietary period there had been twenty-two different governors, yet of these only seven had been appointed by the Proprietors and six by the governor in Charles Town. Nine had been local men who held the office by virtue of their position as president of the council. During the royal period of forty-six years the crown appointed five governors, while four others filled the office temporarily as president of the council. During the entire colonial period of one hundred eleven years, out of thirty-one governors, authorities in London commissioned only a dozen.

Topics in unlimited number and of varying degrees of seriousness were debated between the two factions, and devious means were employed to gain a temporary advantage. The assembly, for example, sometimes attached riders to essential appropriation bills to gain something it wanted. The governor several times summoned the assembly to meet at a time and place inconvenient for delegates from a section that had opposed him—a north-south sectionalism arose after the newly settled Cape Fear region began to rival the old Albemarle. From such an assembly the governor extracted favors in return for concessions. After the backcountry began to fill up, a new kind of sectionalism arose; the east began to realize that it might be overwhelmed by a populous west and it began to adopt means of preserving its control of the assembly. Representation was by county, and as long as the east had a majority of counties, it was safe. The assembly, therefore, was reluctant to create new counties in the west, but it could not always refuse. Often when the assembly was obliged to yield, an old eastern county was divided, so that now there are many very small counties in the coastal plain.

The east also managed to have a voice in local affairs in the western counties. Many of the officers at the county level were appointed by the assembly, and it was only natural that easterners should be selected for these lucrative positions. Nearly every western county seat had a coterie of officeholders more interested in their own welfare than that of the local people whom they should have served. Frontiersmen were convinced that these officials charged excessive fees for entering cases on the court docquet, for recording deeds, and for various other official acts. Taxes were regarded as excessive, and sheriffs and tax collectors demanded prompt payment, often in hard cash rather than in paper money or produce. Cash was scarce on the frontier, and land and personal property were often sold by these appointed officials if taxes were not paid promptly in cash. As often as not, it seemed, friends of the sheriff ended up in possession of many desirable farms when owners could not pay taxes in silver. People on the frontier also resented being taxed for the construction of a provincial capitol and residence for the royal governor. It was a building they likely would never see since it was in far-off New Bern, the capital since 1746. Such a handsome structure would be of no benefit to them. Its very name, Mansion House, suggested that Governor William Tryon had gone too far in the direction of royal living. It was completed in 1771, however, and eventually came to be known as Tryon Palace.

Another cause for discontent in the colony was the Granville District, the northern half of the colony that had been granted to Earl Granville as his portion of the proprietary grant. Although he had no voice in the government, he did hold the land and he collected quitrents on it. He also was empowered to grant land, but his agents in the colony were dishonest and unreliable. Land records were confused and taxes improperly collected. Much of the revenue collected there went into private hands rather than to the government, and residents of the rest of the colony resented having to bear an unduly heavy portion of the costs of government.

Resentful of eastern control over their affairs, suspicious of the honesty of most local officeholders, and confident that they could manage their own government, many people in the backcountry responded with enthusiasm to calls to attend local gatherings at which their problems might be discussed. After several clashes with local officials, the dissatisfied element coalesced into a body which called itself the Regulators, since its members wanted to regulate their own affairs. The objectives were stated quite clearly in a series of Regulator Advertisements that they issued, and their determination was demonstrated in several attacks on county courts and on individual officers. When the assembly meeting in New Bern was threatened, Governor Tryon called out the provincial militia and marched to the center of the Regulator country to quell the rebellion. In a battle fought near Alamance Creek on May 16, 1771, the Regulators were soundly defeated and scattered by the militia. The reform in local government which they so desperately sought was denied them. The west was not to be victorious in its stuggle against eastern control until 1835.

Although the Regulators were not really formidable enemies,

the militia did gain valuable experience in the field. Some of the officers and perhaps a few of the men had seen service during the French and Indian War when the North Carolina assembly, more generous than Virginia had been earlier, appropriated £12,000 and raised a regiment of 750 men to fight on Virginia's frontier. Two North Carolinians played a significant role in the attack on Fort Duquesne in the early winter of 1758. Major Hugh Waddell, a young officer in his twenties, and Sergeant John Rogers, both dressed as Indians, captured an Indian who had recently been inside the French fort. From him they got a description of the defenses inside the fort, which led to its fall. The English then built Fort Pitt about two hundred yards away, and the city of Pittsburgh grew up around the site. English and colonial victories over the French put an end to the almost ceaseless Indian raids of the preceding several years along the frontiers of Virginia and the Carolinas.

The unrest in North Carolina did not go unreported. In 1760 Governor Dobbs informed his superiors in London that his assembly contended that the provisions of the charter of 1663 still prevailed, binding both king and people. He expressed the assembly's viewpoint very well: "The Assembly think themselves entitled to all the Privileges of a British House of Commons and therefore ought not to submit to His Majesty's honorable Privy Council further than do the Commons in England or submit to His Majesty's instructions to His Governor and Council here." Dobbs appealed to the king to strengthen his hand so that he could more effectively "oppose and suppress a republican spirit of Independency rising in this Colony." [5]

This rising opposition did not develop among the mass of people. Most of them were too deeply concerned with trying to earn a living. It did not come from the governor, certainly, nor from his friends—they were loyal to the crown and grateful for their positions. It lay in the hearts and minds of the local planters, merchants, professional men, and the rising class of

5. Saunders, *Colonial Records of North Carolina,* 6:279–280.

officeholders. Dobbs was very perceptive to detect this movement at such an early time, while his superiors in London were very stupid to ignore his plea.

The series of rebellions in North Carolina apparently made little or no impression in England. Many North Carolinians, as the eighteenth century approached its third quarter, had a tradition of more than a century of relatively independent thought and action. Few of them looked to England as the mother country as their grandparents or great-grandparents might have done. Many, of course, were not of English descent anyway. Most North Carolinians were not concerned with the success of the British policy of mercantilism, but only with their own freedom. This they could best manage for themselves without British interference, and they began quite early to resist.

Various acts of Parliament met differing degrees of opposition depending upon what effect they might have in the province. The act most vigorously opposed although without actual violence, was the Stamp Act of 1765. Assemblymen had already expressed their attitude toward taxation by Parliament when they informed the governor in October 1764, following the Sugar Act, that they would regard "new Taxes and impositions laid on us without our Privity and Consent" as a violation of "our Inherent right and exclusive privilege of imposing our own Taxes." [6] The Stamp Act had been under discussion in North Carolina for several months before William Tryon arrived in October 1764 to relieve the aging Governor Dobbs. When the new governor took office the following April, the province was concerned over this act. Speaker John Ashe warned Tryon that the colony would resist its enforcement to the death. Public demonstrations were held at Cross Creek, Edenton, New Bern, and Wilmington. The chief opposition centered in the Lower Cape Fear, however, since Tryon then lived at Russellborough on the outskirts of Brunswick, and because the chief port of the colony was there. When they heard that the act had been passed, the people of Wilmington organized as Sons of Liberty,

6. Saunders, *Colonial Records of North Carolina,* 6:1261.

drank toasts to "Liberty, Property, and no Stamp Duty," hanged Lord Bute (a former prime minister and advocate of the Stamp Act) in effigy, and compelled the stamp agent, Dr. William Houston, to resign. They also warned Andrew Steuart, the public printer, that he had better print the *North Carolina Gazette* on unstamped paper. Tryon became alarmed and called a group of leading merchants into consultation. He offered to pay the cost of stamped paper himself, but they refused to submit. They informed him in no uncertain terms that they regarded this act of Parliament as a violation of their rights as British subjects and were determined to resist to the utmost of their power.

There was no cause to test their intentions until late November, when the English ship *Diligence* arrived with the first shipment of stamped paper. News of her arrival spread rapidly, and armed men from the region hurried to Brunswick to prevent the landing of the paper.

In January two ships arrived without the properly stamped clearance papers, and they were promptly seized by Captain Jacob Lobb of the British cruiser *Viper*, long stationed at the mouth of the river. This aroused the anger of the people even more. Great crowds gathered in nearby Wilmington and signed an association to resist the enforcement of the act. Merchants there refused to furnish supplies for the king's ships, and local officers jailed some members of the crew who came ashore for provisions. Local men set out toward Fort Johnston near Brunswick and they frightened Captain John Dalrymple, the commander, into spiking his guns. They compelled Captain Lobb to release the captured vessels and required public officials to take an oath that they would not directly or indirectly attempt to sell stamped paper in North Carolina.

Almost a month after the arrival of the *Diligence* the stamps were still on board. On the first day of February 1766, more than two months after the stamps had reached the province, Governor Tryon wrote a letter to London about this state of affairs—and he sent the letter off on a ship that sailed without stamped clearance papers. The Cape Fear mob prevented the enforcement of the Stamp Act in North Carolina, thereby successfully denying the right of Parliament to tax the colony. This was eight years before the more famous Boston Tea Party was conducted for the same principle. And in North Carolina no property was damaged or destroyed.

In response to Parliament's retaliatory measures following the repeal of the Stamp Act, Massachusetts in 1768 sent a circular letter to the other colonies, inviting co-operation in concerted measures of resistance. When the letter was laid before North Carolina's assembly by Speaker John Harvey, he was disgusted with the response it received. The colony's "house of commons" declined to take any formal action, contenting itself with merely giving the speaker verbal instructions to reply to it. The house then resolved to send the king "an humble, dutiful and loyal address" appealing to him to intervene with Parliament, and a committee was appointed to prepare it. When Lord Hillsborough, secretary of state for the colonies and a relative of Governor Tryon's wife, heard of this action, he was delighted and reported that it gave "great satisfaction to the King." [7] The committee, however, was influenced by Speaker Harvey, and in addition to making the required appeal to the king it also indicated that North Carolina was willing to co-operate with other colonies. Harvey informed the Massachusetts assembly that the body over which he presided would "ever be ready firmly to unite with their sister colonies in pursuing every constitutional measure for relief of the grievances so justly complained of." [8]

When Parliament chose to punish Massachusetts, Virginia was the first to come to her assistance by proposing a Non-Importation Association to strike at the economic foundations of Great Britain. This document was taken under consideration by the assembly in New Bern, and the members agreed on first reading that it should be approved. At the same time, however, another appeal to King George was made asking him to protect

7. R. D. W. Connor, *North Carolina, Rebuilding an Ancient Commonwealth, 1584–1925,* 2 vols. (Chicago: American Historical Society, Inc., 1929), 1:293.

8. Connor, *North Carolina, Ancient Commonwealth,* 1:294, quoting the *Boston Evening Post,* May 15, 1769.

the colonies from the illegal acts of the Parliament. These acts by the assembly, Tryon announced, "sapped the foundations of confidence and gratitude," and made it his "indispensible duty to put an end to this session." [9] The assembly thereupon was dissolved. Much important business remained unfinished, notably the final approval of the Non-Importation Association. On his own initiative, then, John Harvey called the members together in a "convention" so that they might "take measures for preserving the true and essential interests of the province." [10] Of the seventy-seven members who were present for the assembly, sixty-four promptly gathered in the courthouse in a body entirely independent of the governor. John Harvey was chosen moderator of the two-day session that made North Carolina a member of the revolutionary Non-Importation Association. They signed the record of their action as the "late representatives of the people," and then took steps to see that it was widely circulated in the province. [11]

North Carolina's leaders were clearly prepared to strike out on their own to retain the freedom that they had so long enjoyed. They disobeyed the royal governor in not returning home after he dissolved the assembly, and they took the first step that would eventually lead to the formation of a legislative body of their own creation.

9. Connor, *North Carolina, Ancient Commonwealth,* 1:294.
10. Connor, *North Carolina, Ancient Commonwealth,* 1:295.
11. Connor, *North Carolina, Ancient Commonwealth,* 1:295.

4

Ready Revolutionaries

$\mathcal{OS}$OON after his victory over the Regulators at the Battle of Alamance Governor Tryon left North Carolina to become governor of New York. Following a brief interval when the president of the council, James Hasell, acted as governor, he was succeeded by thirty-four-year-old Josiah Martin. Martin found himself suddenly in a position that required almost every intellectual quality which he lacked. He was stubborn, tactless, and intolerant, and these were certainly not traits to endear him to the people of North Carolina. They were in no mood to endure the petty tyrannies of a provincial governor. Yet Martin had a more exalted idea of the royal prerogative than any of his predecessors, and he insisted that instructions from the crown were of higher authority than acts of the assembly. Royal wishes were binding not only on the governor but also on the assembly. Martin's attitude on this question made the issues of the day perfectly clear to the people: Should they permit their legislature to degenerate into a mere device through which the will of a distant king could be relayed, or should they maintain it as the free, deliberative, lawmaking body into which it had evolved, responsible only to the people of the province? This was a serious subject, and the assemblymen had the ability to recognize its importance and the courage to reply:

Appointed by the people to watch over their rights and privileges, and to guard them from every encroachment of a private and public nature, it becomes our duty and will be our constant endeavour to preserve them secure and inviolate to the present age, and to transmit them unimpaired to posterity. The rules of right and wrong, the limits of the prerogative of the crown and of the privileges of the people are in the present age well known and ascertained; to exceed either of them is highly unjustifiable.[1]

Up and down the Atlantic seaboard other colonies were facing similar questions, and various means were being discussed as to how plans for united resistance might be made. The Virginia assembly in 1773 suggested the organization of a system of intercolonial committees to carry on with each other a "continental correspondence" somewhat in the nature of a great chain letter. Josiah Quincy of Boston visited Wilmington in March and recorded in his journal that he found the popular leaders there heartily in favor of such a plan. When the assembly met in December, it appointed a committee for North Carolina and instructed it "to obtain the most early and authentic intelligence of all such Acts and resolutions of the British Parliament, or proceedings of Administration as may relate to or affect the British Colonies in America and to keep up and maintain a correspondence and communication with our Sister Colonies respecting these important considerations." [2] This was in the same month as the Boston Tea Party, which precipitated a series of parliamentary acts designed both to punish Massachusetts and to reinforce royal authority at the cost of popular liberty.

American response took the form of a call for a continental congress. It was expected that delegates to such an intercolonial body would be chosen by the assemblies, but in North Carolina Governor Martin was determined not to convene an assembly in time. Speaker John Harvey flew into a rage when he heard this

1. Saunders, *Colonial Records,* 9:779.
2. Saunders, *Colonial Records,* 9:741.

and threatened to take action himself, but the calmer mind of Samuel Johnston prevailed to suggest a more logical means. The call for a convention, he persuaded Harvey, should be made to appear to come from the people themselves, so a great mass meeting was quietly arranged to be held in Wilmington. William Hooper presided over it, and it was attended by men from the Cape Fear counties. They agreed that it was "highly expedient" that a provincial congress, independent of the governor, be held. All of the counties were invited to send delegates to convene on August 25 at the Johnston County courthouse about eighty miles up the Neuse River from New Bern. This would be far enough away from the royal governor that he was not likely to interfere. As the time approached, the leaders became bold and changed the place of the meeting to New Bern, under the very nose of the governor. Thirty counties and four borough towns sent delegates to what proved to be the first of five provincial congresses in North Carolina. Only five counties and three towns were not represented.

The action taken by the freeholders in Rowan County at their meeting to select delegates was typical. They first resolved "that we will at all times, when ever we are called upon for that purpose, maintain and defend at the Expense of our Lives and Fortunes, his Majesty's Right and Title to the Crown of Great Britain, and his Dominions in America to whose royal Person and Government we profess all due Obedience & Fidelity." [3] Having made their obeisance to the crown—and there is no reason to doubt its sincerity—they turned to the matter at hand by denying the right of Parliament to tax them or otherwise to exert arbitrary power over them. These isolated frontiersmen then included a phrase that must have been inserted at the suggestion of some outside source: "That the Cause of the Town of Boston is the common Cause of the American Colonies." [4] From there they ranged afield supporting the Non-Importation Association, opposing the slave trade, encouraging

3. Saunders, *Colonial Records,* 9:1024.
4. Saunders, *Colonial Records,* 9:1025.

the raising of sheep, hemp, and flax, supporting manufactures, and finally designating delegates to a provincial congress and authorizing them to select delegates to a "general Congress." In conclusion they resolved that "this Colony ought not to trade with any Colony which shall refuse to join in any Union and Association that shall be agreed upon by the greater Part of the other Colonies on this Continent, for preserving their common Rights and Liberties." [5]

Their purpose, in common with the other freeholders throughout the province, was merely to preserve their ancient rights as British subjects.

The congress assembled in New Bern for a three-day session with seventy-one delegates present and elected John Harvey moderator. It denounced the acts aimed at Massachusetts and declared that the people of that colony had "distinguished themselves in a manly support of the rights of America in general." The proposed calling of a continental congress was approved and they selected William Hooper, Joseph Hewes, and Richard Caswell to represent North Carolina. Although all three had been in the province for a number of years, they were, respectively, natives of Massachusetts, New Jersey, and Maryland. For lack of anything more tangible to offer, the congress pledged the honor of the province in support of whatever measures the national congress recommended.

No more significant action had ever been taken by North Carolinians than the successful calling and meeting of this body. The people learned that there was nothing sacred in a governor's call for an election. They could do it themselves. The freeholders of Pitt County understood this plain fact: "As the Constitutional Assembly of this Colony are prevented from exercising their right of providing for the security of the liberties of the people," they said, "that right again reverts to the people as the foundation from whence all power and legislation flow." [6]

The first Continental Congress sat at Philadelphia from Sep-

5. Saunders, *Colonial Records,* 9:1026.
6. Saunders, *Colonial Records,* 9:1030.

tember 5 to October 26, 1774, for the avowed purpose of agree-
ing on measures to be taken to recover the lost colonial rights
and liberties. For this purpose a nonimportation and nonexporta-
tion association was formed to be enforced by the committee of
safety in each colony. If their cause failed, each delegate stood
to be declared a traitor, so great secrecy cloaked their proceedings. Nevertheless, John Adams later commented that Richard
Caswell was "a model man and true patriot. We always looked
to Caswell of North Carolina." [7]

The women of North Carolina were not to be outdone in the
display of patriotism then so popular. In Edenton on October
25, Mrs. Penelope Barker (wife of Thomas Barker, the province's agent in London) presided at a "tea party" when fifty-
one women of the area solemnly declared that they could not be
indifferent to whatever affected the peace and happiness of the
country. Anxious to demonstrate their patriotism, they signed an
agreement to do everything they could to support the American
cause. This was one of the earliest instances of political activity
by American women. In Rhode Island something similar had
occurred a short while earlier, but it was the North Carolina incident that was noted in London, where newspapers reported it
and a cartoonist depicted the incident in vulgar satire.

Governor Martin, baffled in the attempt to keep his colony
from being represented in the Continental Congress, decided to
make the best of a bad situation and summoned the assembly to
meet in New Bern on April 4, 1775. John Harvey immediately
called the second provincial congress to meet at the same place
a day earlier. The leaders of the popular party intended that the
same men should sit in both bodies, and with few exceptions
that is exactly what happened. Martin was furious and denounced Harvey's actions in two strong proclamations. The
congress showed its contempt of the governor by electing Harvey moderator, while the assembly elected him speaker. The
two bodies met in the same hall; the congress gathered at 9

---

7. John H. Wheeler, *Reminiscences and Memoirs of North Carolina and Eminent
North Carolinians* (Columbus, Ohio: Columbus Printing Works, 1884), p. 105.

o'clock while an hour later it adjourned and immediately reconvened with the same officers and continued business as the royal assembly. Neither body accomplished much. The congress voiced the right of the people to assemble and petition the crown for relief from their grievances, and it also expressed its approval of the actions of the Continental Congress. The assembly accomplished even less because, in addition to electing Harvey speaker, it offended the governor in still another way. It invited the few delegates to the congress who were not also members of the assembly to join in the assembly's deliberations anyway. This was just about as much as the governor could stand, but his proclamations against this strange union were disobeyed. The assembly finally pushed Martin too far when it, too, expressed approval of the Continental Congress' actions. Martin dissolved the assembly on April 8, 1775, and a royal assembly never again met in North Carolina.

Exactly a month later a rumor reached North Carolina that blood had been shed in New England, but it was the middle of the month before letters arrived with the facts of Lexington and Concord. An armed clash was a contingency for which the local safety committees were prepared as they had been at work organizing, equipping, and drilling troops. They were certain that they had not worked in vain when newspapers arrived from London near the end of May announcing that Parliament had declared the colonies to be in a state of rebellion because of the Continental Congress that had been held in Philadelphia the previous September.

This was an eventuality which Governor Martin also had anticipated. He was aware of the loyal sentiments of the Highland Scots, and in March before calling his last assembly he applied to General Thomas Gage at Boston for military stores to equip companies of Loyalists. It was suspected that Martin was plotting to arm slaves, and because of this he was closely watched in the palace at New Bern. Afraid that he would be seized and imprisoned by the local Committee of Safety, Martin fled one night late in May to the security of Fort Johnston at the mouth of Cape Fear River.

With flags flying and drums beating five hundred Cape Fear minutemen announced that they were going to make a formal call on the governor, but not trusting their motives, he fled to the deck of a British sloop-of-war conveniently anchored nearby. With their governor gone, the people of North Carolina were obliged to manage the government as best they could. In this emergency, as they called it, it became necessary to convene another provincial congress. Now every county and every borough town was represented. During the deliberations of this August 1775 congress in the frontier town of Hillsborough, the expression "the common cause of America" was heard over and over. Hillsborough, of course, was in the midst of the former Regulator country, and the session was probably called there as a means of frightening those people, if not into cooperation, at least into nonresistance. This congress laid the foundations for an army, provided for its organization and support and began forming Continental regiments in the state. It also formed a provisional government with a provincial council as the chief executive authority. The assembly, or congress, would continue to be the principal unit of government, however, and the council would be responsible to it.

By December North Carolina troops were sufficiently well organized, trained, and equipped that Colonel Robert Howe and the Second North Carolina Continentals went to assist Virginia troops in driving Lord Dunmore, the royal governor of that colony, out of Norfolk. At the same time 760 men were sent to join South Carolina troops in crushing an impressive Loyalist movement in the western part of that province.

Governor Martin had been working diligently meanwhile to recruit troops in the colony to participate in a joint campaign with British troops that he hoped would restore royal rule in North Carolina. Martin's army included an impressive number of Loyal Highland Scots as well as a body of Black Pioneers, free blacks and slaves recruited for service on British ships in North Carolina waters. In return for their service these blacks were promised freedom and transportation out of the colony. Lord Charles Cornwallis with seven regiments of regulars would rendezvous at the mouth of the Cape Fear River about the middle of February 1776 with 2,000 more British troops from Boston under the command of Sir Henry Clinton. Martin's little army of Loyalists would join them. This plan, the British believed, would enable them to take North Carolina easily and from that secure position move down into South Carolina and Georgia and up into Virginia, quickly occupying the whole south to crush the rebellion in that part of America.

The plan was excellent, of course, but it failed because the Loyalists were too eager and Clinton and Cornwallis were not eager enough. At Martin's command, 1,600 Highlanders led by General Donald MacDonald, a veteran of Culloden, marched out of Cross Creek on February 18 toward Wilmington, and about the same time the Black Pioneers mustered aboard the *Scorpion*. The Whig or Patriot leaders in the area were fully aware of what was taking place because they had intercepted messages passing between Martin and the Loyalists. Colonel James Moore directed the maneuvers that brought Colonel Richard Caswell and Colonel Alexander Lillington with 1,100 minutemen, early on the morning of February 27, face to face with MacDonald's 1,600 Highlanders at Moore's Creek Bridge, eighteen miles above Wilmington. Under cover of darkness, the Patriots removed the floor of the bridge and greased the runners with soft soap and tallow. In the early morning mist, about an hour before sunrise, the Highlanders tried to cross the bridge, but most of them slipped and fell into the creek. Patriots concealed in emplacements just across the bridge opened fire, and thirty Scots were killed. All who could, turned and fled, but many were drowned as they scrambled to get out of the creek, and 850 were taken prisoner. Patriots captured a valuable supply of guns and other military equipment, a large quantity of medicine and surgical supplies, and over a dozen wagons. Patriots pursued the fleeing Scots, and when they entered the town of Cross Creek, a black man led them to a stable where he had seen Loyalists conceal £15,000 sterling.

This splendid victory at the Battle of Moore's Creek Bridge aroused new enthusiasm for the Revolutionary cause. It was clearly understood that North Carolina troops had foiled the British plans when first Clinton and then Cornwallis arrived months later and discovered what had happened. The British sent reconnaissance parties ashore who concluded that they could expect no local support if the army landed. They turned instead to Charleston, S.C., accompanied by Josiah Martin, and North Carolina troops rushed down to help drive them away.

Whether they liked it or not, the people of North Carolina now realized that war had begun. Their appeals to King George for protection from the acts of Parliament had been ignored. The king had sent troops against them and in so doing had violated the compact that had long been understood to exist between king and people. The people owed loyalty to the king in return for which he was bound to protect them. When he no longer did this, he ceased to have any claim on their loyalty. It was through such simple reasoning that many people reconciled themselves to rebellion.

Feeling had reached such a pitch that the next provincial congress, convening at Halifax in April appointed a committee "to take into consideration the usurpations and violences attempted and committed by the King and Parliament of Britain against America, and the further measures for frustrating the same and for the better defense of this province." [8] After deliberating four days, the committee on April 12, 1776, submitted a report that included the formal resolution:

> That the delegates for this Colony in the Continental Congress be impowered to concur with the delegates of the other Colonies in declaring Independency, and forming foreign alliances, reserving to this Colony the sole and exclusive right of forming a Constitution and laws for this Colony, and of appointing delegates from time to time (under the direction of a general representation thereof), to meet the delegates of the other Colonies for such purposes as shall be hereafter pointed out. [9]

8. Saunders, *Colonial Records,* 9:504.
9. Saunders, *Colonial Records,* 10:512.

This document, the Halifax Resolves, was the first official state action for independence, and it was not a declaration for North Carolina alone but a recommendation to the Continental Congress that independence should be declared by all of the colonies through their representatives in the Continental Congress. When this document was presented to the Congress in Philadelphia, other members sent copies to their constituents and urged them to "follow this laudable example." Virginia was the first to do so, and on May 15 the Virginia convention instructed her delegates in Congress to "propose" a declaration of independence. On the 27th the North Carolina and Virginia delegates laid their instructions before Congress, and on June 7 Richard Henry Lee moved "that these United Colonies are and of right ought to be free and independent States." [10] The motion was adopted on July 2, and on July 4, a final draft of the Declaration was laid before Congress and approved. It was signed on behalf of North Carolina by William Hooper, Joseph Hewes, and John Penn, the latter a Virginia-born lawyer who had lived in North Carolina for about two years.

After passing the resolutions of April 12, the provincial congress turned its attention to the formation of a constitution for the state, but two weeks of bitter debate made it clear that the time had not yet come for such an important step. It was agreed to wait until later in the year to try again.

The council of safety, as the old provincial council was now called, had its hands full during the summer and fall of 1776 managing affairs in the state. In the summer it sent 1,400 troops to help defend Charleston against Clinton and Cornwallis. It provided 300 men to aid Virginia in quelling Indian disturbances on her frontier, and General Griffith Rutherford was given 2,400 men for a campaign against the Cherokees who, it was believed, were being stirred up by John Stuart, recent British superintendent of Indian affairs for the Southern Depart-

10. Worthington C. Ford, ed., *Journals of the Continental Congress,* 34 vols. (Washington: U. S. Government Printing Office, 1904–1937), 5:425.

ment. Rutherford's campaign was part of a plan devised by leaders in Virginia, South Carolina, and Georgia. Troops from all four states struck simultaneously to solve a problem that affected all of them. A series of treaties resulted in the containment of the Indians for the time being.

The council was also concerned about Loyalists within the state, particularly those in the Cape Fear Valley. Many suspected Loyalists were required to declare their position. Those who were willing to take an oath of allegiance were permitted to remain. Some suspected persons, however, were forced to give bond for their good behavior. A few whose presence was considered dangerous were paroled within prescribed limits, but some of the most active leaders were imprisoned—some in North Carolina, some in Virginia, and some as far away as Philadelphia.

The adoption of the national Declaration of Independence made it essential that the state have a constitution, so an election was called for October 15 to choose delegates to another provincial congress, which would be expected to draft one. Radicals and conservatives began at once to campaign in an effort to control the congress. Conservatives wanted a government similar to the one they had known all their lives with independent judges, important officers appointed by the assembly, and annual elections for the assembly. Radicals wanted a total change with annual elections for almost every office imaginable.[11] Neither side won a clear victory although a number of known conservatives were defeated and some outspoken radicals elected. At the congress a committee was appointed to prepare a declaration of rights and a constitution. The committee benefited from rather precise instructions from Mecklenburg and Halifax counties in drawing up the declaration of rights, but it also drew freely from similar documents already adopted in Virginia, Maryland, and Pennsylvania. In preparation for drafting a constitution the com-

11. Robert L. Ganyard, "Radicals and Conservatives in Revolutionary North Carolina: A Point at Issue, The October Election, 1776," *William and Mary Quarterly,* 24 (October 1967): 585–586.

mittee wrote John Adams of Massachusetts for advice, which he generously supplied and some of which was accepted. Other sections of the North Carolina constitution were drawn from those of Pennsylvania, New Jersey, and Delaware.[12]

The constitution was short and simple, containing only a bare framework of government and stating the fundamental principles on which it was founded. Details of administration were left to future legislatures. There was no violent break between the new state government and the old colonial one. The constitution provided for a legislature of two houses, a senate and a house of commons; a judiciary consisting of a supreme court, an admiralty court, and county courts; an executive department to be composed of a governor, a council, and whatever other administrative officers might be needed. One radical change was introduced, not in the form of the government but in the spirit of it—the center of political power was shifted from the executive to the legislative branch. Under the colonial government neither the people nor the assembly had had any control over the governor. Now in defining the powers of the chief executive, the committee demonstrated decidedly antiexecutive sentiments. The legislative branch henceforth would have the upper hand. The governor would be the creature of the assembly, elected by it and removable by it. The office was stripped of many former powers, and restrictions were placed on every power that was left. The governor could not take any important step without the advice and consent of the council of state, and he had no voice in the appointment or removal of the councilors. The governor was left the right of initiative, and that, plus the moral influence of the office, might give the incumbent some opportunity for service.

Each county, regardless of population, would have one senator and two commoners. Free men, including blacks, who paid taxes could vote for commoners, but only those owning at least fifty acres of land could vote for senators. To serve in the house

---

12. Earl H. Ketcham, "The Sources of the North Carolina Constitution of 1776," *North Carolina Historical Review,* 6 (July 1929): 213–236.

of commons a man had to own one hundred acres of land in the county he represented while a senator had to own three hundred acres. A governor had to own property worth over £1,000. In accordance with recommendations made in Mecklenburg County, a center of Presbyterianism, the constitution specified that only those who acknowledged the truth of the Protestant religion could hold office. Copied from the Delaware constitution was the provision that no clergyman, while in the exercise of his pastoral functions, could serve in the legislature or on the council.

The constitution, adopted on December 18, 1776, was simply declared to be in force. It was never submitted to a vote of the people. Perhaps the delegates were afraid it would be rejected. Richard Caswell was named governor, and other officers were also selected to serve until their successors could be chosen by the next legislature. These men took an oath of office at Tryon Palace, the first state capitol, on January 16, 1777. The first assembly under the new constitution convened in April, re-elected Caswell and most of the other state officials, and inaugurated the new state government. The radicals won a number of seats in the house of commons, defeating several conservatives who had heretofore played leading roles in the affairs of the day. A few conservatives who might have continued to serve withdrew from public life in disgust. Democracy was in the saddle, and politics ceased to be a game played exclusively by conservative eastern "gentlemen."

After the departure of Cornwallis and Clinton in the spring of 1776, North Carolina was free of the enemy, but her troops, both Continental and militia, were active elsewhere. Colonel James Moore of the First North Carolina Continental Regiment was ordered to join Washington in Pennsylvania early in 1777, but he died while preparing to leave and was succeeded by Francis Nash. Troops under his command took part in the maneuvers preliminary to the Battle of Brandywine in September while a few were in the battle itself. The whole unit participated in the Battle of Germantown in October where Nash, by then a brigadier general, was killed. These North Carolina troops spent the winter at Valley Forge and in the spring played a creditable role in the Battle of Monmouth in New Jersey.

During the years of relative freedom from military action, the hazardous coast of North Carolina proved to be very useful. Ports elsewhere along the Atlantic were either held or blockaded by the British, but stopping the movement of small vessels in and out of the long coast of North Carolina proved to be an impossible task. Geography, for a change, was helpful. There was no reliable source of supplies for British blockaders; their oceangoing vessels could not pursue small coastwise ships through the inlets and into the rivers and creeks; and the treacherous coast off the capes was not known as "the graveyard of the Atlantic" for any frivolous reason. Privately owned ships of North Carolinians were commissioned to carry arms for their own protection as they engaged in trade for the benefit of the country. The state also equipped some ships for the same purpose and even joined with Virginia in operating two large galleys around Ocracoke Inlet. As a result of this activity large quantities of desperately needed supplies were received, but a few merchants also became quite wealthy. Not all ships escaped, of course, and some outward-bound vessels with cargoes of tobacco and lumber were captured by the British.

While the southern states were free of the enemy, the late royal governors of the two Carolinas and Georgia were assuring their superiors in London that a large majority of people in their colonies were Loyalists at heart and wished nothing more fervently than for the British army to come and free them. Sir Henry Clinton, commander-in-chief in America, was not doing too well in the middle states, so he decided to transfer the war to the south. The first blow fell on Georgia, the youngest and weakest of the states, whose defense had been entrusted to Major General Robert Howe, North Carolina's highest ranking officer of the Revolution. In December 1778 a British force landed at Savannah, easily defeated Howe, and within six weeks re-established royal government in Georgia. Howe was recalled and replaced by General Benjamin Lincoln, who felt strong enough by spring to take the offensive. His subordinates were sent out to seize various objectives, but they were all defeated, including General John Ashe, a North Carolinian, who was surprised and routed on the way to take Augusta. Forced to retreat, Lincoln and his troops sought safety behind the defenses of Charleston.

With the approach by sea of a strong British force Lincoln yielded unwisely to the pleas of municipal officials to stay and defend the city. His efforts were to no avail as Charleston fell in May 1780, and shortly South Carolina, like Georgia, was occupied, leaving North Carolina next on the British list. Cornwallis was confident that he could hold the captured territory and readily take his next objective. Had he moved quickly he might have done so, but summer weather arrived early in 1780, and British troops suffered in the humidity and heat of the south. Most of North Carolina, he thought, was already loyal and there was no need to hurry. He sent agents to seek out Loyalists and urge them to work hard, lay in provisions, and remain quiet until the British were ready to march in August or September.

The very completeness of the British victory in South Carolina proved to be Cornwallis's ruin. It supported the exaggerated claims of the loyalty of the people in the south and produced an excessive degree of confidence which the real facts simply did not warrant. The delay, however, gave North Carolina sufficient time to pull her scattered forces together and reorganize them. Partisan leaders such as Griffith Rutherford, William R. Davie, William Lee Davidson, and Francis Locke assembled over a thousand militiamen, mostly from among the Scotch-Irish around Charlotte. They were employed in breaking up foraging parties sent out by the British, but at Ramsour's Mill, near the present town of Lincolnton northwest of Charlotte, they engaged in a battle that broke up a gathering of Loyalists who were making plans to aid the British when they invaded the state. The battle successfully dispersed the Tories, and their assistance was denied the British.

General Washington became concerned about the situation and sent down some Delaware and Maryland troops from his own army. Soon afterwards more troops arrived from Virginia and in late July General Horatio Gates, hero of Saratoga, took command of this southern army. He rashly set out to meet the British before his men were prepared for such a move. As they approached Camden, S.C., in the dark along a narrow causeway, they met the British leaving the town and exchanged a few shots before each side withdrew to wait for dawn. As the sun came up on August 16, 1780, the battle lines of redcoats began to advance on the Americans. Moving across the field, the British fired one volley after another making an impressive and frightening sight. A few of Gates's men stood fast, but others began to fall back, and soon nearly the whole army, including Gates himself, turned and fled. Almost eight hundred Americans, about half of them North Carolinians, were killed and around a thousand captured. Most of the American equipment was also taken.

Once more North Carolina lay open to invasion, and Cornwallis had only to advance to reap the fruits of victory. But again he let the opportunity pass. His delay gave Americans a breathing spell in which to rally their broken forces, and they took full advantage of it. The militia once again was rounded up and joined by some troops from Maryland and Virginia. When Cornwallis broke camp on September 8 and set out for Charlotte, he soon discovered that his flanks were almost constantly harassed by alert partisan bands that moved quickly, did all the damage they could, and disappeared into the countryside. So effective were they that it took Cornwallis seventeen days to cover 70 miles. In Charlotte, on October 3, Governor Josiah Martin issued a proclamation announcing the triumph of the British army and the restoration of royal government. However seriously Martin took his own premature proclamation, Cornwallis must have known that it was foolish. It had not taken him a whole week he reported, to discover that he was in the "hornet's nest" of the Revolution. He said that he found Charlotte to be "an agreeable village but in a damned rebellious country" and that the people there were more hostile to England than any he had found in America. He was in a hotbed of Scotch-Irish

Presbyterians who had long memories of the English who had driven their fathers from their pleasant homes in Ulster.[13]

When Cornwallis set out from Camden, he sent Colonel Patrick Ferguson, one of his best and most trusted officers, with about four thousand Loyalist militiamen to protect the left flank of the main army from attack by over-mountain men—Patriots such as Joseph and Charles McDowell, Isaac Shelby, and John Sevier from the newly settled region beyond the mountains. Ferguson pushed into North Carolina, and from Gilbert Town in newly formed Rutherford County, he sent word that unless the over-mountain men dispersed and ceased further resistance, he would cross the mountains, hang their leaders, and destroy their settlements by fire and sword. This was all the challenge Shelby and Sevier needed. They called their neighbors to arms and set out to silence Ferguson. On the way they were joined by other militiamen from various parts of North Carolina and some even came from Virginia.

Ferguson made fun of the motley army until he heard how near it was, and then he hurried a messenger off to Cornwallis for aid. Forced to seek protection, he turned and took up what he regarded as a safe refuge on the southern slope of King's Mountain a short distance across the boundary in South Carolina. From camp there he boasted that all the rebels in hell could not drive him away. He must have forgotten, if he ever knew, that he was now dealing with men who were accustomed to climbing real mountains, not a mere hill in the piedmont like King's Mountain. Reaching the foot of the little ridge in mid-afternoon, October 7, 1780, the over-mountain men were divided into three columns for a prompt assault. From three different points they advanced in turn. When Ferguson returned to his mountaintop position from repulsing one group, he was immediately faced by another attack from a different direction. Ferguson used a silver whistle to assemble his men so the Americans

13. Walter Clark, ed., *State Records of North Carolina,* 16 vols. numbered 11–26 following the *Colonial Records* (Winston and elsewhere: M. I. & J. C. Stewart [and others], Printers to the State, 1895–1905), 15:172.

had no trouble in spotting him. His situation was already clearly hopeless when he was killed by a shot through the heart, and his second in command promptly surrendered.

The battle lasted about an hour. The victory was complete. Ferguson's corps was completely wiped out. The British lost over nine hundred men. This remarkable achievement cost the Americans only twenty-eight killed and sixty-two wounded. It was a magnificent victory—the first encouraging sign since the fall of Charleston. It was hailed as a turning point of great significance. British General Clinton reported that it threw South Carolina into confusion and rebellion against the newly established royal authority there and totally disheartened the Loyalists. It also upset Cornwallis's plans and made his position in Charlotte untenable. He felt that his friends had deserted him, and it was clear that fresh swarms of Americans were pouring into the region. He ceased to dream of conquering North Carolina and instead, on October 12, abandoned Charlotte in some disorder to take up a position in Winnsboro, South Carolina.

North Carolinians demonstrated that they had both the strength and the spirit to defend their country. What they needed most was competent leadership. The Continental Congress had tried its favorites—Howe, Lincoln, and Gates—to no avail, so George Washington was asked to select a commander. He chose Nathanael Greene, Rhode Island-born Quaker, who took command at Charlotte early in December. He found only the shadow of an army, poorly equipped and generally untrained, but with the help of good subordinates and his own inspiring presence its weaknesses were repaired. Greene perhaps knew Cornwallis's mind better than Cornwallis himself did, and he executed a movement in which Cornwallis unwittingly cooperated to the fullest. Greene cleverly lured Cornwallis into pursuing him across piedmont North Carolina during the cold and bleak weeks of January 1781. Greene hoped to draw the British as far away as he could from their base of supplies, wearying them at the same time, and then at just the right moment turn on them and destroy them if possible. If not, the infliction of whatever damage he could would be enough.

When the British set out from South Carolina, Colonel Banastre Tarleton pursued a segment of Greene's army commanded by General Daniel Morgan. Morgan took up a position at Cowpens with the Broad River at his back (so his men could not retreat) and waited for Tarleton. The British arrived early in the morning, January 17, expected to drive the Americans head over heels into the river. They took no precautions and were surprised to come up against unexpectedly stubborn resistance. The militia in Morgan's front line fired very effectively and fell back to be replaced by a bayonet charge. At that point mounted troops swept onto the scene from the side and attacked the British flanks. Tarleton and his men turned and fled in panic, but only about 270 ever found their way back to camp. Over 900 were killed, wounded, or captured. The loss of this excellent corps, following so soon after Ferguson's defeat, was a blow from which the British in the south never recovered.

With Cornwallis seldom more than twenty-five miles behind, Greene's men behaved splendidly in the face of adversity. They were drenched with constant rain and sleet, and the roads were often knee-deep in mud and ice. The men were compelled to wade waist-deep through flooded creeks. Tents and blankets were scarce and food was inadequate, but with Greene himself sharing their hardships the men pushed on. Near the middle of February Greene crossed Dan River into Virginia and let his army rest. Here they were joined by additional troops who had been inspired by what had just happened and full of anticipation for what was clearly about to happen.

While Greene was in Virginia, Cornwallis went to Hillsborough where he tried but failed to recruit troops and gather supplies. He had abandoned most of his heavy equipment when passing by Ramsour's Mill, and a little farther along, when marching through the area settled by the Germans, he lost many of his Hessian mercenaries. They deserted and settled down to a comfortable life among new-found friends. As a matter of fact, some of his English-speaking soldiers also deserted and settled down among new-found friends along the way.

When the two opposing armies finally faced each other at

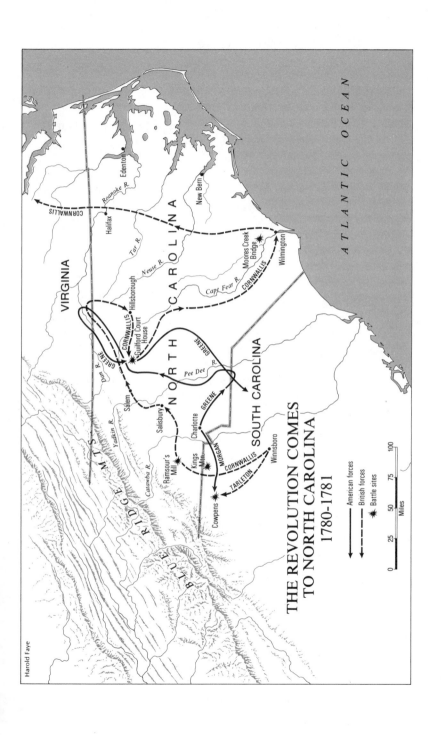

Harold Faye

THE REVOLUTION COMES
TO NORTH CAROLINA
1780-1781

American forces
British forces
★ Battle sites

Miles
0   25   50   75   100

ATLANTIC OCEAN

VIRGINIA

NORTH CAROLINA

SOUTH CAROLINA

BLUE RIDGE MTS.

Edenton
New Bern
Halifax
Roanoke R.
CORNWALLIS
Tar R.
Neuse R.
Hillsborough
CORNWALLIS
Guilford Court House
GREENE
Cape Fear R.
Moores Creek Bridge
CORNWALLIS
Wilmington
Pee Dee R.
GREENE
Dan R.
GREENE
Salem
Yadkin R.
Salisbury
Catawba R.
Ramsour's Mill
Charlotte
GREENE
Kings Mtn.
MORGAN
CORNWALLIS
Winnsboro
TARLETON
Cowpens

Guilford County courthouse on March 15, Greene's force numbered slightly over 4,400, more than half of whom had never been in battle, while Cornwallis commanded 2,253 men, of whom about 2,000 were seasoned veterans. Fighting was fierce on both sides, particularly between the British regulars and the Continentals. Twice the British were turned back with heavy losses, but Cornwallis rallied them himself. After the second time he brought up fresh troops and prepared for a final assault, but by then Greene was satisfied with the damage he had already inflicted, and, determined to preserve his own army, he withdrew, leaving Cornwallis in possession of the field. It was a costly victory for the British, and after it they were weaker than ever.

Nothing was left to do but to move as decisively as possible to repair his losses, so Cornwallis marched through the length of North Carolina to Wilmington, which had been taken by Major James H. Craig a few weeks earlier. As soon as Greene was certain of Cornwallis's movement, he returned to South Carolina to begin freeing that state from the British. Cornwallis was reported to have been deeply hurt that Greene did not consider his army worth pursuing. The British were able to get little in the way of supplies and reinforcements in Wilmington, so Cornwallis had to consider what his alternatives were. It was obvious that he could not take North Carolina, so he thought about returning to South Carolina and beginning all over again. When it occurred to him that that would be admitting defeat, he decided to bypass North Carolina. After taking Virginia it would be a simple matter to return at his leisure to take and hold North Carolina. Preparing to depart, Cornwallis proclaimed the restoration of royal authority in the colony and turned over the ''restored'' government to Josiah Martin even though the area in which he might effectively operate hardly exceeded the narrow confines of the little town of Wilmington. Martin must have been thoroughly chastised by his experiences in the state, and shortly after Cornwallis left, he said that he was ill and boarded the first ship bound for England.

The British marched out of Wilmington on April 25 in the direction of Virginia. Loyalists and other camp followers plundered farms and plantations along the way, and it was observed that smoke-blackened chimneys marked their route. In Virginia Cornwallis went to Petersburg where he began an unsuccessful pursuit of Lafayette to the north. He retired to Richmond and then moved down the penninsula to Williamsburg. Expecting assistance from the British fleet in Chesapeake Bay, he moved to Yorktown but there was bottled up by American and French forces. On October 19 he surrendered and for all practical purposes the American Revolution was over.

The events of the past few years that led to this occasion wrought a remarkable change in North Carolina. From isolation and introspection her people turned to co-operation and concern on a scale completely out of keeping with her past record. Except for the effective flurry of opposition to the Stamp Act and the casual assertion of support for the rights of Massachusetts, few North Carolinians had ever given any indication that they were aware of problems beyond the bounds of their own colony. Suddenly, however, the Edenton Tea Party, the Halifax Resolves, and the Battle of Moore's Creek Bridge demonstrated a new interest and energy. This new spirit, effective though it was, cannot be said to have been indigenous. It flourished under the leadership of men who came into North Carolina from elsewhere. As has already been seen, the three signers of the Declaration of Independence for the state were born in other colonies but had moved to North Carolina between two and twenty years earlier. The first governor of the new state was a native of Maryland. The second had moved from Virginia, and the third was born in Ireland. Revolutionary firebrand John Harvey admittedly was a native of the state, but his successor, Samuel Johnston, was Scottish-born. The list might be expanded indefinitely to include men from other states as well as from Britain, but suffice it to say that the rank-and-file North Carolinian responded to this leadership. Whether they consciously willed it or not, the citizens of the state rose to the cause, played significant roles, and for many years afterwards boasted of what they had done. The Revolution briefly roused the state from its lethargy and instilled in her people a temporary sense of pride. Unfortunately the change of character was short-lived.

5

Independent Carolinians

*T*HE departure of the armies of Greene and Cornwallis left North Carolina at the mercy of many loosely organized, undisciplined bands of armed men, Patriot and Loyalist alike. For more than a year they carried on a relentless civil war, and the state was the victim of about as much pillage, murder, and general disorder as later followed the Civil War. These events largely explain the bitterness many people felt toward the Loyalists, most of whom lived in the Cape Fear River Valley.

The most notorious raider was David Fanning who held a commission as colonel of the Loyal militia from Major Craig in Wilmington. Fanning's activities in North Carolina exceeded those of William ("Bloody Bill") Cunningham in South Carolina. As a partisan leader he was unexcelled on either side in the Carolinas, and as historian Samuel A. Ashe said, "Had he been on the Whig side, his fame could have been more enduring than that of any partisan officer whose memory is now so dear to all patriots." [1] Fanning was said to have had all the dash and daring of Thomas Sumter, the dispatch of Francis Marion, and the resourcefulness of William R. Davie, Patriot leaders of partisan bands who operated effectively against the British in both Caro-

---

1. Samuel A. Ashe, ed., *Biographical History of North Carolina,* 8 vols. (Greensboro: Charles L. Van Noppen, Publisher, 1905–1917), 5:93.

linas. Fanning, however, lacked the moral character that raised these men above his level. He was uneducated and suffered from a disease called the scald head (*porrigo*) which became so offensive that he did not eat at the table with his family and finally had to wear a silk cap all the time so that even his closest friends never saw his head uncovered. Fanning was characterized as crafty, treacherous, cruel, and vindictive. In later life, after he had fled to Canada, he wrote an autobiography in which he boasted that he spared neither age nor sex in warring on his enemies.[2]

Often during the war he led bands of Loyalists on raids in the Carolinas, terrorizing whole regions of both states. He usually commanded his own independent band but sometimes he worked in connection with the marches of Cornwallis or other British leaders. On one occasion he attacked the town of Pittsboro, where a court martial was about to be held, and among his 53 prisoners he took a colonel, a major, a captain, and three members of the General Assembly. His most notable raid occurred about two months later, however, when he dashed into Hillsborough on September 12, 1781, ran out the small force guarding the town, and captured about 200 prisoners including Governor Thomas Burke. He took Burke directly to Wilmington and turned him over to his friend Major Craig, the British officer who had occupied Wilmington in January 1781.

From Wilmington Burke was sent to Sullivan's Island in Charleston harbor where the British had a prison camp. Since Burke was not a soldier, he was regarded as a political prisoner and therefore not eligible for exchange. He was, in fact, held as a hostage for the safety of Fanning. When Burke protested the rough treatment he encountered, he was paroled to another island where he found that he had gained nothing. Here most of his neighbors were Loyalist refugees from North Carolina who regarded him as the symbol of the government responsible for their exile. Every day he was subjected to indignities, insults,

2. David Fanning, *The Narrative of Colonel David Fanning* (Richmond, Va.: Printed for Private Distribution Only, 1861), 92 pp.

and threats of injury, and on one occasion shots were fired into the room that he occupied; although Burke was untouched, one man was killed and another wounded. Burke's appeals to the British commander in Charleston were treated with such indifference that he concluded he had been paroled among these people as part of a scheme to get rid of him in such a way as to relieve the British of any blame for his death. Brooding over his unhappy fate, Burke finally reasoned that having given his word of honor in exchange for protection, the refusal of the British to protect him released him from his moral if not his legal obligation to remain there. In January, therefore, he escaped and returned home to resume his duties as governor. Through the kindness of General Nathanael Greene, Governor Burke offered to secure the release of any British officer in American hands whom the British might designate in exchange for himself. The British refused, wanting only Burke. Burke, of course, refused to give himself up, and shortly afterwards he learned that many American officers, including General Greene, condemned his action in violating his parole. A man's word was sacred, of course, and if he broke it, he was truly disgraced. Burke ceased his attempts to negotiate and, at the conclusion of his term of office, retired to his home near Hillsborough with his wife and young daughter. The humiliation of having broken his parole hung over him for the next two years until he died at the age of 36.

Major Craig evacuated Wilmington on November 18, 1781, removing the last British troops from North Carolina, but the internal strife continued until the departure of Fanning the following May. Nearly a year passed, however, before formal notice was taken of the conclusion of the war. On April 19, 1783, Governor Alexander Martin, a man of varied experience during the Revolution and unrelated to Royal Governor Martin, addressed the legislature on the subject of American independence.

Since the last meeting of the Legislature a Train of great and interesting events have intervened in our political system, which, added to those of the preceding year, have under Almighty God led at length the power of the United America to the summit of her wishes. . . .

The enemy after reiterated attempts to subjugate the Southern States, baffled and defeated in almost every enterprise, compelled to retire into the circumscribed limits of the garrisons of Charleston and Savannah in despair of continuing a fruitless War, have successively abandoned those posts and withdrawn their army, thereby yielding to the States of South Carolina and Georgia the full possession and Sovereignty of all their territories. . . .

With impatience I hasten to communicate the most important intelligence that has yet arrived in the American Continent. His Britannic Majesty . . . acknowledged the United States of America free, Sovereign and Independent, and for himself, his Heirs and Successors relinquished all Claims to the Government, proprietary and Territorial rights of the same. . . . For this most happy and auspicious event, which, involves in it a most precious inheritance for ages and all the blessings that can flow from Independent Empire, with the most lively and heart-felt joy, I congratulate you and thro' you all my fellow-citizens of the State of North Carolina. . . .

On the causes of this great dismemberment of the Empire of Great Britain, by which her first great pillar has been removed and her late might fabrick shaken to the centre, may States and Kingdoms look with awe and tremble for themselves.

Nothing now remains but to enjoy the fruits of uninterrupted Constitutional Freedom, the more sweet and precious as the tree was planted by virtue, raised by the Toil and nurtured by the blood of Heroes. To you, Gentlemen, the representatives of the free, Sovereign and Independent State, belongs the Task, that in sheathing the Sword, you soften the horrors and repair those ravages which war has made with a skillful hand, and thereby heal the wounds of your bleeding Country. Our late revolted Citizens who, through ignorance and delusion, have forfeited their lives but are endeavouring to expiate their crimes by new proofs of fidelity, have fresh claims to your Clemency on this happy occasion. . . .[3]

There were numerous problems, internal as well as external, that had to be solved, however, before Governor Martin's antici-

3. Clark, ed., *State Records of North Carolina*, 16:773–775.

pated golden age could begin. It was up to the assembly to set the priorities. Its first efforts were directed toward providing for the veterans of the war, and many tracts of public land in the west beyond the mountains were surveyed and granted to them. Land had been promised to men who enlisted in the Continental line for the duration of the war. Secondly, through the assistance of General Greene, North Carolina secured the release of prisoners still held by the British, and finally, the assembly turned its attention to the former Loyalists. Governor Martin's strong plea for clemency prompted the legislature to pass a generous Act of Pardon and Oblivion. Nevertheless, exempted from its provisions were those who had accepted commissions and served in the British army, those whose deeds during the Revolution had been so disturbing to the state that they had been cited by name in acts of the assembly confiscating property, those who had left the state with the British armies and not returned within the year prior to the passage of this act, persons guilty of deliberate and willful houseburning, murder, and rape, and three men in particular: Peter Mallet, Samuel Andrews, and David Fanning. Fanning's record, of course, is well known; Peter Mallet was wrongly suspected of disloyalty, but when the truth was known, his name was removed from the act; and Samuel Andrews was a Loyalist officer who served with Fanning after having taken an oath to support the state. It was official policy to forgive and forget what the Loyalists had done, but enforcing such an act was another matter. In many communities these people were never forgiven. Loyalists who returned, expecting to resume their positions in the community, often found themselves ostracized socially and politically, and some of them once more left North Carolina, going to Canada or Florida. In many neighborhoods it was not until a new generation was born and reached adulthood that relations returned to anything like normal. During the War of 1812 against the British, however, recruiting officers reported that their rolls were quickly filled by young men from the heart of the former Loyalist country along the Cape Fear River when a new generation took advantage of an opportunity to demonstrate where their loyalties lay.

Bitter political differences also plagued the newly independent state. Because of the nature of the issues involved, personal feelings were sometimes violently expressed. Currency was one of the bothersome questions, and while some people wanted more paper money, others longed for a stable monetary system. Some people felt that debts owed in Great Britain before the war should be forgotten, while others regarded this as dishonest and immoral. The state's policy with respect to public land was also debated: some people thought the state should dispose of western land to escape the expense of protecting it, while others wanted to sell it or develop it to help pay the public debt. Many people were hostile to the courts and were convinced that they could never get justice under the judges and lawyers who seemed to be in control.

Opposing forces in the state developed into embryonic political parties. One group, called the Radicals, was the party of the debtor class. They demanded more paper money, further confiscation of Loyalists' property, outlawing of British debts, and cession of the western lands. The Conservatives, on the other hand, advocated the opposite in every case.

Still another matter of dispute was the location of a state capital. New Bern was too far east to be convenient for many people, but because of the rivalry among other potential sites, particularly Tarboro, Fayetteville, and Hillsborough, no agreement could be reached. Finally, in desperation, the assembly decided to refer the question to a convention called to meet in Hillsborough in 1788 to debate the new federal constitution. That body adopted an ordinance calling for the capital to be located within ten miles of Isaac Hunter's tavern in Wake County. This had long been a popular stopping place for judges and lawyers traveling the circuit, and it was said that their decision was made because of the good rum punch served at the tavern. The assembly received the convention's recommendation, but three years passed before an agreement was reached to appoint a commission to locate the precise site. Finally in 1792, the state purchased a thousand acres from Joel Lane near the Wake County courthouse and soon laid out in the wilderness a well-planned city named Raleigh, for Sir Walter Raleigh. There were four main streets 99 feet wide and all others were 66 feet. Four public squares, each four acres in size, were reserved in the four quarters of the city while a fifth, in the center, was reserved for the new capitol, the cornerstone of which was laid later in 1792. The building, a three-story brick structure, was plain at first, but a few years later it was enhanced by a covering of stucco and the addition of classic porticos and a cupola. Inside, a significant work of art graced the building. Space had been reserved on the first floor under the dome for a statue of George Washington, and Thomas Jefferson's advice was sought concerning a sculptor. He recommended an Italian, Antonio Canova, regarded as the world's foremost sculptor, and in due time, thanks to transportation by the young United States Navy, a brilliant white-marble statue of a seated Washington, attired in a Roman toga, was installed. This was promptly acclaimed as the most precious work of art in America, and many travelers through the south made a point of visiting Raleigh to see it.

In 1786 before the national constitution was drawn up, a North Carolina state court handed down a significant opinion that was to have a place in American jurisprudence. The assembly in 1785 passed an act prohibiting courts from hearing suits for the recovery of property when the title to that property was derived from the confiscation laws. Under these laws, passed in the face of urgent wartime conditions, the property of many Loyalists was sold for the dual purpose of driving undesirable residents out of the state and also providing necessary funds for prosecuting the war. Title to this property was guaranteed by the state. Nevertheless, Mrs. Elizabeth Bayard of New York, daughter of Samuel Cornell, a Loyalist merchant of New Bern before the war, brought suit for the recovery of property in New Bern that Spyres Singleton had purchased from the commissioner of confiscated property. The case was called at New Bern in May 1786, and an impressive array of lawyers appeared. Abner Nash, representing Singleton, cited the law of 1785 and moved that the suit be dismissed. Mrs. Bayard's lawyers, chief of whom was James Iredell, opposed the motion. Citing the

Declaration of Rights, a part of the state's 1776 constitution guaranteeing jury trial "in all Controversies at Law respecting property," her lawyers argued that the law of 1785 violated the state constitution and, therefore, was null and void. The court was impressed by this argument and declined to dismiss the action. It ruled unanimously that the act of the legislature in 1785 was clearly in conflict with the constitution and therefore must "stand as abrogated and without any effect." This decision in the case of *Bayard* vs. *Singleton* had far-reaching influence. It was the first reported case in which an act of a legislature was declared unconstitutional, thus becoming a precedent for one of the fundamental principles of American constitutional law.[4]

None of the states supported the national government with much enthusiasm under the Articles of Confederation. There were many reasons for this, among them was the fear of small states that they would be overwhelmed by the larger states. Maryland even refused to ratify the Articles until assured that Virginia would surrender her claim to the lands northwest of the Ohio River. North Carolina, with western lands extending to the Mississippi River, was one of the large states and was therefore frequently pressed to relinquish control of the region beyond the mountains to Congress. The idea was discussed in the state from time to time and various proposals were made by which she might comply with the wishes of the small states. In the fall of 1782 it was hinted by some of the state's leaders that this might be accomplished if the ceded lands could be disposed of so as to reduce the state's share in the national debt; if the state's quota of Continental expenses was credited with the total expense of the Indian expeditions of 1776–1777; and if the territory released ever became a separate state, that it must accept a portion of the public debt in proportion to the value of the land it contained. In 1783 it was pointed out that there probably would be little land left to cede once the state had finished making grants to Revolutionary War veterans. The subject remained a live issue, nevertheless, and in April 1784, the month after Virginia

4. Connor, *North Carolina, Ancient Commonwealth,* 1:395–396.

ratified a deed ceding her western lands to the United States, the General Assembly of North Carolina made a conditional offer to do the same thing. There were strings attached, to be sure, but two provisions were very generous and forward-looking, while the third was an indication of the uncertainty that prevailed in the state over the whole question. The ceded land, the assembly said, must be considered as a common fund for the use and benefit of the whole nation. Second, if a state was ever created in the ceded territory, it must be "a distinct republican state" and have the same rights and powers as the other states. The third proviso was that the offer terminated in one year if Congress did not accept the cession, while in the meantime North Carolina retained sovereignty over the area.

Almost at once objections were raised. Political leaders said that the state's credit should be well established before she became so generous with valuable resources. The state debt ought to be paid before anything was done by North Carolina that might help reduce the national debt. It was also pointed out that the act contained no reference to the cost of the Indian expeditions during the war. When the legislature met in October, only six months after the tentative cession offer had been made, the act was repealed. Since the option given the national government still had six months to run, the assembly was severely criticized. Legislator Allen Jones remarked: "We cannot agree in a political capacity to do that which would dishonor us in a private action." [5]

During the period April to October 1784, steps were taken in the western region of North Carolina to organize an independent government as the State of Franklin. This was among the earliest of the separatist movements beginning to appear along the frontier. Vermont was about to break away from New Hampshire, while Kentucky County in Virginia was soon to follow. Discussion of the Franklin movement set people to thinking about the changes that would surely come, and they concluded

5. Archibald Henderson, *North Carolina, The Old North State and the New,* 2 vols. (Chicago: Lewis Publishing Company, 1941), 1:385.

that there was nothing magic in being one of the original thirteen states. The bonds that tied states together, ever so loosely at this time, were capable of expansion.

Scotch-Irish families from piedmont North Carolina moved beyond the mountains to settle the region where the legislature created the counties of Washington, Sullivan, Greene, and Davidson between 1777 and 1783. In 1784 the legislature chartered Nashville as the seat of Davidson County, afterwards to become the capital of Tennessee. These people were independent by nature, many had fought against the Loyalists at King's Mountain, and they soon resented the arbitrary power that North Carolina appeared to exercise over them. When word reached the frontier that North Carolina had offered to cede that region to the central government, they set about to organize their own state government. After calling for elections, holding conventions, and going through other formalities which they persisted in even after North Carolina withdrew the offer to cede the land, they drew up a constitution modeled on the one of their mother state. A memorial to Congress seeking admission to the Confederation as an equal of other states was not approved. Nevertheless, Franklin was an effective state. Elections were held and an assembly convened. John Sevier was elected governor while sheriffs took office and collected taxes. North Carolina exerted a steady pressure on the people of the region to give up their pretense of statehood. By forgiving the people their overdue taxes, by granting favors to some of the local political leaders, and by threatening to use force, North Carolina undermined the government. In 1787 people in those four western counties elected representatives to the North Carolina legislature. On March 3, 1788, when Sevier's term of office expired, there was no legislature to elect a successor, and the State of Franklin collapsed. In August 1789 Sevier was elected to the North Carolina senate from Washington County.

The peaceful solution of this problem disappointed England, France, and Spain, as they anxiously stood on the sidelines waiting for the American states to begin fighting among themselves. These foreign nations who knew the region well had expected to move in and pick up the pieces. Citizens of other frontier communities took heart from the ease with which a government had been formed and realized that in time they would succeed where these people had temporarily failed.

In 1790, the year after North Carolina finally ceded her western territory to the new United States, that region, together with Kentucky, which Virginia had ceded in 1786, was organized as "The Territory South of the Ohio." Four years later the region was divided, the southern portion becoming the Territory of Tennessee, and in 1796 Tennessee was admitted to the Union as a state.

The Articles of Confederation, ratified near the end of the Revolution, were recognized as inadequate in many respects, and a convention that met in Philadelphia in May 1787 devised a new form of government. It was this body that produced the Constitution of the United States. North Carolina delegates were Alexander Martin, Richard Dobbs Spaight, William R. Davie, Hugh Williamson, and William Blount. Blount and Spaight were natives of the state, Martin and Williamson were natives of New Jersey and Pennsylvania, respectively, while Davie was born in England. Except for Martin all were in favor of a strong central government.

In the Convention North Carolina delegates generally sided with the large states, but on several occasions they made concessions to the small ones. They voted with the small states, for example, to provide equal representation in the Senate rather than representation based on population. Williamson mentioned that he and his colleagues accepted equality in the Senate on condition that money bills originate in the lower house. North Carolina also contributed to the rejection of a combination of wealth and population in determining representation in the lower house; it was Williamson who moved that it be based on free and slave population. The antislavery interests were opposed to counting slaves at all, while South Carolina and Georgia demanded that they be counted equal to whites. North Carolina, contrary to her own best interests in gaining a larger congressional delegation, supported the $3/5$ compromise by which five blacks were counted equal to three whites. This was a generous move on the part of the state, since she had around 100,000 slaves, only slightly fewer than South Carolina but more than three times as many as Georgia.

The idea of providing for impeachment of officers was first suggested by Williamson. He moved, and it was seconded by Davie, that the executive be removable on impeachment and conviction of malpractices or neglect of duty. And in the course of events a native North Carolinian, Andrew Johnson, became the only president to be impeached. After a committee had recommended a ¾ vote, Williamson proposed the ⅔ vote necessary to override a presidential veto in Congress.

When word of the new Constitution reached the state, forces of opposition and support polarized. Small farmers in the backcountry were almost universally opposed, while the people of the east, especially those who lived in the towns, favored it. This was the same division that had marked the Radicals and Conservatives, and now party names came into use. Conservatives who favored the new Constitution came to be called Federalists because they believed that a strong federal government would protect property, stimulate trade, stabilize the currency, and pay the national debt. On the other hand, the Anti-Federalists were content with conditions as they were, particularly the freedom that each state enjoyed in managing its own affairs.

Opposition to the Plan of Government, as the Constitution was called, formed in North Carolina even before the Convention finished its work. Hugh Williamson wrote home urging friends to elect legislators favorable to the idea of a strong central government. Yet in spite of this suggestion, Radicals gained a majority in both houses. Nevertheless, when the legislature met in November 1787, it called for a convention in Hillsborough in July 1788 to determine whether North Carolina would approve the new government. The text of the Constitution had already appeared in the *State Gazette of North-Carolina* of October 4, 1787, but the legislature also ordered it printed as a pamphlet for wider distribution so that still more people could read it. The campaign to elect delegates to the convention was hotly contested. James Iredell, a native of Sussex County, England, but a resident of North Carolina for twenty years, was one of the most vigorous supporters of the new form of government. He wrote several pamphlets in its support and he and Davie collaborated on another. These were widely read both in the state and elsewhere.

Among state leaders who were opposed, Willie Jones was perhaps the most vocal. He was a native of Virginia, educated at Eton College in England, and a resident of North Carolina for about thirty-five years. In spite of his aristocratic background he was not a Federalist. He advocated "an independent state democracy administered along fraternal lines and with just so much connection with the other states as to insure peace between them." [6] The Anti-Federalists had a majority of one hundred in the convention, and as a matter of economy Jones moved on the third day that a vote be taken. Iredell objected and Jones yielded. The burden of the debate was thrown on the Federalists who were forced to answer penetrating and embarrassing questions. Jones and his friends opposed the potential arrogation of power by the proposed new government as reflected in the words "We the people." Why not "We, the delegates of the people" or "We, the states," Jones and his friends asked. It was clear that a consolidated government was intended. Judge Samuel Spencer, another Anti-Federalist, inquired why there was no bill of rights, and later he showed concern about the operation of a system of federal courts within the bounds of the state. Anti-Federalists also opposed the right of Congress to levy direct taxes, fearing that the poor people of the state would be crushed by the burden of federal taxes. They also feared the arbitrary action of countless appointed federal officials far removed from any control by the people.

North Carolina declined by a vote of 184 to 84 to adopt the United States Constitution in August 1788. The convention rec-

6. Blackwell P. Robinson, "Willie Jones of Halifax," *North Carolina Historical Review,* 18 (April 1941): 147.

ommended that a bill of rights be added to it and it also proposed more than twenty-five amendments. Since eleven states had already ratified, it was obvious that North Carolina's action would not prevent the formation of the new government. Jones commented that Thomas Jefferson had expressed the hope that several states would decline to approve the Constitution and thereby call attention to the need for amendments. This, it seems, explains what lay behind much of the opposition. That North Carolina expected to join the new nation in due time may have been revealed in the convention's resolution calling on the state to collect customs duties on imported goods at the same rate as that set by Congress. Duties so collected were turned over to the new national government.

New York and Rhode Island had not yet ratified the Constitution but New York soon did so. North Carolina and Rhode Island, however, remained outside the Union. This was an embarrassing situation for the Federalists, and they launched a campaign of education to reverse the decision of the Hillsborough convention. A flood of petitions convinced the assembly in November 1788 that a second convention on the same subject was in order. The Anti-Federalists were overwhelmed, and a resolution was passed calling for a convention to meet in Fayetteville on November 16, 1789.

Two events occurred in the spring of 1789 that made the work of the Fayetteville convention a bit easier. In May the new Congress took up the question of amendments to the Constitution, and in June Iredell and Davie, at their own expense, published the debates of the Hillsborough convention. They had had the foresight to employ a reporter to record the debates, realizing all along that whenever they spoke, they were speaking for the record.

The debates of the second convention were not reported. Everything that needed to be said had already been said in Hillsborough. Delegates had read those debates and made up their minds how they would vote before leaving home. This time the Constitution was ratified by a vote of 195 to 77.

For a long time it was said in North Carolina that the Constitution was rejected because it did not have a bill of rights and that it was accepted only after the first ten amendments had been adopted. The second convention was called, however, six months before Congress took up the question of amendments. The proposed amendments were then submitted to the states in September, but when the Fayetteville convention organized, not a single state had acted on them. North Carolina, therefore, approved the identical document on November 16, 1789, that it had rejected on August 4, 1788, but now it was apparent that the Bill of Rights was about to be added. Rhode Island held out until May 29, 1790. North Carolina ratified the ten amendments on December 22, 1789, but the amendments did not become effective until December 15, 1791. The state's delay in 1788 undoubtedly accomplished what Jefferson had sought in dramatizing the need for a bill of rights. It also meant that North Carolina had no voice in the election of George Washington as the first president and, of course, was not represented in the first session of the first Congress when the new government was inaugurated.

The state had emerged from the Revolution relatively unscathed by the British, but the Loyalists' activity during the war left scars so strong that years would be required to erase them. Other problems posed by a heavy state debt, vast tracts of western land, and a people sharply divided along economic, social, and political lines demanded the attention of the state's leaders through the final years of the eighteenth century and into the next. Because of her occupation with such internal questions as these, many of which were the result of a government that left a large portion of the people virtually unrepresented in the legislature, North Carolina began to turn inward and appeared to national observers to be withdrawn from the world and asleep.

6

The Sleep of the Innocent

NORTH CAROLINA accepted the federal Constitution more or less on faith yet with great confidence that the pending Bill of Rights would protect her and her people from the rash actions of a government that was remote from local control. Her uncertainty grew out of long years of experience with an even more remote power in London, but the anticipated guarantee of many of the same rights that were mentioned in the Declaration of Rights in her own state constitution was assuring enough that she was willing at least to give the new government a trial. Since Federalists in each of the states had been responsible for the adoption of the Constitution by their states, it was they who inaugurated the new government. Federalism flourished briefly even in North Carolina. Both senators and three of the five congressmen that she sent to the second session of the first national Congress were Federalists. When they took their seats, they discovered that Alexander Hamilton's program to form a strong national government was being discussed. This was not to their liking nor, they reasoned, would it be to their constituents'. Hamilton's plan to centralize power in the hands of the federal government distressed them, and they were disturbed by the tendency of the Federalist party to support a loose interpretation of the provisions of the Constitution. Such a policy would place more power in the hands of national officials than North Carolinians thought necessary or desirable.

Reaction against Federalism was demonstrated in the state by the refusal of members of the House of Commons in 1790 to take an oath to support the federal Constitution. The legislature also passed a vote of thanks to a state court of equity for refusing to obey a writ of the federal district court ordering the transfer of a case from state to federal jurisdiction. Since United States senators were elected by the General Assembly, that body also undertook to instruct the senators in their duties as the state's representatives. The state legislature clearly distrusted and feared the federal government. North Carolinians had a long tradition of resenting and even rejecting orders issued by outsiders, and they regarded the threat of federal directives as potentially just as oppressive as any that had come from England during the colonial period.

This feeling was not confined to the Republicans, as the old Anti-Federalists under the leadership of Thomas Jefferson were now being called. William R. Davie and Samuel Johnston, long-standing Federalists, also became concerned. Even James Iredell, whose appointment to the Supreme Court by Washington in 1790 was a source of pride to the state, quickly became suspicious of the growing power of the national government. He pointed out that the course the government appeared to be taking was not one that he had anticipated in 1788 or 1789. Justice Iredell's dissenting opinion in 1794 in the case *Chisholm* v. *Georgia* took issue with his Federalist colleagues who held that a private citizen of one state could sue another state in federal court. Iredell maintained that each state was still sovereign as to all powers that it had not specifically delegated to the federal government, and he described the federal Constitution as a compact between sovereign states. Iredell's view was widely hailed throughout the young nation, and it led to the adoption of the Eleventh Amendment depriving federal courts of jurisdiction in cases against a state by a citizen of another state.

The further decline of Federalism in the state was hastened by the death of some of its old defenders. A few moved from North

Carolina to other states for a variety of reasons, not the least of which was their search for a more compatible political climate. Republican use of the patronage removed still other Federalists from the state, as in the case of William R. Davie, who was appointed by President Jefferson to negotiate an Indian treaty, and John Steele, who retained his position of comptroller of the United States treasury.

One of the most significant steps taken by North Carolina in the late eighteenth century came as a result of a directive in the 1776 state constitution. Article XLI directed that "all useful learning shall be duly encouraged and promoted in one or more universities." It was a nearly verbatim extract from the constitution recently drawn up by Pennsylvania. At the beginning of the Revolution there were only nine colleges in the thirteen states and of them only the College of Philadelphia (later the University of Pennyslvania) was nonsectarian. The idea of the state university was a new concept, and the University of North Carolina was the earliest to be established. After several attempts to carry out the constitutional directive, a bill introduced by William R. Davie was passed by the General Assembly in 1789 with the aid of men who had recently secured the adoption of the federal Constitution. Its preamble noted that "in all well regulated Governments it is the indispensable duty of every Legislature to consult the Happiness of a rising generation, and endeavour to fit them for an honourable discharge of the social duties of life, by paying the strictest attention to their education." [1]

The Board of Trustees met promptly and began laying plans for the institution. A site was selected near the center of the state where two important roads crossed, where there were springs of clear water, and where local farmers consented to give a substantial area of land. An old Anglican chapel at the crossroads known as New Hope Chapel Hill gave the site the name of Chapel Hill. The cornerstone of the first building was

1. R. D. W. Connor, ed., *A Documentary History of the University of North Carolina,* 2 vols. (Chapel Hill: University of North Carolina Press, 1953), 1:23.

laid on October 12, 1793, and formal opening exercises were held on January 15, 1795. The course of study was intended to prepare young men for lives of service to their community, the state, and the nation. The university graduated countless young men who became governors, not only of North Carolina but also of nearly every other southern state and of others as far away as Oregon. Congressmen, cabinet members, ambassadors, and one president, James K. Polk, are numbered among the alumni. After a few years the effects of university training were reflected in many new programs inaugurated and successfully operated in the state.

In anticipation of the opening of the university several private preparatory schools were established in the state to qualify young men for college. Shortly after it opened, the university also established a school of its own adjacent to the campus where young men might remedy deficiencies in their earlier education that had been discovered by the college "masters," as faculty members were called. A number of the university's early supporters were men of strong Federalist sympathies, and the new institution soon acquired a reputation as a hotbed of Federalism. Because of this, Republicans in control of the state legislature attempted to remove some of the sources of income enjoyed by the university. Their action was appealed to the courts of the state, and in the case of *University* v. *Foy* the power of the legislature to strangle the university was denied. The university, although chartered by the legislature, was established under a section of the state constitution, an authority higher than the legislature. The legislature could not withdraw support or deny further support for an agency created by the will of the people. This decision preceded by nearly twenty years the better known Dartmouth College Case in which the same basic principle was upheld.

Despite its good record in providing leaders in its early days, the University of North Carolina catered to the elite. Opportunities for preparatory education were available only to the children of weathy families. Since higher education could be had only outside the state prior to 1795, it undoubtedly was with the full knowledge that they were benefiting their own pocket-books when elitest legislators pushed through the bill to charter the university. Sending their sons to a university in the state would be less expensive than sending them away. The trustees who planned the course of study surely knew who their patrons were, but it was their hope, nevertheless, that the faculty might instill a philosophy of public service in the rich young men who came under their influence. In this the trustees and faculty were successful. Many of the early professors were graduates of Princeton and Yale, and they brought new ideas and ideals to the future leaders of the state. Although it may have been established to serve the wealthy, the university became the source of dynamic leadership that benefited a wide range of people.

North Carolina's intellectual life received a further stimulus in the waning years of the eighteenth century with the establishment of the first in a series of influential newspapers. The first newspaper within her bounds began publication in 1751. James Davis, a printer enticed to the province from Williamsburg, Virginia, in 1749 opened the first printing press in the colony when he was employed by the government to print official matter. As time permitted, he was allowed to print for the public as well. In the period before the American Revolution there were only two other presses in North Carolina, but by the end of the century about twenty-five printers had worked at one time or another, including some who printed in French, German, and Gaelic. Congressman Nathaniel Macon, a conservative Republican, is credited with the establishment of the partisan press in the state, however. In Congress he was impressed by the diligence of an Englishman, Joseph Gales, who was working as a shorthand reporter. Gales had owned a newspaper and printshop in England, but his support of the local working class and his concern for broadening the suffrage had gotten him into trouble. He was obliged to flee his native country, and he arrived in Philadelphia in 1795 with his family. He established a newspaper there and soon was outspokenly critical of a number of national policies that also displeased North Carolina congressmen, Nathaniel Macon among them. At Macon's urging

Gales was persuaded to leave Philadelphia for Raleigh, the new capital of North Carolina, and establish a newspaper there to combat Federalism in the state. The first issue of his new paper, the *Raleigh Register,* appeared on October 22, 1799. The newspaper that Gales sold in Philadelphia moved to the new capital when it was established in Washington and there it became the *National Intelligencer.* As soon as he could afford to do so, Gales purchased an interest in the Washington paper, and his son, Joseph, Jr., joined the staff as congressional reporter. In 1810 the younger Gales became sole owner, and under his guidance it soon achieved a national reputation for its broad coverage and its accuracy. The Raleigh paper immediately upon its establishment became the mouthpiece of the Jeffersonian Republican party in the state, and in due time with the national renown of his son's paper in Washington and his own good paper in Raleigh, the two men enjoyed a reputation for journalistic excellence. Joseph, Jr., arranged to secure news reports from the north ahead of his competitors and by special courier rushed them down to Raleigh so that the *Raleigh Register* often published national news a week or more ahead of other papers in the state. Extensive files were preserved of both newspapers and they have been widely used by historians of the early and mid-nineteenth century. From the Galeses' day to the present, North Carolina has had a long run of good newspapers, many of which attracted national attention. The state also has produced some outstanding journalists, among whom are Edward R. Murrow, Tom Wicker, Charles Kuralt, Lou Harris, and Josephus and Jonathan Daniels, father and son.

When Republicans came to power, they set about to reform the system of courts in North Carolina. Previously court had been held only once or twice a year at district court towns; there were six such towns at first, but the number increased from time to time. In 1806 a state law created superior courts in every county, but this was opposed by lawyers who were accustomed to riding the circuit with judges, picking up clients at each session. In some places public meetings were held, with people sometimes defending and sometimes attacking the new system.

One of the backcountry Republicans who defended the old system was Felix Walker, a rising young politician who later became famous for a frivolous reason. As a congressman he was once making a long and boring speech of interest to no one except, by some stretch of imagination, a few of his constituents back home in the mountains of Buncombe County, North Carolina. When he was chided about his performance, Walker replied that he was merely "talking for Buncombe," and from that remark the word "bunk" was added to our language. Everything he said had clearly been just a lot of "bunk," his fellow congressmen concluded.

A continuing problem that had its origins in the eighteenth century concerned the Indians in the extreme western region of the state. Griffith Rutherford's campaign during the Revolution had quieted them for a time, but in 1784 when Samuel Davidson moved into the Swannanoa River Valley, he was immediately murdered. The next year a small band of settlers was established there with little difficulty. Thereafter followed the steady belligerent push of pioneers, and the arrival of friendly traders, missionaries, teachers, and Indian agents. Reduced hunting grounds and the exposure to a more comfortable agrarian economy changed the pattern of Indian life. The invasion of whites could not be resisted, and late in 1785 United States commissioners and Cherokee Indian representatives agreed on a division of land. The main valley of the French Broad River was to be left to the Cherokees, but land along the Swannanoa River nearly to the site of Asheville, as well as elsewhere in the region, was opened to whites. This included the territory of all or most of five modern counties. Within two years North Carolina was ignoring the treaty and granting land that lay in the Indians' territory. In 1791 the treaty was revised to the white man's benefit, a pattern that was repeated again and again until 1835 when Indians, as individuals, were required to take out land grants just as whites were instead of having free range over large tracts. From time to time the question was raised whether North Carolina or the United States held title to land released by Indian treaties in which federal commissioners participated. In cases heard before both state and federal courts it was established that Indians had the right of occupancy only; and although the state employed federal agents in making treaties, land released by Indians reverted to the state. Under President Jackson a federal policy was implemented of moving Indians to remote places beyond the Mississippi. General Winfield Scott was sent into the mountains and established his headquarters in eastern Tennessee to round up the Cherokees and march them away. He had under his command about 7,000 troops to find about 3,500 Indians.

Under the leadership of an old man named Tsali (or Charley) about a thousand Indians revolted against the inhumanity of the soldiers. An agreement was reached that if Tsali surrendered, a plan would be worked out to permit his followers to remain. Whether Tsali surrendered or was betrayed is debatable. Nevertheless he and a few of his relatives were executed, and the rest of the rebels were permitted to remain. They were granted United States citizenship, and arrangements were made by William Holland Thomas, their white chief, to purchase land for each family. This was the origin of the Qualla Boundary or Cherokee Indian reservation still maintained in southwestern North Carolina.

The Cherokee tribe is the only one in the state to retain its language and culture, but Indians of unknown heritage are found in many places. There are at least one hundred Indians in twenty-six of the state's one hundred counties, and a total Indian population of 44,406 in the whole state. Only the states of Arizona, California, New Mexico, and Oklahoma have a larger Indian population than North Carolina. In 1971 the state legislature created a Commission of Indian Affairs to study and recommend ways in which Indian citizens of the state might be assisted. The commission also co-ordinates the distribution of federal funds in the state.

During the first decade of the nineteenth century Americans were aware that British agents continued their friendly contacts with Indians on the frontier. From British forts in Canada guns and ammunition found their way into Indian hands. This was a disturbing thing, of course, and it took on new significance when viewed in the light of events on the high seas during a war between England and France. Each of these nations began searching American ships on the pretext of looking for their own nationals. Britain did this frequently, and in pretending to take her own she actually took some American citizens. Attempts at negotiation failed, and war seemed inevitable. American resistance to war was strong, but it was finally worn down and war was declared in June 1812. An alliance of congressmen called War Hawks was largely responsible, and one of these was a native North Carolinian and an alumnus of the university—William Rufus King. King later moved to Alabama, was minister to France and to Russia, and became vice-president of the United States in 1853. The War of 1812 was not popular, and as in the later war in Vietnam, there were many outspoken critics. Newspaper editors in the state were divided with some condemning the war and others supporting it, sometimes enthusiastically. Descendants of Highland Scots, of course, enlisted readily. The state also furnished a handful of national heroes. Lieutenant Colonel Benjamin Forsyth, a regular army officer, was killed in the fighting at Odelltown near the Canadian frontier, and like General Nash of the Revolution he became a hero to the people at home. The state granted a ceremonial sword and $250 annually for seven years to James Forsyth, his eight-year-old son. Otway Burns, commander of a merchantman before the war, became one of the best known privateers in the war, bringing in many cargoes of great value and terrifying British shipping up and down the Atlantic coast. Captain Johnston Blakeley, a native of Ireland who was brought to North Carolina as an infant, attended the university briefly before enlisting in the navy after his family's fortune failed. He served under such notables as Dale, Preble, Decatur, and Rodgers, and during the War of 1812 he commanded several important ships. Operating in the North Atlantic and in the English Channel, Blakely sent home a number of prize ships but finally disappeared at sea without a trace. In gratitude for his service, the State of North Carolina provided funds for the education of his only child, a daughter, and gave her a handsome silver tea service. After the death of the last member of the family, the tea service came back to North Carolina and is now held by the North Carolina Museum of Art.

In August 1814, after landing from ships anchored in Chesapeake Bay, British troops marched into Washington and set fire to the Capitol, the president's house, and the executive office. Dolley Payne Madison, wife of the president and native of Guilford County, North Carolina, paused long enough before fleeing the executive mansion to cut a portrait of George Washington from its frame and roll it up for safekeeping. She also managed to gather up the mansion silver and various presidential papers.

The final notable American hero from the state was General Andrew Jackson, whose brilliant victory at the great Battle of New Orleans on January 8, 1815, often pictured in the movies and on television, came a little over two weeks after a treaty of peace was signed but, of course, before the news of it reached the United States. Jackson dramatically repulsed the British, who lost over 2,000 men including their general, Sir Edward Pakenham, while the Americans lost just 71.

The conclusion of the War of 1812 found many parts of the country poised for progress. Liberal ideas prevailed during a period of prosperity that saw industrial growth, educational advancement, and the development of better means of transportation. This, regrettably, was not true in North Carolina. No state in the Union at that time was less receptive to liberal ideas. Although modest signs of progress were evident just before the war, they quickly disappeared. The legislature, tightly controlled by a wealthy class, was unwilling to support a progressive program because it would have to finance it. The common people were poorly educated, and ignorance then, as now, tended to perpetuate itself. Legislators echoed a common sentiment that they picked up from their poor constituents—"what was good enough for grandpa is good enough for us." Early-nineteenth-century leaders of the state, more interested in their own pocketbooks than anything else, simply refused to give serious consideration to any program of public betterment.

For a very short while it appeared that North Carolina might develop a balanced economy with both industry and agriculture. In 1813 Michael Schenck and Absolom Warlick, descendants of German settlers in the piedmont, built a cotton mill two miles east of Lincolnton, the first in the state and perhaps the second in the south. Before long the Battle family also built one on the Tar River at Rocky Mount in the eastern part of the state. Soon more than forty thousand looms in widely scattered parts of the state produced over seven million yards of cloth. This exceeded the total output of both woolen and cotton goods from Massachusetts, but this was a record that soon toppled.

A turning point was reached after the cotton gin was patented in 1794. In 1790 no cotton was exported from the United States, but the availability of Eli Whitney's invention, whereby the seed could be easily separated from the fiber of the cotton, greatly increased the demand. North Carolina along with the other southern states began to devote more and more acres to cotton. Previously only patches had been planted and that was chiefly for home use. In 1794, after the cotton gin had been available for about a year, slightly more than a million and a half pounds were exported, but the next year five million pounds were shipped.

The commercial production of cotton meant several things. First of all, local industry declined as the demand grew for cotton that could be so easily grown in the state. Secondly, the demand for slave labor increased rapidly; heretofore it appeared that slavery was declining. And finally, the demand for new land became a serious problem. Four of the most important crops—corn, wheat, cotton, and tobacco—grew best on new land, and except for tobacco, which remained largely a product of the coastal plain in North Carolina, their production moved into the backcountry as long as any fertile land was available. Getting the most from agriculture meant a steady movement from old fields to new ones. Nature took over abandoned fields in a regular pattern of broomsedge and then pine trees, and after about twenty-five years the land could be cleared and worked again. Many men understood the importance of maintaining the fertility of their fields. Washington, Jefferson, and Edmund Ruffin in Virginia were looked upon as progressive, scientific farmers. North Carolina also had such men, some of whom corresponded with Jefferson and other outstanding agriculturists. Nathaniel Macon, Thomas Ruffin, Josiah Collins, Jr., Henry and Thomas Burgwyn, Abisha Slade, and Kenneth Raynor were among them, not only corresponding to enlarge their knowledge but also writing for agricultural journals, organizing agricultural societies, and going about to demonstrate what they had learned. Such men, however, were rare.

As slave labor was found to be most profitable for the cultivation of cotton and tobacco, other crops were neglected. Food and forage that might easily have been produced at home were often imported, and of course nearly all manufactured goods were. Paul Cameron, a large plantation owner of Orange County, happened to be at the railroad station in Raleigh when he saw wagons there unloading hay from the north for stock in the county as well as in town. Butter from Orange County, New York, he observed, was being sold in his own Orange County.

Because slave labor was available the year round, it was considered more profitable to use it in the fall and winter to clear new fields rather than to fertilize the old. This system produced large areas of eroded land while it also wasted vast tracts of woodland. Such a bleak situation faced many farmers, when they no longer owned any reserve land, that they fled the state.

There were other causes of distressing conditions that prevailed in the state. The old problems of inadequate transportation and other means of communication survived from the colonial era. Landowners who controlled the legislature were reluctant to provide tax support for public education. Instead academies were chartered, exempt from taxation but dependent largely on local generosity for their support, to provide a modest education for those whose parents could pay tuition. The inadequacy of this system was reflected clearly in the census of 1840, when it was revealed that after more than sixty years of independence one-third of the adult white population of North Carolina could neither read nor write. Members of the planter class could afford to educate their own children, and they saw no need to educate others. Laborers generally had no need for education, and if everybody was educated, they reasoned, who would do the work of the world?

Extravagance throughout the nation after the War of 1812 resulted in a panic in 1819, and the severe depression that followed produced widespread suffering in North Carolina. The price of cotton fell by half, land values quickly dropped twenty percent, and bad crops and low prices added to the misery. Economic conditions quickly killed the modest industry that remained.

Any one of these conditions alone may have done so, but it was certainly the combination of unfortunate circumstances that drove thousands of people to leave the state. In 1790, at the time of the first census, North Carolina ranked third in population—only Virginia and Pennsylvania were larger. Between 1800 and 1810 the state narrowly held fourth place, and by 1830 it had dropped to fifth. In 1820 there were only seven towns in the state with more than a thousand people, and five of them had more slaves than free people. The total urban population was just over 16,000, of whom 7,500 were white and 8,800 black. The lack of cities or even modest towns as trading centers contributed to the backwardness of the state. Persons with goods to sell or merchants who wanted to stock their shops were usually obliged to go outside the state. Lack of trade clearly was a serious obstacle to the development of the state.

Between 1815 and 1850 the state was drained of one-third of its population. In 1815 it was estimated by Archibald D. Murphey, an attorney and legislator of uncommon ability, that 200,000 North Carolinians had migrated to Tennessee, Alabama, and Ohio. In 1829 a newspaper correspondent in Asheville reported that from eight to fifteen wagons passed through that town every day bound for the west. Another observer noted that in the 1830s and 1840s on some days he had seen as many as two thousand slaves cross the bridge over the Yadkin River headed south. The editor of the *Greensboro Patriot* one day in 1845 counted nineteen wagons from Wake County passing through Greensboro on the way to the west. The 1840 census revealed that 32 of the 68 counties in the state had lost population. The 1850 census, the first to give figures on interstate migration, revealed the amazing fact that 31 percent of all the natives of North Carolina then living in the United States were living in other states than North Carolina. Because of her indifference to education, neglect of natural resources, reluctance to levy taxes for any public service, and general backwardness, the state had driven away 405,161 people of whom two-thirds were white. About 58,000 had moved to states in which slavery was prohibited, probably in order to escape its evils.

The reluctance of the legislature to levy and collect taxes was merely a reflection of the attitude of a majority of the people in the state toward the proper function of government. Government at best was regarded as a necessary evil; but if it maintained order, protected life, and safeguarded the rights and interests of property, it had done enough. There was a widespread aversion to taxation and a general lack of interest in public works. The legislature, dominated by landowners and slaveholders, encouraged such attitudes. It was happy to avoid taxing either land or slaves.

Political conditions, of course, contributed significantly to the sleepy conditions that prevailed in the state. Political power under the inadequate constitution of 1776 was centered in the least progressive region—the coastal plain. The state had a representative democracy in form, to be sure, yet in practice this was not true. Equal county representation and the reluctance of the legislature to create new counties as the center of population moved out of the east meant that the government was controlled by a small minority of the people, and these were people with a special interest. In 1790 approximately 62 percent of the people lived in the east. Fifty years later only about 49 percent lived there. The population of the east increased a mere 53 percent during that half century but the west increased by 156 percent. Despite the great growth of the west, the east retained its control over state government. In 1830, for instance, there were 64 counties in the state. Of these 36 were east of Raleigh and contained only 41 percent of the voting population, yet they elected 59 percent of the members of the assembly. The voting population of these eastern counties was less than 10 percent of the total white population of the state, yet this 10 percent elected a majority of the legislators by whom laws were made and the governor and other state officials chosen.

Frequently, in order to get new counties created and try to equalize representation, the west resorted to the scheme of selecting the names of popular living eastern leaders for proposed new counties in the hope of getting the support of their friends and admirers. This explains why so many counties in the western part of the state bear the names of eastern politicians. When the assembly yielded, however, it nearly always divided an eastern county so that the west never really gained much in the process. Between 1777 and 1823, 33 new counties were formed; of these 18 were in the west and 15 in the east.

The government of North Carolina remained undemocratic both in form and in spirit. It was tightly controlled by a landed aristocracy, an ultraconservative group that often held the common people in contempt. The legislature grew increasingly indifferent to growing pleas from the west for internal improvements in the form of better means of transportation, for schools, and for constitutional reform. The situation in due time became so thoroughly oppressive that thinking men, those with an inner sense of state pride that could not be contained, began to speak out. They soon discovered that their concerns were also those of others, and from a very small beginning a movement burgeoned that could no longer be stilled by reactionary politicians.

7

Up and Away

WHILE most North Carolinians pursued their own interests, little concerned over the plight of their state, a few men from both east and west had the vision to anticipate the day when conditions would be different. Their activity was ultimately responsible for the rise and development of democracy in the state, and this made possible a liberalized political organization, a system of public schools, improved transportation, and a variety of humanitarian reforms including better care for the poor and aged, the insane, the blind, deaf, and mute, and better treatment of prisoners. Between 1815 and 1840 they laid foundations for the impressive progress witnessed in North Carolina before 1860. The most influential leader was Archibald D. Murphey, 38 in 1815. Judge William Gaston, 39, and president of the university, Joseph Caldwell, 42, also played significant roles. David L. Swain, who became governor in 1832 at the age of 31, and William A. Graham and John Motley Morehead, later governors, were active in the final stages of this movement. Charles Fisher from Salisbury and Edward B. Dudley from Wilmington, both born in 1789, and Bartlett Yancey from Caswell County, four years their senior, had parts to play soon after the movement got under way.

Murphey, born in Caswell County in 1777 and a 1799 graduate of the university, where he also taught for a brief period, was an attorney, a judge, and a member of the General Assembly. He was deeply disturbed by the conditions he observed in the state as he traveled to hold court. Writing to his friend Thomas Ruffin from Fayetteville in April 1819, Murphey said:

> I know ten times as much of the Topography of this Circuit, as the Men who have lived here fifty Years. I had no Idea that we had such a poor, ignorant, squalid Population, as I have seen. Who that sees these People, and those of the Centre and the West, can wonder that we wish to have a Convention [to amend the constitution]? In the Towns are found decent and well informed Men in Matters of Business, Men who look well and live well. But the Mass of the Common People in the Country are lazy, sickly, poor, dirty and ignorant. Yet this is a Section of the State upon which the Hand of Industry would soon impress a fine Character. [1]

Murphey had been aware of such conditions for years and as a member of the legislature had unsuccessfully sponsored legislation to alleviate them. He prepared brilliant reports on the educational needs of the state, and he made recommendations for meeting them. He informed himself of Thomas Jefferson's educational plan in Virginia, he was aware of Pennsylvania's activity, and he had read of the systems of schools in Switzerland and in England. From all of these he drew plans for his native state. Education was not the state's only need, of course, and he introduced legislation designed to provide a system of internal improvements that clearly would have led to agricultural and industrial growth. He certainly was aware of the proposals for national roads, canals, and water transportation made by Secretary of the Treasury Albert Gallatin in 1808, and such features were embodied in his own plan for tying the rivers of the state together by canals and turnpikes. Murphey's reports on education and internal improvements were published and widely read, and many people gradually began to realize what benefits would result from the implementation of his programs. Murphey was a dreamer and an idealist, however, rather than a practical politi-

1. William Henry Hoyt, ed., *The Papers of Archibald D. Murphey,* 2 vols. (Raleigh: North Carolina Historical Commission, 1914), 1:138.

cian, so he was unable to persuade the legislature of the value of his ideas to the point of adopting them and appropriating money to implement them. President Caldwell supported Murphey, and he, too, published pamphlets on these subjects. One of Caldwell's most popular ones dealt with education, and it contained very practical directions for organizing local school committees and planning a course of study; it even had floor plans for a schoolhouse.

The writing of a history of the state was another of Murphey's ambitions. He believed that the people would take pride in their state and have ambition and hope for the future once they understood their past and how they had come to their present sad condition. He sought funds from the legislature for copying documents from British archives, but no appropriation was made. The assembly contented itself with granting him permission to hold a lottery to raise funds for this purpose, but the lottery was not very successful. He was not discouraged, however, and proceeded to draw up a detailed outline and to write at least one chapter. He also discussed his plans with some of the state's leaders, securing their promises of assistance through interviews and the use of their papers. In another respect, Murphey was ahead of his time. He favored the draining of swampy lands in the east as a means of improving the health of people who lived nearby, as well as providing new and fertile land for farming. He advocated the return of free blacks to Africa or their resettlement in free territories. He succeeded in getting favorable action on a bill abolishing imprisonment for debt in 1820, but it was repealed the following year. In 1829 near the end of his life, Murphey, himself, was imprisoned for twenty days when he could not complete payment of a debt he had incurred for the purchase of land.

It became apparent, in the face of the failure of his projects to win support in the legislature, that the first battle to be won was that of constitutional reform. Democratic western counties gave him the most support, but their voice in the state capitol was not strong enough to prevail. The question of reform had first been raised by others, when Murphey was just ten years old, and it

NORTH CAROLINA

A photographer's essay by Bruce Roberts

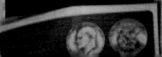

Photographs in sequence

Dirt road near Maxton.
Commercial fishermen on trawler out of Morehead City.
Hang-gliding over Jockeys Ridge, Nags Head.
Skiing on Sugar Mountain.
Surfer off Cape Hatteras.
Shadrack Mace, mountain chairmaker and furniture builder.
Postmistress handing out mail in general store, Valle Crucis.
Mountain man and team between Boone and North Wilkesboro.
Picking cotton near Laurinburg.
Stringing tobacco leaves for flue-curing.
View from Grandfather Mountain in the Blue Ridge.
Pioneer homestead, North Carolina entrance to Great Smoky Mountains
    National Park, Cherokee.
Chatham County Courthouse, Pittsboro.
Downtown Charlotte at dusk.
Low clouds in mountains near Boone.

was mentioned at least twice on the floor of the assembly before Murphey became a member in 1812. When a petition arrived from Rutherford County militia officers in 1816 urging the calling of a constitutional convention, it was referred to a committee of which Murphey was chairman. He made this the excuse for presenting before the legislature a clear and objective review of the history of the state constitution, pointing out the injustices that had developed in its application since 1776. Inequality of representation was the chief flaw of government, he said, and militated against the first principle of a republican system of government. " 'That a Majority should govern,' is one of those first Principles. The Condition of the State has so changed since the Constitution was adopted, that this Principle no longer Operates," he pointed out.[2]

On this subject, as on those of education and internal improvements, he was pessimistic. He said now as he had said before in speaking of other bills: "It will be rejected, but it will draw the public Mind to the Subject." [3] The time was not yet ripe for the realization of his dreams and he understood that. He was merely laying the groundwork, pointing the way, educating the people.

The political situation in North Carolina during the early years of the nineteenth century was completely stagnant. With the final disappearance of the Federalists after the War of 1812, the Republican, or Democratic-Republican, party prevailed, and personal politics flourished. It was not unusual for men to serve long periods of time in elective offices. There were several members of the assembly who held their seats for over twenty years, while one approached thirty. It was a common occurrence for certain families to dominate an office or even a group of offices for long periods as did the Hawkins family in Warren County, the Arringtons in Nash, the Battles, Clarks, and Tooles in Edgecombe, the Speights in Greene, and others elsewhere. The absence of party competition and the influence of large land-

---

2. Hoyt, *Papers of Archibald D. Murphey,* 2:58.
3. Hoyt, *Papers of Archibald D. Murphey,* 1:91.

owning families were largely responsible for backward conditions in the state.

Because she was out of sympathy with many national practices, North Carolina ceased to show any real interest in national politics. Virginia and New York appeared to have an unbreakable hold on affairs in that arena, and North Carolina fell under the domination of Virginia. Some of North Carolina's leaders were natives of Virginia, and they and others sold cotton and tobacco in Virginia markets, while many of the planter class in the northern half of the state went regularly to Virginia for the horse racing season. Social and economic ties brought political imitation in their course. The poorer class was too preoccupied with its own daily affairs to show any interest in events beyond the neighborhood.

In the minds of most North Carolinians Nathaniel Macon personified Republicanism, and people were content to follow his lead. They knew that he had declined a commission during the Revolutionary War and served instead as a private, afterwards refusing to accept any pay or the grant of land for which he was eligible. His long record of public service began in 1780, when he was elected to the first of four terms in the General Assembly. He was also elected to two terms as a member of the council of state, after which in 1785 he was elected to the Continental Congress but declined to serve. Elected to the United States House of Representatives in 1791, he served until 1815 and was speaker during the years 1801–1807 for much of Jefferson's presidency. Macon supported Jefferson in his negotiations for the Louisiana Purchase, and Macon and his Virginia friend John Randolph successfully maneuvered the bill for this purpose through the House. Macon advised Jefferson against the president's attempts to impeach Supreme Court Justice Samuel Chase, but Jefferson persisted. Chase was acquitted, and Jefferson thereafter for a time found Macon's presence irritating. Eventually, however, he recognized Macon's fine qualities when he called him "the last of the Romans." During the period of estrangement Macon supported Randolph in an intraparty struggle with Jefferson. Macon was identified with the faction known as Quids and he was not re-elected to the speaker-ship.

In 1816 Macon moved from the House to the Senate where he served until 1828, being president *pro tem* from 1826 until his retirement. In speaking, Macon was brief and had no patience with showy oratory. He believed that both governments and individuals should avoid debt. He thought that annual sessions of the legislature were essential for democratic government. He was scrupulously honest and open in his actions and favored strict economy in government. In brief he possessed all of the traits which most North Carolinians admired in a man and which they liked to think that they all possessed. Macon's opposition to the impeachment of Chase had demonstrated his support for an independent judiciary. In opposing the Missouri Compromise of 1820, which he regarded as a surrender by the South to the North, he predicted that the region south of the James and Cumberland rivers would form an independent republic. This also appealed to his constituents.

Like most North Carolinians, Macon lived a very simple life. Although he owned several thousand acres of land, he had a very simple house. His clothes were well made of good material, but they were old-fashioned. Although he lived until 1837, he continued to dress in the style of 1776.

Signs of a further split in the Democratic-Republican party began to appear prior to the presidential election of 1824. William H. Crawford of Georgia was favored by Macon and appeared to be the most "Southern" candidate. He was also Virginia's favorite. Charles Fisher of the western town of Salisbury began secretly to organize the opposition, and soon discovered that Andrew Jackson, with strong North Carolina connections, was popular in the western counties and in the Albemarle Sound region where Jackson's stand on the General Survey Bill was acclaimed. The "People's Ticket" developed by Fisher and his friends produced a revolt against the old party by its large vote for Jackson in those two sections of the state. Jackson led in electoral votes nationally but did not gain a majority, so the election was thrown into the House of Representatives, where

Adams was chosen. It was this election that contributed to the split of the old party into two factions at the national level—the National Republicans and the Democratic-Republicans, or Jackson men. At the election of 1828 the eastern politicians supported Jackson, too. Jackson was elected and served from 1829 to 1837, but in North Carolina the west was disappointed that he did not support internal improvements.

The action of two North Carolinians may have been important in Jackson's switch on the question of internal improvements and perhaps even for his choice of his successor as president. Jackson appointed his very good friend John H. Eaton, a native of North Carolina but then a resident of Tennessee, to his cabinet as secretary of war. To be secretary of the navy he appointed John Branch, also a North Carolinian. A few weeks before the appointment Eaton married Margaret (Peggy) O'Neal Timberlake, widow of "a dissipated purser of the navy" who was reported to have committed suicide because of his wife's conduct. She was described as "a witty, pretty, saucy, active tavern keeper's daughter," who freely bestowed her favors on guests at her father's tavern.[4] Peggy Eaton was not socially acceptable to the wives of other cabinet members, and under Mrs. Branch's leadership they shunned her company, refusing to invite her to their dinners and other entertainments. Jackson took this as a personal affront and thought it was a plan to discredit his administration. Martin Van Buren, a widower and secretary of state, was cordial to Mrs. Eaton, however, and he quickly found favor with Jackson. The president parted ways with the vice-president, John C. Calhoun, whose wife was among those refusing to associate with Peggy Eaton. Jackson ceased to look with favor on internal improvements, a special interest of Calhoun's, and soon came around to Van Buren's view—opposition. Since Mrs. Branch was one of the most vocal opponents of Peggy Eaton, Jackson asked for her husband's resignation, which he promptly received. Two other members of the cabinet

4. James Parton, *Life of Andrew Jackson,* 3 vols. (New York: Mason Brothers, 1860), 3:184.

also soon resigned. Van Buren rose rapidly in Jackson's favor and was his handpicked successor at the end of his own second term.

Jackson's clear opposition to internal improvements which both the western counties and the Sound region in North Carolina favored contributed significantly to the split in the Republican party in the state. A new national party, the Whigs, was formed in 1834, and it quickly attracted extensive support in North Carolina. Jackson's followers came to be called Democrats.

At the state level the new Whig party needed to do more than just oppose Jackson. It needed a viable program that would attract support, so it quickly adopted the causes that Murphey had so long espoused—constitutional reform, public schools, and internal improvements. On the first of these the other two depended. Numerous attempts already had been made to secure the passage of bills for a constitutional convention, but they were always defeated on a strictly sectional vote. Westerners resorted to mass meetings at which the subject was discussed and opinion sounded. Unofficial polls taken at elections clearly revealed a great public interest in the question. The refusal of the legislature to act on the wishes of westerners led many newspapers, including some in the east, to lend editorial support to the cause. Public sentiment reached the point of defiance, and revolution came to be mentioned. In Salisbury, the editor of the *Carolina Watchmen* warned that if the legislature of 1834 did not take some positive steps in the direction of constitutional reform, the people of the west would set about to secure an improvement in government for themselves. The editor admitted that this was a dangerous course, but with such virtuous people as those who lived in his region and with the spirit of their fathers during the Revolution still fresh in their minds, he felt confident that their hopes would be met one way or another.

About this time several events occurred in the state that brought unexpected support to the west. The capitol burned on June 21, 1831, and almost before the ashes had cooled, people of Fayetteville set to work to try to have the capital moved there. Raleigh was still only a village, they pointed out. The state had no large trading center, but if the capital were moved to Fayetteville, at the head of navigation on the Cape Fear River, that town would develop into a flourishing metropolis. Since the capital had been fixed by an ordinance of the 1788 convention, it could be changed only by another convention, so the supporters of Fayetteville were willing to call one. The west, of course, won favor with Fayetteville by also advocating the move from Raleigh. Even though Fayetteville was not successful in its efforts, it was grateful to its new western friends for their support.

The other incident which brought the west unexpected assistance came in 1833, when the legislature appointed William Gaston to be a justice of the supreme court. Gaston, a resident of the eastern town of New Bern, was a highly respected lawyer and judge, clearly very well qualified except in one respect—he was a Roman Catholic. The state constitution provided that only those who believed the truth of the Protestant religion could hold office in the state. Gaston's friends, anxious to have this stigma removed, leaving no doubt as to his eligibility, were also willing to support a call for a convention.

It was fortunate for the people of the west that they had a sympathetic governor at that critical juncture. He was, in fact, a westerner, only the third from his section to hold the office since the Revolution and the first Whig. David L. Swain, a native of Buncombe County, an alumnus of the university, and the youngest man ever to be governor of the state, was highly respected because of his even temper, his intellectual ability, and his splendid character. He was a strong advocate of the program of Murphey, who died in 1832, the very year that Swain became governor. The new governor had the knowledge of politics that Murphey lacked, and this knowledge, combined with his office, made him an effective leader.

In 1834 as his last term in office began, Swain addressed the legislature in very plain language on the subject of constitutional amendment. In due time a bill calling for a convention to amend the constitution was introduced and passed the house by a vote

of 66 to 62 and in the senate by 31 to 30. In both houses the
support of the county and borough delegates from Cumberland
County, the site of Fayetteville, and from Craven County, the
home county of William Gaston, was critical.

The convention met in Raleigh in 1835 with a great many
outstanding leaders of the state as delegates. Nathaniel Macon,
77 and retired, was chosen president more for the honor than for
any political implication. Governor Swain addressed the convention, bluntly mentioning revolution if the needs of the west
for adequate representation were not met. The convention settled down to work and produced amendments that established a
senate with representation by districts determined by taxes paid
into the state treasury and a house of commons based on population. Biennial instead of annual sessions of the legislature, a
two-year instead of a one-year term of office for the governor
with eligibility for two successive terms, a popular election of
the governor, and the substitution of "Christian" for "Protestant" in the religious qualification article were proposed. Free
blacks were disfranchised by a very close vote, borough representation was abolished, and some legislative duties were
shifted to local courts. Simple means of amending the constitution in the future were also devised. These amendments, when
submitted to a referendum of the electorate, were approved by a
strictly sectional vote—the west overwhelmingly in favor and
the east equally as strongly opposed. This was the first time a
question of concern to all the people had ever been submitted to
them.

Although the Board of Internal Improvements had been established in 1819 and the Literary Board in 1825, both with invested funds for eventual use, neither had fulfilled the hopes of
the people of the state who badly needed both transportation and
schools. The creation of these boards and funds appears to have
been merely a screen behind which the reactionary legislators
might hide. When approached on such subjects, they could
point to these initial steps and urge their constituents to wait pa-
tiently until funds were sufficient for work to get under way.

Murphey's program of education had helped arouse the people from their lethargy and set the stage for the period of progress that soon opened. Other influences were also at work, of course. A worldwide democratic movement was producing more liberal constitutions in new states being admitted to the Union; the suffrage was being broadened elsewhere; and the Catholic Emancipation Act in England was not unnoticed in the state. School systems were being developed in many other states. Hospitals for the care of the insane were being opened, and one of the national leaders in this field, Dorothea Dix from Massachusetts, visited North Carolina, where she played a leading role in securing passage of an act to establish a state insane asylum. In seeking an engineer to direct the internal-improvements program, a committee visited similar projects already under way in other states and was duly influenced by what it observed. Soon various programs were under way in North Carolina, and young men, new to the political scene, rapidly assumed positions of leadership.

A Whig governor was elected, and that party remained in power until 1851. In 1840 a handsome capitol in Greek Revival style, begun in 1833, was completed with money appropriated on several occasions. Today this building is regarded as one of the finest and best-preserved examples of a major civic building of its style. It was adequate for all agencies of state government until 1888, when the supreme court moved to its own building. In the years since, the expansion of government has resulted in the erection of buildings over several blocks in various directions from the capitol. In 1963 the General Assembly occupied the State Legislative Building and soon afterwards all of the council of state except the secretary of state abandoned the old state capitol for one of the new modern office buildings. In 1977, at the beginning of a new administration, the governor's office returned to the capitol, now restored as nearly as possible to its original condition.

Railroads came to be recognized as far superior to turnpikes and waterways for meeting the state's needs. A group of farmers from several piedmont counties met at William Albright's farm in Chatham County in 1828 and agreed that a rail line running east and west through the middle of the state would serve best for getting goods to market. Unfortunately this group and others like it controlled very little capital or credit. Money was to be found in the towns, and that is where the successful plans were laid. The legislature that convened in December 1835 revised the charter of an inactive group in Wilmington formed two years before, and with this new incentive it pushed rapidly ahead to build a railroad from Wilmington to Weldon on the Roanoke River near the Virginia line. When it was completed in 1840, the 161½-mile railroad was the longest in the world. Yet it served only the heart of the coastal plain, not the backcountry, moving goods between two of the state's most important navigable rivers, the Roanoke and the Cape Fear. The same General Assembly that spurred this activity also chartered a company to construct a railroad from Raleigh to Gaston, just a few miles west of Weldon. Both lines connected with Virginia railroads. Frederick Law Olmsted of New York, going from Gaston to Raleigh in 1853, noted that some new equipment had been added to the line, but the train he happened to be on was old. He occupied what he described as "a full-length lounge, on which, with my overcoat for a pillow, the car being warmed, and unintentionally well ventilated, I slept soundly after dark." He commented that trains had smoking rooms and water-closets, so, he added, "why not sleeping, dressing, and refreshment rooms? With these additions, and good ventilation, we could go from New York to New Orleans by rail without stopping; as it is, a man of ordinary constitution cannot go a quarter that distance without suffering serious indisposition." [5]

The first railroads in North Carolina were undertaken by private corporations that secured their capital from private subscriptions. This same plan was tried elsewhere, but in none of the states was it totally successful. Government assistance was essential to provide sufficient capital. About the time these lines were being laid a surplus developed in the federal treasury

5. Frederick Law Olmsted, *A Journey in the Seaboard Slave States* (New York: Dix & Edwards, 1856), p. 318.

largely because the protective tariff was so high. This was shared with the states, and North Carolina received her first installment early in 1837. She promptly aided the Wilmington-based railroad company, and a few years later the Raleigh and Gaston line also received aid.

Westerners were chagrined that they had no rail service, so they began discussing plans for a line from Charlotte to Danville, Virginia, with a southern extension to Columbia, South Carolina. When easterners heard of this, they were concerned that the two neighboring states might benefit from western trade, so easterners themselves pushed the formation of the North Carolina Railroad Company to build a line from Goldsboro, along a part of the Wilmington and Weldon line, through Raleigh to Charlotte. The bill passed and it was soon called "North Carolina's declaration of economic independence." [6] This line, generally following the route of an ancient Indian trading path, passed through the middle of the state, and the small towns along its route began to grow rapidly. Today they form the Piedmont Crescent with Raleigh as its eastern point, Burlington, Greensboro, Lexington, and Salisbury lying between, and Charlotte at the western point.

The surplus federal revenue that North Carolina received fattened the Literary Fund as well, and a system of public schools following Murphey's plan very closely was adopted early in 1839. The legislature divided the state into districts and established schools in each, supported by county taxes as well as by income from the Literary Fund. Although not a compulsory plan, 61 of the 68 counties adopted it, and within a year more than 630 schools served the state. Since local boards managed the schools, the system was far from uniform, but with the creation of a state superintendent of public schools in 1852, conditions began to improve. As superintendent, Calvin H. Wiley almost single-handedly developed the system of public schools in the state into the best in the nation before the Civil War. The

6. Hugh T. Lefler and A. R. Newsome, *North Carolina, The History of a Southern State* (Chapel Hill: University of North Carolina Press, 1973), p. 366.

Boston Post of May 1, 1856, commented favorably on Wiley's annual report for 1855 mentioning particularly the superintendent's "largeness of views" and his zeal and energy in his accomplishments. As a part of his work he formed a statewide teachers' organization and began publication of a quarterly journal to further the professional growth of teachers in the state. He and other concerned leaders prevailed upon the convention that took North Carolina out of the Union on May 20, 1861, to leave the Literary Fund untouched. During the war the legislature was tempted to draw upon the fund for military purposes, but Wiley always succeeded in saving it. The schools continued to operate under his direction until 1866.

In 1851 Superintendent Wiley issued the first edition of his *North Carolina Reader,* an anthology designed to teach young people the history, geography, and literature of North Carolina, and it went through six editions before 1874. He also was responsible for the addition of a special supplement on the state to Mitchell's *Intermediate Geography* published in Philadelphia in 1856. In every classroom he installed a state map and a chart containing concise information about North Carolina. The practice of exposing all pupils in the public schools to a well-planned course on the history of the state, its geography, and government was instituted almost from the beginning of the system of public schools. For generations thereafter North Carolinians were made aware of their heritage, and the broad knowledge that nearly every North Carolinian had of the state often drew comments of amazement from outsiders. In recent years, however, this policy was dropped by the State Department of Public Instruction and "units" on North Carolina were made optional in general courses devoted to United States history.

Murphey's many concerns had included the "unfortunates" for whom the state provided so inadequately. The poor of a community might receive a modest amount of aid from concerned neighbors, and some counties had poorhouses, but in most places the county court "farmed out" the poor to someone who would care for them at a very low rate, perhaps in return for their labor. The deaf and dumb were often regarded as mentally retarded, and, as in the case of the blind, no means existed in the state for training or educating them. Prisoners often were badly treated, and, as Murphey well knew, men and women frequently received jail sentences for frivolous reasons. Perhaps the insane, however, evoked the most sympathy. Many were confined in county jails and received very little attention. Others were confined to rooms or even chained to beds in their homes or maintained in a small but secure building nearby. Virginia had a private hospital for the insane by 1773, while South Carolina had one in 1822. There also were two state-supported hospitals for the insane in Virginia in 1848.

Citing lack of money, the North Carolina legislature rejected various bills introduced to provide help for the poor, handicapped, and insane before 1835. At the insistence of Joseph Gales and Joseph Caldwell, who were acquainted with the good work of the Pennsylvania Institution for the Deaf and Dumb, a group organized to provide instruction for North Carolina's deaf and dumb, bringing William D. Cooke, principal of such an institution in Virginia, to Raleigh in 1844 to develop a school. The school succeeded so well that Governor John Motley Morehead urged the legislature to establish a state school for the benefit of such afflicted people. In the spring of 1845 the state opened a school for persons between the ages of eight and thirty, adding a department for the blind in 1851.

As early as 1825 the legislature expressed concern over the lack of facilities for the care of the insane when it called for the collection of information on the subject. Two years later, concluding that the cost would be prohibitive, it was suggested that a state prison and asylum might be combined. Not until 1844, when Governor Morehead mentioned the insane and other people who needed state facilities, did the matter come to be seriously considered. Four years later Dorothea Dix of Boston and New York spent three months in the state investigating the treatment of a variety of unfortunate people. The mentally ill, she urged in North Carolina as she had done in other states, should be removed from the dungeons to a state hospital for proper treatment. ''Short excursions, resort to the workshops, carpentering, joining, turning [and] the use of a good library, are aids in advancing the cure of the patient,'' she pointed out.[7] A bill to this effect was introduced in the legislature, but at first it seemed likely to be lost in the mass of legislation bogged down in the disputes between Whigs and Democrats.

While she was in Raleigh, Miss Dix frequently called on Mrs. James C. Dobbin, incurably ill wife of an effective political leader. Her visits cheered and comforted Mrs. Dobbin, and a few weeks later Mrs. Dobbin, on her deathbed, sought assurance from her husband that he would support the legislation Miss Dix so ardently desired to establish a mental hospital. Four days after his wife's death Dobbin made what was described as a great emotional speech which united all factions in the legislature and secured passage of the bill. Taxes were levied for a hospital to accommodate 150 patients, and construction began in 1853.

During this impressive period of social reform and growth, economic and industrial changes also occurred. One of the most significant and certainly the most publicized was the development of gold mining on such a large scale as to attract attention around the world. A little gold was found during the colonial period, but in 1799 in the bed of a stream in Cabarrus County in the western piedmont the children of John Reed discovered a seventeen-pound nugget of gold. It was used as a doorstop in the Reed home for several years before being identified as gold. In the years before 1848 a mine on Reed's farm was reported to have yielded gold worth $10 million. The discovery of gold before 1820 in a number of nearby counties was mentioned in newspapers in Washington, New York, Boston, and elsewhere in the United States as well as in Europe. This brought a flood of speculators to the state. Development companies, using improved methods of mining, were formed. Native and foreign engineers arrived at the many new mines opened throughout the piedmont, and boom towns developed. In addition to native

7. Guion G. Johnson, *Ante-Bellum North Carolina, A Social History* (Chapel Hill: University of North Carolina Press, 1937), p. 712.

workers others of English, Welsh, Cornish, Scottish, Irish, Spanish, Swedish, German, Swiss, Polish, Austrian, Brazilian, Turkish, Mexican, Hungarian, Italian, and Portuguese origin found employment. Slaves were also frequently employed in many jobs. In one mine alone it was reported that workers spoke thirteen different languages.

In 1831 Christopher Bechtler, a German, opened a private mint at Rutherfordton that he and his sons and nephews continued to operate until 1857. In addition to very fine coins with a higher gold content than those of the United States mint, they made many kinds of jewelry for men as well as for women. North Carolina ranked as the nation's leading gold-producing region until the gold rush in California in 1849. Late in 1837 the United States established a branch mint in Charlotte, which continued to operate until 1861, when it was taken over by the Confederate government. After the Civil War it opened again but for assaying only and finally closed in 1913. The Bechtlers' mint, the branch mint, and the mint in Philadelphia together produced over $17.5 million in coins from North Carolina gold.

North Carolina in many respects was on the threshold of true greatness on the eve of the Civil War. Her natural resources were great and beginning to be tapped, while her people were alert to industrial and agricultural opportunities. As factories and mills opened, the agricultural scene changed through diversification. A great many mainline and subsidiary railroads had been laid while turnpikes and plank roads provided transportation in nearly every part of the state. Illiteracy was declining and more newspapers were being published. Native authors were being read. More people were beginning to travel outside the state and to return with ideas for changes and improvement at home. National disputes between the North and the South over the extension of slavery and the old question of the rights of the states under the federal government soon brought an end to the state's progress, however, and many years passed before conditions permitted a resumption of the program begun with such promise just before the middle of the nineteenth century.

8

A State Forced Out
of the Union

B Y 1860 most North Carolinians realized that trouble was brewing and that there was little they could do to avoid it. Sectional differences had steadily worsened for many years over the question of slavery, especially the right of Congress to control the expansion or abolition of slavery in new states. The first serious threat of national disruption over the issue was resolved in the Missouri Compromise of 1820, admitting that state as a slave state and Maine as a free state. Much of the South regarded the compromise as a defeat because slavery was prohibited in that part of the Louisiana Purchase north of 36° 30'. Senator Macon opposed it at every stage. Senator Montfort Stokes and six of the state's western congressmen, on the other hand, voted in favor because of the antislavery sentiment in the region they represented. For a generation afterwards states were admitted to the Union in pairs to retain the precarious balance in the Senate between slave and free states.

The state was far from unified over the question, however, as there were many who were strongly opposed to slavery. On the other hand there were 34,658 slaveholders most of whom defended the system. In North Carolina various abolition, manumission, and colonization societies existed with more than forty branches and over 1,600 members. Their agents received over 2,500 slaves, many of whom were sent to free states or territories or abroad. Levi Coffin, a Quaker from Guilford County who moved to Indiana and afterward to Ohio, was largely responsible for the organization of the Underground Railroad, which helped slaves to make their way secretly out of the state. Quakers sometimes had small secret rooms in their houses where slaves were hidden until they could be safely sent on their way. North Carolinians had close connections with receptive organizations in Indiana, and there was frequent passing between the two states.

In 1850 Congress effected a new "compromise" by which, among other provisions, California was admitted as a free state, breaking the equal balance of slave- and free-state representation in the Senate, but the South secured a national fugitive-slave law that was expected to result in the return of runaway slaves. The North accepted the parts of the compromise that pleased it, but effectively disregarded the fugitive-slave law, much to the distress of the Southern states.

In 1860 North Carolina had a white population of just under 630,000 and a black population of 361,522, of whom 30,463 were free. Of the other Southern states only Virginia had more free Negroes. In all of the South there were 300 owners of 300 or more slaves, and these 300 were probably millionaires. Of this number there were only three in North Carolina. The census of that year revealed that there were 85,000 farmers in the state, but fewer than 27,000 of them owned any slaves at all. Among the slave owners in the coastal plain about one in twenty owned as many as twenty slaves, while in the piedmont only about one in fifty had that number. Slave owners clearly constituted a small minority in North Carolina, yet they composed a special-interest group with political influence completely out of proportion to its voting strength. It was they, in large measure, who by a close vote, had disfranchised free Negroes at the constitutional convention of 1835. Nevertheless by 1860 the law held that a master no longer owned a slave "body and soul" but only the slave's labor. The slave had the obligation to work, while the master was obliged to feed, clothe, and care for him. These were the terms of a kind of employer-employee relationship.

A North Carolina historian, Professor Archibald Henderson, pointed out in retrospect that an analogy existed in the free states where an employer bought the labor of the employee for regular wages. A mutual obligation also existed there, and it might be defined by a formal contract or by free choice. There were planters concerned about the welfare of their workers just as there were Northern industrialists with concern for the community where their businesses existed. The cruel and arrogant master in the South was matched by the driving and despotic millowner whose workers were bound to him by what Edmund Ruffin called "slavery to want." Apologists for slavery, as Henderson observed, "were on firm ground when they contended that the differences between the voluntary servitude of the masses of industrial workers and the involuntary servitude of the Southern Negroes consisted in a larger degree of economic and social security for the black slaves." [1]

Slavery was not only an economic issue, it was also a moral and social issue. Attempts to restrict its movement into new states reflected the attitude of a large number of Americans most of whom, but by no means all, lived in the North. Hinton Rowan Helper, native of Davie County, North Carolina, held strong antislavery sentiments. He was the author of a very influential book, *The Impending Crisis of the South: How to Meet It,* published in New York in 1857. He was extremely critical of slave owners to whom he applied such terms as "tyrants," "slaveocrats," and "lords of the lash." But his sympathy lay with the poorer whites, not with the slaves. Slavery, he wrote, was a curse that prevented the economic development of the South, and he used statistics in what has been called an unfair and unscholarly way to demonstrate his thesis. Largely because of his words against slavery his book was adopted by the Republican party in 1860 as a campaign document, and over 100,000 copies were circulated. In the South it was regarded as

1. Henderson, *North Carolina, Old North State,* 2:192–193.

inflammatory with the potential to incite poor whites to rise against the slave-owning class. Helper's extreme hatred of Negroes was disregarded by the Republicans, however, and Congressman John Sherman of Ohio endorsed the book. It thereby became the subject of extended angry debate resulting ultimately in Sherman's defeat in his bid for the speakership. In the South the book was condemned, and to own a copy or to read it became a criminal offense. Although Helper's book was clearly an appeal to class hatred, much of what he pointed out was correct.

Many North Carolinians became alarmed in November 1860 at the election of Abraham Lincoln, the Republican candidate, by a minority of the total popular vote although he had a majority in the electoral college. Governor John W. Ellis was advised by his friends to be cautious but firm. W. W. Holden, editor of the influential *North Carolina Standard* in Raleigh, urged the people of the state to "Watch and Wait." Many old Whigs who followed the "states' rights" line maintained that the right of revolution was reserved to the states, but they felt that W. A. Graham, a slave-owning Whig lawyer, former United States senator, secretary of the navy, and governor of North Carolina, was right in maintaining that "the necessity for revolution does not yet exist." [2] Governor Ellis soon after the middle of the month told the legislature that Lincoln's election did not at that moment pose a threat, but

> . . . an effort to employ the military power of the General Government against one of the Southern States would present an emergency demanding prompt and decided action on our part. It can but be manifest that a blow thus aimed at one of the Southern States would involve the whole country in civil war, the destructive consequences of which to us, could only be controlled by our ability to resist those engaged in waging it. [3]

2. Henderson, *North Carolina, Old North State*, 2:211.
3. Noble J. Tolbert, ed., *The Papers of John Willis Ellis*, 2 vols. (Raleigh: State Department of Archives and History, 1964), 2:513.

Ellis firmly advocated secession, but he expected that force would be used to try to hold the Union together. He therefore advised that steps be taken to resist, but when he suggested that a state convention be held, he was running ahead of the sentiment of his constituents. During the final two months of 1860, public meetings were held in a great many counties where every imaginable point of view was expressed. North Carolinians were disturbed about national events, although they had no clear vision of what action they should take. Real affection was expressed for the Union at the same time concern was demonstrated over the possible use of force by the national government against the Southern states. After South Carolina seceded on December 20, a wave of enthusiasm for secession swept North Carolina, yet when the legislature recessed for Christmas two days later, no action had been taken. Many old-time Whigs still hoped that the sectional differences might be resolved peacefully.

Shortly after the first of the new year citizens of Wilmington were rebuffed when they sought the governor's approval of their plans to seize Fort Caswell and Fort Johnston at the mouth of the Cape Fear River. Ellis wanted to do nothing to antagonize the federal government so long as the state remained in the Union, but on January 8 without official authorization, some men of the Cape Fear region aided by state troops seized the forts anyway. Governor Ellis promptly ordered them returned to federal control.

By the first of February seven states of the Lower South had seceded, and on the fourth, in Montgomery, Alabama, a provisional constitution for the Confederate States of America was adopted. What the border states would do was questionable. William Gilmore Simms of South Carolina felt in late February that Virginia, Maryland, Kentucky, Tennessee, North Carolina, and Missouri might form a "Middle Confederacy." [4] As a

4. William Gilmore Simms, *Letters,* 5 vols. (Columbia: University of South Carolina Press, 1952–1956), 4:330–331.

border state between the United States and the Confederate States, North Carolina could no longer waver. The General Assembly in late January called for a referendum on the question of a convention to consider secession and at the same time to elect delegates in case the convention question carried. State Senator Jonathan Worth, desperately anxious to preserve the Union, urged his constituents to vote against a convention but at the same time to vote for Union men as potential delegates. W. W. Holden, on the other hand, who was also for the Union, favored a convention but also urged the election of Union men. In the balloting, the convention proposal lost by just 651 votes in a heavy turnout; 78 unionist and 42 secessionist delegates were elected to attend if the convention had won.[5]

Virginia called upon the border slave states to send delegates to a peace conference in Washington on February 4, and the North Carolina legislature elected five men, a majority of whom were unionist in sympathy. After three weeks of work the recommendations of the conference were submitted to Congress, but nothing came of them. In effect, they were ignored.

At the same time the legislature selected delegates for the Washington conference, it also elected representatives to go to Montgomery, Alabama, to witness the formation of the Confederate government. These men reported that they discovered little to suggest that there was any love for the old Union left anywhere in the South. David L. Swain commented on the large number of native North Carolinians who represented their adopted states in Montgomery, and he was impressed by the significant roles they played in forming the new government. He described them as men of wealth, intelligence, and respectability, and their support of the Confederacy made an impression on North Carolinians at home.

Following the inauguration of Lincoln on March 4, 1861, the United States Senate remained in executive session to discuss the question of protecting federal property in the seceded states.

5. Joseph Carlyle Sitterson, *The Secession Movement in North Carolina* (Chapel Hill: University of North Carolina Press, 1939), p. 223.

On the 15th, Senator Stephen A. Douglas from Illinois, supported by Senator Thomas L. Clingman from North Carolina, offered similar resolutions concerning the evacuation of all forts in the seceded states except those at Key West and Tortugas. Although the resolutions were tabled, Lincoln did not deny current reports that the forts, including Fort Sumter at Charleston, S.C., were to be evacuated. Shortly afterwards the president was prevailed upon to reconsider any such plans he might have had, and Federal ships were soon en route to Charleston. Word of this triggered the firing on Fort Sumter by Confederate forces, and on April 12 the fort fell. On the 14th Lincoln called on all of the governors of states still in the Union to furnish 75,000 troops to assist in restoring the Union. The very real possibility existed that North Carolina might be invaded by Federal troops if the state refused to make troops available to the United States. Such reasoning convinced unionists in the state that all hope for reconciliation had been dashed. In reply to the telegram seeking troops, Governor Ellis telegraphed Lincoln's secretary of war:

Your dispatch is recd. and if genuine which its extraordinary character leads me to doubt I have to say in reply that I regard the levy of troops made by the administration for the purpose of subjugating the States of the South as in violation of the Constitution and a gross usurpation of power. I can be no party to this wicked violation of the laws of the country and to this war upon the liberties of a free people. You can get no troops from North Carolina. I will reply more in detail when your call is received by mail.[6]

Virginia passed an ordinance of secession on April 17, as did Arkansas on May 6. On the following day in Nashville, the legislature of Tennessee declared independence of the coercive Federal government and soon joined the Confederacy. The North Carolina legislature was called into special session on May 1 prior to which the governor directed the seizure of forts, arsenals, and other Federal property in the state. Governor Ellis

6. Tolbert, *Papers of John Willis Ellis,* 2:612.

promptly offered the services of "our" mint in Charlotte to coin money for the Confederacy. He also responded to an urgent request of the Confederacy by sending state troops for service in Virginia. Since he could not lawfully draw on the state treasury for their transportation, however, he asked that the Confederate government provide the necessary funds.

Congressman Zebulon B. Vance's comments on his feeling during these troubled times undoubtedly represented those of countless other men and women who had been fervently loyal to the United States all of their lives. It was Lincoln's call for "volunteers to suppress the insurrection" that changed the situation instantly. It was because of that that "Union men had every prop knocked out from under them." At the very moment he heard this news, Vance said,

> I was canvassing for the Union with all my strength; I was addressing a large and excited crowd, large numbers of whom were armed, and literally had my hand extended upward in pleading for peace and the Union of our Fathers, when the telegraphic news was announced of the firing on Sumter and the President's call for 75,000 volunteers.
>
> When my hand came down from that impassioned gesticulation, it fell slowly and sadly by the side of a Secessionist. I immediately, with altered voice and manner, called upon the assembled multitude to volunteer not to fight against but for South Carolina. I said, if war must come, I preferred to be with my own people. If we had to shed blood I preferred to shed Northern rather than Southern blood. If we had to slay I had rather slay strangers than my own kindred and neighbors; and that it was better, whether right or wrong, that communities and states should get together and face the horrors of war in a body—sharing a common fate, rather than endure the unspeakable calamities of internecine strife.[7]

The legislature set May 13 as election day for delegates to a state convention that would assemble on May 20. Lincoln had placed a blockade along the coast of the state even before the

---

7. Glenn Tucker, *Zeb Vance, Champion of Personal Freedom* (Indianapolis: Bobbs-Merrill Company, Inc., 1965), pp. 105–106.

legislature convened, leaving it little choice on the question of secession. When the convention met, it rejected a rather lengthy document that described the reasons and principles that justified secession because of Lincoln's unconstitutional and coercive actions. Instead, it passed a simple ordinance repealing the one of 1789 by which the state had joined the Union in the first place. Thereupon, the ordinance proclaimed, the state resumed "full possession and exercise of all those rights of sovereignty which belong and appertain to a free and independent state." [8]

Jonathan Worth, unionist Whig, predicted that secession would produce a number of sectional governments that would require "the cartridge box instead of the ballot box" to preserve them. He disapproved of secession, of course, but he also opposed the provocative action taken by the Lincoln administration. The president, he said, "showed want of common sense" in deciding to reinforce Fort Sumter. He placed the blame for the ultimate break in North Carolina squarely on Lincoln because it was he who "made us a unit to resist until we repel our invaders or die." To his own family, however, he confessed: "I think the South is committing suicide, but my lot is cast with the South and being unable to manage the ship, I intend to face the breakers manfully and go down with my companions." [9]

It was Worth's belief that if Lincoln "had withdrawn the garrison of Fort Sumter on the principle of military necessity and in obedience to what seemed to be the will of Congress . . . this state and Tennessee and the other states which had not passed the ordinance of secession, would have stood up for the Union." However, at this very critical time, he ordered an expedition to Fort Sumter. Just as North Carolinians on the eve of the Revolution felt that King George had ignored their pleas, many now were convinced that Lincoln had done the same thing. "All of us who had stood by the Union," Worth said, "felt that he had abandoned us and had surrendered us to the

8. Sitterson, *Secession Movement,* p. 247.

9. Joseph G. deR. Hamilton, ed., *Correspondence of Jonathan Worth,* 2 vols. (Raleigh: Edwards & Broughton Printing Co., 1909), 1:144.

tender mercies of Democracy & the Devil.'' [10] The state held out as long as possible and was, in fact, next to the last one to leave the old Union and join the Confederacy.

North Carolina's role during the Civil War and her relations with the Confederate government bore most clearly the imprint of the character of one man—Zebulon Baird Vance. A native of the mountain county of Buncombe, an alumnus of the University of North Carolina, an attorney, and colonel of the Twenty-sixth Regiment, he was elected governor of the state in 1862 through the action of old-time Whigs and former unionists. He was just 32, and it was his energy and ability, his devotion to the state, and his charisma that made possible the organization and direction of a diverse and independent-minded people during the war. His efforts were successfully directed toward industrializing the state, revolutionizing agriculture, and recruiting and equipping troops. Civil authority, he was convinced, should not be subordinated to the military, so he spent his best efforts in keeping the courts open, schools operating, and railroads running. He was intent on protecting the rights of citizens against arbitrary actions by the government. Vance never gave the Confederate government the support he had given the United States before the war; he and Governor Joseph E. Brown of Georgia were noted for their lack of co-operation with the administration of President Jefferson Davis.

The Confederacy, historian Frank L. Owsley has written, died of states' rights. The political system of the South broke down ''under the weight of an impracticable doctrine put into practice in the midst of a revolution.'' If the leaders had granted the Confederate government as much freedom as the Federal government had during the war, defeat would have been almost impossible. Such leaders as Vance, however, could not wait ''to try out their theories and air their differences'' and they thereby ''sowed dissension among the people and destroyed all spirit of cooperation . . . between the states and the Confederate government, and, at times, arrayed local against central gov-

10. Hamilton, *Correspondence of Jonathan Worth,* 1:147.

ernment as if each had been an unfriendly foreign power." [11]

Vance on numerous occasions felt slighted by President Davis, who appeared not to respond quickly enough to the governor's messages. The governor suspected that his former unionist position made Confederate officials reluctant to trust him. He blamed this, or the fact that the state waited so long to secede, for the failure of the state's officers to be given high rank in the Confederate army, and for Confederate refusal to provide troops in sufficient numbers to protect the state from enemy raids. Vance once wrote the Confederate secretary of war that "the history of the war has been a succession of calamities in North Carolina. . . . I shall not pretend to say that our defense is intentionally neglected, but that it is very poorly provided for is a fact too patent to deny." [12]

The work of Confederate conscription officers in his state rankled Vance, too. He maintained that he had the right to exempt from military service all whom he considered essential to the functioning of state government. "God forbid," he once wrote, "that the rights, honor, and the existence itself of the States should rest only upon the grace and mercy of a bureau of conscription." [13] It was at Vance's insistence that the Confederate congress modified the exemption laws to include anyone whom a governor of a state deemed essential for the administration of government, and he then took full advantage of the law. In some cases even workers in factories where cotton and woolen goods were being made under state contract secured this boon.

Their governor was not only protecting North Carolinians from arbitrary acts of Confederate officials but also maintaining state sovereignty. He had the welfare of his people at heart in other respects, as well. It was his duty to see that troops had the necessary food, clothing, and equipment, and he was anxious

11. Frank L. Owsley, *State Rights in the Confederacy* (Chicago: University of Chicago Press, 1925), pp. 1–2.

12. Richard E. Yates, "Zebulon B. Vance as War Governor of North Carolina, 1862–1865," *Journal of Southern History,* 2 (February 1937): 53.

13. Yates, "Zebulon B. Vance," p. 62.

that the civilian population suffer as little as possible. When domestic resources were exhausted, Vance sent agents abroad, and soon the state was engaged not only in shipping cotton and other produce abroad for sale and buying supplies for home consumption, but also in operating a fleet of ships through the Federal blockade. By such valiant efforts Vance clothed North Carolina soldiers and by the end of 1864 had a surplus of 92,000 uniforms in storage. The state made only limited efforts to share with the Confederate government her surplus of uniforms and other goods badly needed by Confederate forces in the field. At the end of the war state warehouses were raided by men from both sides and were rapidly emptied. State-operated salt works on the coast provided that essential commodity for the people of the state, and corn and pork were distributed by the state to soldiers' families and other needy people.

Vance's concern for the people was repaid by their gratitude and devotion. It was this as much as anything that enabled Vance to hold the support of the majority of North Carolinians when a peace movement was organized by W. W. Holden and others.

In terms of manpower, however, North Carolina was generous to the Southern cause. With one-ninth of the total population of the eleven Confederate states, North Carolina furnished between one-sixth and one-seventh of all Confederate soldiers. Her total contribution of 140,000 men was considerably greater than her voting population. The state lost over 11,000 killed in battle, while about 24,000 died of disease and 30,000 were wounded. The state's total loss was greater than that of any of the other Confederate states.

In addition to enlisted men and officers in all of the ranks from lieutenant general down, three Confederate cabinet officers were from the state. At different times Judah P. Benjamin, Thomas Bragg, and George Davis were attorneys general, and Benjamin was also secretary of war and secretary of state. Benjamin was a native of the West Indies but some of his early years had been spent in Wilmington. Christopher Memminger, Confederate secretary of the treasury, was a native of Germany, but he had a summer home in the mountains of the state and is buried there.

Lincoln's attempt to blockade Southern ports even before North Carolina seceded was damaging, of course, and evading it tested the courage and ingenuity of seamen. Although dangerous, blockade-running was exciting, profitable, and patriotic. North Carolina's chief port, Wilmington, proved to be especially useful because its unique entrance at Cape Fear was protected by a strong fort and because it lay almost due west of Bermuda and straight north of Nassau on New Providence Island. Both of these British islands became centers of trade between Confederate shippers and British merchants, to the financial benefit of all. By the middle of June many fast-sailing, low-built ships painted dark colors began to run frequently. Agents representing London firms opened offices and warehouses to receive cotton, tobacco, and other products of the South. Some merchandise was sold for gold, but more was exchanged for goods badly needed at home—guns and ammunition, cloth, tools, coffee, sugar, fresh fruit, for example. Wine, china, fine gloves, bolts of silk, lace, and other luxuries were also brought in. After just a few trips the owners of ships cleared enough profit that no real loss was suffered if their ship then fell into enemy hands.

From Wilmington most ships sailed at night and stayed as close to shore as possible to blend with the background of trees, presenting no silhouette against the sky. About ten minutes at full speed would carry a ship through the actual blockade, and an hour more would put her out of range of the Yankee squadron. As Confederate blockade-runners neared their destination, they usually encountered more United States vessels conducting what virtually amounted to a blockade of a neutral harbor. Confederate ships were frequently chased into port after which Union and Confederate vessels docked alongside each other, and officers and men stayed in the same hotel.

Captain John Newland Maffit proved to be one of the most skillful blockade-runners in the business. About dusk one day early in 1862 he sailed from Nassau for Wilmington, and at daybreak next day found himself in the company of three Federal cruisers. He gave his ship all the power possible and pulled away from the enemy as they fired after him. A few hours later he discovered two more ships just ahead sailing straight for him, but by running a zig-zag course he escaped them. Soon he sighted a Spanish ship on fire. He sent a man aloft to keep a sharp watch for the enemy while he sent an officer over to help extinguish the flames. The Spanish captain thanked him graciously, and Maffit continued his course for Wilmington inwardly pleased at the thought of what the two New England women aboard the troubled ship would have done had they known they were being saved by a Rebel blockade-runner.

By that evening Maffit was seventy miles southeast of his destination when he ordered full steam ahead for sixty miles and then for the last ten carefully picked his way through the blockade. Shore lights were out, and precise navigation was absolutely essential. Maffit and his pilot knew the coast well, and the currents of the Cape Fear River could easily be read. He knew he was near shore and soon heard seven bells strike from a ship just ahead of him. It was high tide. He could make out two Federal warships anchored on either side of the channel. He intended to dart between them hoping not to be noticed so he ordered full speed ahead. The sound of a rocket flare going up told him that he had been discovered, and a voice from a nearby speaking trumpet ordered: "Heave to, or I will sink you!" "Ay, ay, sir!" he replied. And in an unusually loud voice he shouted to his crew: "Stop the engines!" This was a dreaded command and the end seemed near, but by this time the momentum of Maffit's ship had carried her beyond the two warships where a boarding party was making ready to take the Confederate vessel. From one of the Federal ships the command came: "Back your engines, sir, and stand by to receive my boat." Captain Maffit in a low voice said to his engineer: "Full speed ahead, sir, and open wide your throttle-valve!" [14]

14. James Sprunt, *Tales and Traditions of the Lower Cape Fear River, 1661–1896* (Wilmington: LeGwin Brothers, Printers, 1896), pp. 166–174.

In the darkness the Federal ships thought their prey was backing up, and with a boarding party out their gunners were in no position to fire. When they discovered how they had been tricked, they began firing, but Captain Maffit was then under the guns of Fort Fisher at the mouth of the river and safely home. On board were nine hundred barrels of powder, so a hit could easily have blown his ship out of the water.

In 1863 Maffit was at sea for eight months during which he destroyed about $10 million worth of enemy shipping. At the end of the war he searched for a Southern port still open into which he could bring his ship; but when he found Galveston, Charleston, and Wilmington all closed, he sailed for Liverpool where he turned his ship over to the British. Shortly afterwards he was licensed to command a British merchant steamer and for two years plied regularly between Liverpool and Rio de Janeiro. Only after his ship was sold to the Brazilian government did he return home to settle in the country near Wilmington where he died in 1886.

A number of places along the coast and in the eastern coastal plain were taken by Federal forces quite early in the war, but the remainder of North Carolina was generally free of enemy action until near the end of the conflict. It was word of the approach of Union General William T. Sherman that struck terror in the hearts of those who believed their homes lay in the path of his march. Sherman's decision to use military force against civilians just as against the military was implemented in Mississippi, perfected in Georgia, and continued in South Carolina. From Columbia, left in ruins, he headed for Goldsboro by way of Fayetteville where he expected to get supplies for his weary men and to destroy North Carolina's rail connections with the east. Orders were issued to regulate foraging parties, but they were widely disregarded, and roaming bands of soldiers—"bummers" they were called even by a member of Sherman's own staff—were guilty of almost every outrage imaginable.

On March 3, 1865, the Federal army broke camp at its last stop in South Carolina and anticipated a rather cordial welcome on the far side of the state line that it would soon cross. Like the British during the Revolution, the men had been led to believe that many loyal North Carolinians were anxiously awaiting the arrival of a liberating army. Sherman was just as disappointed in what he found as Cornwallis had been. The weather proved to be very much like that which had greeted His Lordship as he chased Greene across the state. On the very day the Yankees entered the state torrential rains began and the roads soon resembled canals. Water flowing over mud made them almost impassable for wagon trains and troops. Mules dragged the wagons along only with the help of soldiers tugging at ropes in front and turning wheels by brute force. An Ohio soldier wrote home that "Such a wild scene of splashing and yelling and swearing and braying has rarely greeted mortal eyes and ears." [15]

In North Carolina these Northern troops found something they had never seen before, and it delighted them. Tall, stately pine trees which had been boxed to collect rosin for turpentine made a scene that reminded some of the nave of a cathedral. The bare trunks were like magnificent columns while the spreading branches high overhead formed a ceiling. The soldiers quickly discovered that a match applied to the dripping rosin would set fire to a whole forest creating an awe-inspiring sight throughout the night leaving a pall of smoke over the countryside the following day. Their glee in such entertainment knew no bounds, and their officers were unable to control them. Vast tracts of longleaf pines were wantonly destroyed.

Union cavalry under General Judson Kilpatrick set out to prevent Confederate General Wade Hampton, who was in front of Sherman, from getting to Fayetteville first. Kilpatrick moved around and camped along a road ahead of Hampton, expecting to surprise him when he passed on the morning of March 10. Confederate horsemen arrived earlier than anticipated, and Kilpatrick, dressed only in his underwear, abandoned the warm bed

15. John G. Barrett, *Sherman's March Through the Carolinas* (Chapel Hill: University of North Carolina Press, 1956), p. 123.

of a "lady" companion, and without the comfort of a saddle
mounted the nearest horse and rode off into the swamp. Embar-
rassed by what had happened, Kilpatrick later denied that any
such event occurred. His version reported that as was his custom he left his headquarters in his slippers about daybreak to attend to his horses when he was surprised. Hearing this version,
a Confederate soldier who was present said that he presumed
Kilpatrick to be the only general from Joshua to the nineteenth
century who, only partially dressed, would leave a warm room
in cold weather to see his horses fed a hundred yards away.

Fayetteville was occupied and plundered by the first wave of
troops before Sherman could station guards to protect private
property. Here he replaced his sick and feeble mules and horses
with animals taken from the surrounding countryside and here
he also divested himself of large numbers of white refugees and
blacks who had been following his army. He referred to these
people as "twenty to thirty thousand useless mouths. They are
dead weight to me and consume our supplies." [16] Setting out
for Goldsboro, Sherman anticipated no delay, so he was surprised at the small community of Bentonville to discover that
General Joseph E. Johnston and General W. J. Hardee had
gathered scattered Confederate forces to resist the movement.
The attack began on March 19 and completely surprised Sherman, whose Fourteenth Corps was almost defeated before it was
reinforced late the next day. On the 21st Sherman was on the
scene with his entire army and the Confederate forces withdrew
to Smithfield. Union forces, twice those of the Confederates,
were almost defeated in the bloodiest battle ever fought in North
Carolina. Burning farmhouses as they went, the invading troops
moved on to Goldsboro and from there on April 10 headed
toward Raleigh. On the night of April 11 news of General Lee's
surrender at Appomattox was received, and a joyous spirit pervaded the army as it moved on the state capital. A Confederate
locomotive bearing peace commissioners dispatched by Gover-

16. Barrett, *Sherman's March*, p. 137.

nor Vance arrived at Sherman's headquarters. No agreement could be reached on the suspension of hostilities, but Sherman promised to protect state and municipal officials. Before the army reached Raleigh the governor and the Confederate forces evacuated the city. General Johnston reported to President Davis, who was in Greensboro, and when Johnston learned of General Lee's capitulation, he knew that further resistance was useless. Johnston persuaded Davis to let him send a dispatch to Sherman, then in Raleigh, asking for a suspension of hostilities.

The message was received on April 14, and Sherman arranged a meeting with Johnston at a point about midway between the two armies. At James Bennett's farmhouse a few miles west of Durham the two generals met on April 17 and 18. Sherman knew that Johnston's surrender was not a military necessity and that he might not accept harsh terms, so he acceded to terms acceptable to the Confederate general—an armistice that might be terminated on forty-eight-hours notice, Confederate arms to be deposited in state arsenals, and the troops disbanded. When state officials took an oath of allegiance, their government would be recognized by the United States, federal courts re-established, and political and civil rights restored to the people. A provision for general amnesty was also included. President Davis approved the terms for the Confederacy, but they were rejected in the North. General U.S. Grant ordered Sherman to reopen negotiations on the same basis as had prevailed when General Lee surrendered at Appomattox. Davis was opposed and directed General Johnston and his mounted troops to escape to renew the fighting. Johnston, aware of the hopelessness of the situation, declined to do so and met Sherman again at the Bennett place. This time on April 26, 1865, a purely military surrender took place with no other provisions considered.

Sherman's superior, Secretary of War Edwin M. Stanton, implied that the general had disobeyed orders and that for a payment in gold he might be permitting Jefferson Davis to escape. Sherman was furious and spoke of Stanton as a "mean, scheming, vindictive politician who made it his business to rob military men of their credit earned by exposing their lives in the service of their country.'' [17]

Angry at Northern politicians in general and the press in particular, Sherman came to regard the defeated Confederates and the soldiers of his own army at his best friends. He wrote Chief Justice Salmon P. Chase that in case of war against a foreign enemy he would not hesitate to mingle with Southerners and to lead them in battle. In much the same tone he wrote to his wife that ''the mass of people south will never trouble us again. They have suffered terribly, and I now feel disposed to befriend them—of course not the leaders and lawyers, but the armies who have fought and manifested their sincerity though misled by risking their persons.'' [18]

Sherman was recalled from his command in Raleigh and on April 29 he boarded a train and left, knowing that he had done his best to shorten the road to reunion. If the initial terms to which he agreed with Johnston at the Bennett place had been accepted in the North, the people of the South would have resumed the place in the Union that they had held in 1860, and many of the trials of Reconstruction would have been unknown.

17. Barrett, *Sherman's March,* p. 206.
18. Barrett, *Sherman's March,* p. 206.

9

After the War

*C*ONGRESS rejected President Andrew Johnson's moderate plan that would return the Southern states to the Union. Congressmen in those days were not as generous toward those "conquered" in war. Twentieth-century programs of financial assistance to help defeated nations rebuild their devastated land would have been considered preposterous. Punishment became the watchword; humiliation was the objective; and obedience to congressional directives was essential if the Southern states expected to return to the Union—and on the latter point they had no choice but to return on the conditions dictated by Congress. The threat of eradication of state lines and total rearrangement of states was made. The loss of land and other property was as much a possibility as the loss of the franchise, which did come very quickly for some.

Lincoln as early as December 1863 announced a very moderate plan to restore the Southern states to the Union. As soon as ten percent of the men who could vote in 1860 took an oath to support the United States Constitution and the Emancipation Proclamation, they could form new state governments. This lenient plan was abandoned under congressional pressure, however, and Lincoln's successor, Andrew Johnson, adopted another one that was almost but not quite as generous. His plan required the seceded states to repeal their secession ordinances,

144

to abolish slavery, and to repudiate Confederate debts. Presidential pardon would be granted to most of the former leaders of the South. In Louisiana and Arkansas new governments were established under these guidelines by December 1865. Nevertheless, when Congress convened near the end of that month, the newly "reconstructed" states were denied admission. Thaddeus Stevens of Pennsylvania was largely responsible for the rejection of Johnson's plan. He and other congressmen questioned the nature of a military victory that returned their old enemies to office, especially to Congress, and they rejected Johnson's plan by instituting a second Reconstruction of their own.

As a means of testing the sincerity of the South, the Fourteenth Amendment to the Constitution was drawn up and required to be ratified by a state seeking to return to the Union. To many in the North it appeared that the South, while recognizing the end of slavery and granting technical freedom to the Negro, intended to keep blacks in a state of serfdom. The Fourteenth Amendment was intended to prevent this. It defined United States citizenship, an omission in the original Constitution, and also contained provisions for the protection of citizens' civil rights and individual liberties against any action by the states. By giving the national government authority to intervene in the states' treatment of their citizens, this amendment clearly was in conflict with the Tenth Amendment that reserved to the states all powers not delegated to the United States by the Constitution. This was clearly a thrust at the old ideal of states' rights, but once adopted, the Fourteenth Amendment superseded the Tenth. Secretary of State William H. Seward, on July 28, 1868, declared the new amendment ratified, although it had the approval of just the twenty-three Northern states and Tennessee—considerably less than the three-fourths prescribed in Article V of the Constitution. In determining the number of states necessary to ratify, Seward discounted the Southern states still not readmitted to the Union. In addition to the ten Southern states, the amendment was rejected by Delaware, Kentucky, and Maryland, while California took no action on it. Later, of course, as a part of the requirements for readmission to the Union, Southern states ratified.

Many white Southerners regarded the new amendment as humiliating and degrading. Many who had served in state and local government before the war were now ineligible for office under its terms, and concerned citizens of North Carolina spoke out in opposition to it. Although they were too young to vote, members of the senior class at the University of North Carolina in 1866 found a way to express their personal feelings about the situation. In great secrecy they prepared engraved invitations to their commencement ball and sent them out before the faculty knew what they were doing. Named on the elaborately engraved invitation as honorary managers of the ball were President Jefferson Davis, Governor Zebulon B. Vance, General Robert E. Lee, and several other notable Confederate officers. The next year the students had an opportunity to demonstrate their feelings again when President Johnson attended commencement. He was, after all, a native of Raleigh and for that reason moderately acceptable. Members of the Dialectic Literary Society approved honorary membership for him. On the other hand, the Philanthropic Society refused the same honor to U.S. General Daniel E. Sickles, military commander of the district in which North Carolina lay.

In the congressional election of 1866 men of radical views were victorious, and it became quite clear that further hard times were ahead for the South. Some realistic Southerners, accepting defeat of their cause, began to feel that perhaps they had gone a bit too far with their clearly haughty attitude toward their recent and not yet placated foes. Early in 1867 something of a proposed compromise plan originated in North Carolina. It was called "The North Carolina Plan of Adjustment" or "The New Confederate Movement" and proposed to Congress among other things that if no disabilities were imposed upon white suffrage, in return the states would accept total enfranchisement of blacks. Even though it was endorsed by the governors of Alabama, Florida, Mississippi, and South Carolina, and by a number of congressmen from Arkansas, North Carolina, and

Texas, Congress never seriously considered it. The new Congress promptly passed reconstruction acts overturning the state governments recently established under President Johnson and dividing the South into military districts each under the supervision of a general.

A new registration of voters under terms to be implemented by the Fourteenth Amendment was ordered, to be followed by the election of delegates to conventions that would draw up new constitutions for the Southern states. This would result in new governments in the hands of "loyal" men and the readmission of Southern states to the Union with the seating of their representatives and senators. North Carolinians who anticipated that they were about to be disfranchised began frantically to call upon General Sickles for instruction as to how they might remove their disabilities. They wanted to be eligible to participate in the formation of the new government for their state. Spur-of-the-moment decisions were made by the general: those who had been drafted into the Confederate army were not disqualified and neither were those who took local office during the war to prevent a more volatile "rebel" from holding it or to keep themselves out of the army. In some instances, however, a federal district attorney had to make a ruling. Because registrars and inspectors of elections had to demonstrate that they had never been disloyal to the United States, it was difficult to find election officials. Sickles was reluctant to appoint blacks, so he sought out North Carolinians who had served as Union soldiers.

Delegates of both races and varied political views were elected to the constitutional convention with Republicans in the majority. Daniel R. Goodloe, editor of the *Union Register* in Raleigh and a native-born Republican totally free of the taint of having supported the Confederacy, wrote very frankly to Charles Sumner of Massachusetts, leader of the Radical Republicans, concerning the delegates to the convention.

> As you may well suppose, with the former governing class of the people disfranchised, the delegates are for the most part inferior in intelligence and character. Thirteen [actually fifteen] of them are persons of African descent—only one of whom, a Pennsylvanian has

any education worth speaking of. He is a Methodist preacher, and seems to be a man of good character. Two others,—natives,—without much culture, show considerable talent for speaking. Others are barbers, and two or three, literally, *field hands*. About twenty-seven of the delegates are recently from the North, and not of the most disinterested characteristics. . . . You may imagine, that the best Constitution in the world, if made by such men, would be unsatisfactory to the majority of the people. . . . The difficulty about electing better Men is partly due—perhaps Mainly due, to the disfranchisement of the governing class; but also in great degree to the ignorance of the negroes. They are the dupes of the lowest and meanest demagogues. The basest men are the most popular among the negroes, because the basest men will bid the highest for their votes— [1]

There were 120 delegates at the convention that gathered in Raleigh on January 14, 1868. The 15 blacks, with a single exception, were all natives of the state. Of the 105 whites, 13 were Conservative, a newly formed group of former Whigs and Democrats, and 92 Republican. Of the latter, 74 were prewar residents of the state, most of whom were also natives. There were, therefore, only 18 genuine "outsiders" or carpetbaggers among the white delegates. Plato Durham, 27, a native of Rutherford County, and John W. Graham, 29, of Hillsborough, son of former Governor William A. Graham, were spokesmen for the Conservative element. William B. Rodman, 51, of Washington, moderate Republican, was also an effective leader who spoke for North Carolina rather than for party or faction. All three of these men were alumni of the university, Confederate veterans, and practicing attorneys. Calvin Cowles, Republican president of the convention, was 47, a merchant from the mountain county of Wilkes, and son-in-law of W. W. Holden. Because of a physical disability he had not served in the war. The most influential carpetbagger was Albion W. Tourgée, 29-year-old native of Ohio, Union veteran and a graduate of the Univer-

---

1. William A. Russ, Jr., "Radical Disfranchisement in North Carolina, 1867–1868," *North Carolina Historical Review*, 11 (October 1934): 279.

sity of Rochester, who in 1865 had moved to Greensboro, where he soon began publishing a newspaper.

The constitution prepared by this group of men proved much better than most North Carolinians conceded until recently. As the basis for government in the state, it has survived in large measure to the present time. It was the only one of the Southern constitutions to withstand the attacks of the Conservatives who tried to emasculate it when they returned to power.

The Declaration of Rights from the 1776 constitution was virtually unchanged except that it was somewhat broadened. The basic agencies of government from the prewar period were also retained. Otherwise the constitution was modernized to conform to the political trends of the day. The judicial system was overhauled and the ancient distinction between suits in equity and actions at law abolished. The convention adopted a code of civil procedure and greatly simplified the system of courts in the state. The legislature would no longer appoint judges; instead they would be elected by the people. Largely at the insistence of Tourgée, who had a sound knowledge of the operation of county government in Pennsylvania, a new form of local government was devised. Townships created in the counties became the basic units of local government. Legislative appointment of county justices, the practice of the past, was abandoned in favor of local election of county commissioners. Tourgée appreciated the role of democracy in local government in the North, and he credited its absence in the South with suppressing free thought and free speech, with degrading labor, encouraging ignorance, and establishing an aristocracy.[2] With the support of Conservative members of a committee of which he was chairman, the control of schools in the state was placed in the hands of township committees.

Significant constitutional changes were also made at the state level to give the government of North Carolina a more progressive and democratic tenor. Henceforth the governor would be

2. Otto H. Olsen, *Carpetbagger's Crusade: The Life of Albion Winegar Tourgée* (Baltimore: Johns Hopkins University Press, 1965), pp. 97–98.

elected by the people to a four-year term; some of his powers were also increased, but he still was denied the veto—the governor of North Carolina today being the only one to whom this authority is yet denied. The memory of unhappy relations with colonial governors persisted. Other state officials, heretofore appointed, would be elected in the future, and in some cases terms of office were extended. Although some ex-Confederates believed they would have to demonstrate proper repentance, in general universal suffrage was extended to all males. Property qualifications for voting and officeholding were abolished, a provision that many people in the state advocated as early as 1842. Representation in the senate would no longer be based on taxes paid into the state treasury, as provided in the 1835 revisions, but on population. The legislature would meet annually. Provisions were made for a uniform state system of taxation, and the fiscal powers of the legislature were limited with respect to levying taxes and borrowing money.[3]

Because Tourgée was particularly concerned about certain humanitarian reforms, he assisted the chairman of the Committee on Punishments, Penal Institutions, and Public Charities in several proposals. As a result, the new constitution made the state more responsible for the needy. Another matter which was the cause of extensive dispute, even among the Republicans, concerned the purpose of criminal punishment. Tourgée believed that its objective should be to reform as well as to punish, but those who did not agree felt that a criminal's experience with the law should serve as a deterrent to others. The death penalty, he believed, should be pronounced only to punish wilful murder, but both Republicans and Conservatives agreed that it should apply to other offenses as well. Tourgée was never won over to that point of view and he hoped that the death penalty might be abolished by petition to an early legislature. The use of the whipping post, stocks, and branding was prohibited.

3. John L. Sanders, "A Brief History of the Constitution of North Carolina," in John L. Cheney, Jr., ed., *North Carolina Government, 1585–1974* (Raleigh: North Carolina Department of the Secretary of State, 1975), pp. 796–797.

The oath to be taken by voters and officeholders was one of the most widely debated and hotly contested topics of the convention. Insofar as disfranchisement of Confederates was concerned, the radicals were strangely moderate in their wishes. No one, the majority report specified, should be disqualified for rebellion, although a few extremists in the convention proposed to try to identify and deny the vote to anyone who had inflicted unusually cruel punishment on United States soldiers during the war. These same extremists would have applied the criteria of the Fourteenth Amendment to prospective voters in the state and would require prospective registrants to take an oath never again to support the principle of secession in the state. In their opinion, voters should also acknowledge acceptance of the civil and political equality of all men. All of these restrictions were rejected. One delegate wished to see registrants take an oath pledging devotion to the Union, and opposition to its dissolution. Each prospective voter should also swear that he had no sympathy for those who had favored secession, and that he, himself, had never supported or sympathized with those who did support sedition or defection. These proposals, however, were never put to a vote.

The majority report, which was readily accepted, provided that the legislature should pass a registration law under which a voter had only to swear to obey the laws and to abide by the constitutions of the state and the United States. A similar oath was required for officeholding.

Although it was not even a constitutional issue, the question of relief for debtors was one of the most bitterly debated topics to come before the convention. A similar question had been raised in North Carolina after the Revolutionary War with respect to debts owed in Great Britain. Rodman worked diligently to restrain the convention delegates in 1868 from declaring all debts invalid. Prewar debts were due after the Civil War just as they were after the Revolution.

Having completed its work, which included the granting of the ballot to all blacks and denying it to no white men, just as the North Carolina Plan of Adjustment had proposed in 1867, the convention concluded its work with an address to the people, saying in part:

> It is an undeniable monument to the wisdom, and equity, and magnanimity, of the Union people of North Carolina, that in three years after the close of a bloody and devastating civil war, in which wrongs and outrages were endured that can never be forgotten, they have framed a Constitution, in which not a trace of animosity or vindictiveness can be found; in which the wrongs of the past are ignored for the sake of the peace of the future, and all who are now true to their country, are invited to participate in its government. Such wise forbearance is certain of its reward in the approval of reflecting men now, and of all posterity.[4]

By order of General E. R. S. Canby, Sickles's successor, both the constitution and the officers for which it provided were to be voted on at the same time. Ballots for officers might be cast by all who would be qualified under the constitution just as if it had already been approved—that is, all males, black and white. Only those qualified to vote under the restrictions of the national reconstruction acts, however, could vote on the constitution itself. On this question Canby, in effect, disfranchised those who would soon be enfranchised by the new constitution, while he enfranchised those who would not be so privileged until it was adopted. This was not in violation of the reconstruction acts, of course, but by this means he secured the election of legislators and state officials acceptable to Congress, and Congress approved the new constitution on June 25, 1868, readmitting North Carolina to the Union.

During the meeting of the convention the whole range of political opinion came up for lengthy debate. The resulting decisions, especially the one regarding the oath, resulted from compromise and adjustment rather than from the forcing of a particular point of view. Professor Joseph S. Ferrell of the Institute of Government at the University of North Carolina at Chapel Hill, who is making a fresh study of the work of the

4. *Journal of the North Carolina Convention of 1868* (Raleigh, J. W. Holden, 1868), pp. 484–485.

convention, describes what came out of the meeting as "a loose and uneasy confederation of groups organized under the Republican banner, struggling to make some accommodation with Washington while at the same time preserving as much of the heritage and tradition of North Carolina as was consistent with the end of slavery." The reaction in the convention among the opposing factions was a mirror of the complex political life of that day. "I see their intellectual descendants today," Ferrell observes, "organized under different party labels but little changed in political and social philosophy by the passage of a century. What came about from the convention was a peculiarly North Carolinian way of arriving at and preserving political stability." [5]

Countless people from the victorious North showed up in the South for many reasons—to aid the blacks, to profit personally from the unsettled conditions, to hold office, to enjoy the milder climate which they had discovered as soldiers, and for various other reasons. They were often called carpetbaggers because it was believed that they could carry all of their personal possessions in a type of popular luggage called a carpetbag. Southerners who joined the carpetbaggers in support of Republican policies were called scalawags. The Freedmen's Bureau, established in 1865 as a federal agency to assist blacks in adjusting to their new condition and to provide food, clothing, land, education, and other necessities, brought in many more Northerners—men and women. Many of these people used the newly enfranchised blacks to gain control not only in the state but also in counties and local communities. There was also an army of occupation, but the army seldom sparked any friction or discontentment in the South. The army, in fact, in some places looked with dismay at the antics of many conscienceless civilians as they pursued their own selfish aims. There were exceptions, of course, in many communities. In North Carolina Tourgée's ability was recognized, and he had many friends. So did William Henry Snow, who moved to the state from Vermont and be-

5. These comments are based on recent conversations with Mr. Ferrell.

came the guiding spirit in the program of industrialization for Greensboro and High Point. And there were others who found ready acceptance in their new homes.

Old line Democrats and former Whigs had banded together to oppose what they regarded as the radical version of Reconstruction being implemented in the state. For party harmony they called their party the Conservative party, but it was basically the prewar Democratic party. Opposing it was the state's Republican party, organized in Raleigh in March 1867 with William W. Holden at its head. Holden's political ambitions had been frustrated in his old party and he became embittered. During the war he began a peace movement, but Governor Vance, because of his popularity with the people, had been able to quell it. Holden was appointed governor under President Johnson's plan of reconstruction, but he was replaced by Jonathan Worth at the first postwar election. For a brief time it appeared that the state's problems were nearing an end, but when Worth's two-year term ended, the new constitution was in effect. Holden was then elected by the new Republican party, which had the support of the newly enfranchised blacks. During his administration fraud, deceit, and dishonesty flourished. Public funds were wasted and a heavy state debt incurred. Under the leadership of carpetbaggers and scalawags the state participated in a variety of railroad-development schemes that were of primary benefit only to those who controlled them; massive stock frauds were perpetrated.

In 1870, following the withdrawal of federal troops from the state, the Democratic party returned to power and eventually repudiated almost half of the state debt of $30 million. Fortunately the Eleventh Amendment, which had grown out of James Iredell's dissenting opinion in the case of *Chisholm* vs. *Georgia,* prevented individuals of other states from suing North Carolina. The agency employed by the Conservatives to help bring about their return to power was the Ku Klux Klan. Although it was not understood at the time, the Klan was maintained largely for political purposes—to defeat the radical Republicans. The Klan was a secret organization formed in

Tennessee soon after the war, and by late 1867 or early 1868 it had spread into North Carolina. It grew in membership and activity until about 1871, when it began to decline after the return of Conservative control to government. The Klan existed in part to counteract the influence of a Republican organization, the Union League, which controlled blacks. The Union League saw that Negroes supported the Republican ticket. The Klan's purpose, however, was not merely to prevent the Negro from voting but to keep him "in his place" as well.

The Klan in the state was well organized. Colonel William L. Saunders of Chapel Hill was believed to be its head, and there were district and community officers throughout the state. Local groups were known as "dens," and members of a den in one county might go to another county to carry out an assignment where the possibility existed that local men might be recognized. There were other organizations with many of the same objectives; the Constitutional Union Guard and the White Brotherhood were both smaller than the Klan, but many of their members also belonged to the Klan.

The Klan uniform generally was a flowing white robe concealing the wearer's face. Members rode horses and made calls after dark, their activity ranging from simple warnings through threats and whippings all the way to murder. Blacks, of course, were most often their victims, but whites who collaborated with carpetbaggers or who flaunted their affiliation with the Republicans were not immune. Sometimes Klan members made it known that they were simply seeing justice done when reputed criminals or persons suspected of criminal action were punished. Klan members also meted out what in their opinion was justice to the guilty who were not convicted in court. Nevertheless, behind the varied activities of the Klan lay the ultimate objective of denying Republicans the controlling voice in government.

Terrorism reached a peak in the piedmont counties of Alamance and Caswell after the fall elections of 1868, when it was discovered that these two were among the few counties in the state where Republicans' strength had increased. Clearly if local

Conservatives were to return to power at the 1870 election, desperate action was necessary. During a single twelve-month period in the county of Caswell alone two white men were whipped and one was killed. Six blacks were whipped, one shot, one killed, and the property of another destroyed. In addition, countless members of both races were frightened and threatened. What took place may have been somewhat more drastic than elsewhere, but it was by no means unique. Local Republican leaders in Caswell County and elsewhere sought aid from Raleigh. In the face of such unstable and tense conditions Governor Holden became alarmed. It was perhaps at his suggestion during the sitting of the legislature late in 1869 that Republican Senator T. M. Shoffner of Alamance County, a county adjoining Caswell, introduced a bill giving the governor the power to suspend the writ of habeas corpus and authorizing him to use the militia to suppress lawlessness in counties where civil authorities were unable to maintain order. The Klan greeted Shoffner's bill with defiance and laid plans to hang him. He either heard of this or suspected what was about to happen, and when Klansmen gathered "to suspend Shoffner's writ of habeas corpus" the Alamance County native fled to Indiana, a place well known in North Carolina as offering refuge to abolitionists and escaped slaves before the war.

The one man in Caswell County believed by the Democrats to be most responsible for Republican growth was John W. Stephens, a native of nearby Guilford County, who was known as "Chicken" Stephens from his having killed a neighbor's chickens in a fit of anger when they strayed onto his property. It was also believed that he had murdered his own mother. In Caswell County he was a "detective" for Governor Holden and the trusted confidant of Tourgée in getting out the Republican vote. He openly associated with blacks and was suspected of inspiring them to burn a number of barns, destroy crops, steal livestock, and in other ways contribute to the unrest that plagued the community. Many thought they had evidence that he, himself, had burned a local hotel and a row of brick shops.

Nevertheless, Stephens's Republican friends elected him to represent the county in the state senate.

For his countless dastardly deeds Stephens was tried *in absentia* by the Ku Klux Klan. Members later maintained that his actions were carefully investigated and that at the trial he was represented by diligent defenders. As was expected, he was found guilty of the crimes of which he was accused, and the sentence of death was imposed. Stephens may have heard rumors of the trial or he may simply have expected that his luck was about to run out. At any rate, he took out a large life insurance policy, fortified his house which stood near the courthouse, and armed himself with three pistols.

On May 21, 1870, Democrats held a convention in the courthouse to nominate candidates for the August election, and a host of experienced white political leaders spoke. Stephens was present trying to persuade a former Democratic sheriff to become a candidate on the Republican ticket. Later in the day the former sheriff signaled Stephens to meet him on the ground floor for a conference. The next morning Stephens's body was found in a locked room in the courthouse. He had been murdered in the clear light of day in a public building occupied by a great many people. It was a "perfect" crime. The facts of the case were only revealed in a letter written in 1919 and opened in 1935 after the death of the last witness. As long as they lived, the lips of the participants were sealed. Republicans, of course, investigated the case, did everything they could to solve the mystery, and took testimony from thirty-five men and women, black and white, who were presumed to have knowledge of the deed. Although friends and companions of the unknown murderer were called to testify, the murderer himself was never questioned. His friends, including those who witnessed the deed, kept the secret.

Republicans of both races as well as a number of Klansmen quietly departed, and a Democratic victory in August resulted. Governor Holden, however, was unwilling to surrender to the forces of violence or to see party strength drained from the county. With the advice of members of his party, he concluded that military force would have to be applied. Federal occupation troops had been ineffective so he decided to use the militia. Since the regular state militia might be reluctant to act in this situation and Negro militiamen would only add to the unrest, the governor called on President Grant and the acting secretary of war, W. T. Sherman, for assistance. George W. Kirk of Jonesboro, Tennessee, late colonel of the United States Army and prior to that a deserter from the Confederate army, was sent with some enlisted men of unionist sympathies from the mountains of Tennessee. The three hundred men ranging in age from fifteen or sixteen up to seventy composed Kirk's force. They were untrained and described locally as vagabonds and uncivilized. One of them, on a hot summer afternoon, took off all his clothes and bathed at the town pump near the courthouse in Yanceyville and then proceeded to wash his clothes. On another occasion, when a team of horses approached pulling a threshing machine, all Kirk's troops fled. When they were rounded up, one of them explained that they thought it was a cannon.

The Kirk-Holden War, as this little episode is called in spite of the fact that no actual fighting took place, occupied the attention of North Carolina from mid-July until early December 1870. Holden gave Kirk a lengthy list of men in the area to be arrested and held for trial. In a letter of July 26 to Chief Justice Richmond M. Pearson, Holden stressed the fact that his purpose was merely to "suppress the insurrection." Civil authority had broken down and justice could not be served by the courts, he pointed out. "The civil and the military are alike constitutional powers," the governor wrote, "the civil to protect life and property when it can, and the military only when the former has failed." [6] Men arrested under suspicion of having subverted justice in the county would stand trial before courts martial, Holden directed, and not in the civil courts. The privilege of habeas corpus would be denied the accused.

6. William S. Powell, *When the Past Refused to Die, The History of Caswell County, 1777–1977* (Durham: Moore Publishing Company, 1977), p. 246.

Colonel Kirk sent squads of men around the county to bring in the men wanted by the governor. No time was wasted as the first man was picked up the very day the army arrived. Former Sheriff Frank Wiley, who had called Stephens to the fatal conference, was high on the list, of course, and a squad was promptly dispatched to bring him in. He was found working in a tobacco field. His horse that he was working was unhitched, and Wiley was ordered to mount it. His request for an explanation was met by curses and threats, and when he asked to consult a lawyer, the soldiers knocked him down with a fence rail and again ordered him to mount. As soon as he recovered enough to do so, he did as they ordered. He was then tied and whipped with switches as the motley crew rode toward Yanceyville, where he arrived with a bloody back.

These arrests, in which men were often cruelly treated, were also sometimes pathetic, and on one occasion humorous. Captain John G. Lea recorded that the youthful soldier sent to bring him in "begged me all the way to Yanceyville not to let anybody shoot him. He also asked me to let him get behind me. He then unslung his gun and so we went into town. The guard begged me to let him come to my house and work for me, saying he did not expect to find so many kind people and that he would be glad to live in the neighborhood; that he had been brought down from the mountains, not knowing where he was going nor what he was to do, or what sort of people he would be among." [7]

Some of Kirk's prisoners were held in the county seat while others were sent to nearby counties or to Raleigh. Among them were a former congressman, a member of the legislature, a sheriff, several attorneys, businessmen, planters, and other prominent citizens.

Even before the arrival of Kirk's army, leading members of the Klan realized that the purposes for which they had organized had generally been accomplished. The murder of Stephens marked the turning point in Klan activity and dissolution of the

7. Powell, *When the Past Refused to Die*, pp. 246–247.

organization was urged by the members. Conservatives (or Democrats) who were arrested during the period of military rule wasted no time in taking steps to gain their freedom. Publicity helped, of course, and the sympathetic state press reported details of the treatment received by these men. Governor Holden's denial of habeas corpus was made much of. Holden explained to Chief Justice Pearson that he was convinced no state court would have enough courage to convict men charged with Klan offenses—only military courts would do so.

Applications for writs of habeas corpus were made, nevertheless, by prominent Conservative lawyers representing the incarcerated enemies of Holden. When the chief justice issued a writ directing Kirk to release a particular prisoner, he refused saying that he could obey only the governor. The attorneys then sought an order from the judge to arrest Kirk and to send a sheriff to do so. Fearing a confrontation between a sheriff and the militia, Pearson declined to order a sheriff to bring in Kirk, but he did issue a writ for his arrest. In suspending the habeas corpus, Pearson believed, the governor had exceeded his authority, even that granted by the Shoffner Act, and he readily issued writs for all of the prisoners arrested by Kirk on order of the governor. Pearson took no steps to see that the writs were complied with as this, he said, was outside the jurisdiction of the court. In ignoring the writs, Holden committed a grievous error. Attorneys for some of the prisoners appealed to the federal district court claiming that their clients had been denied their liberty without due process of law as guaranteed by the Fourteenth Amendment ratified just two years before. The judge was prepared to hear the evidence and, if he deemed it sufficient, to hold the accused. Since the state had no evidence at all that it could present, nearly all of the prisoners were released. White men had been freed by the constitutional amendment designed primarily to protect blacks. Holden appealed in vain to his friends in Washington, but none of the men on his list ever faced trial.

At the election in August the Democrats prevailed. A broad shift in political power was about to take place and the old leaders of the state began to prepare themselves. In September Holden disbanded the militia and in November declared the insurrection at an end. Kirk fled the state to escape prosecution for falsely arresting North Carolina citizens. The legislature convened in November, and soon a resolution was introduced to impeach Governor Holden. Charging him with high crimes and misdemeanors in office, a committee from the house appeared before the senate to carry out the intent of the resolution. Eight articles of impeachment were drawn and presented, and the trial got under way on February 2, 1871. After seven weeks, during which 113 witnesses appeared for the governor and 57 against him, he was found guilty on six charges, expelled from office, and declared forever ineligible to hold public office in the state. Governor Charles Robinson of Kansas had been impeached in 1862, but the charges against him were rejected; Holden was the first governor to be convicted.

One of the standing objectives of the Conservatives was the repeal of the 1868 constitution; so when they gained control of the legislature in 1870, they gave the people of the state an opportunity to vote on the question. It must have been with considerable chagrin that the assemblymen learned the question lost by 9,245 votes. But they still held an ace up their sleeves. The legislature could initiate amendments and by approval of two successive sessions adopt amendments to be submitted to a vote of the people. By this means they secured approval in 1873 of eight changes which, among other things, restored biennial sessions of the General Assembly, transferred control of the university from the State Board of Education to the legislature, abolished various new state offices, and repealed the prohibition against repudiation of the state debt. They wanted more, however, and in 1875 on their own initiative, as was their prerogative, they called a constitutional convention. That convention, the last ever held in the state, remained in session for five weeks in the fall with 58 Conservative, 58 Republican, and 3 independent delegates. The 1868 constitution escaped basically unchanged, but thirty amendments were approved, most of which were the results of events of the period since 1865. Secret societies were outlawed and so was the carrying of concealed weapons. Compensation for legislators was specified. A Department of Agriculture, Immigration and Statistics was established; persons guilty of a felony or other infamous crimes were denied the vote; and the marriage of whites and blacks was prohibited. A section provided that "the children of the white race and the children of the colored race shall be taught in separate public schools, but there shall be no discrimination made in favor of, or to the prejudice of, either race." Justices of the peace would in the future be appointed by the legislature; and control of county government, in effect, was placed in the hands of legislators—this to prevent control of local government by blacks in those eastern counties where they constituted a majority. And there were other changes of lesser and varying significance.

Federal troops finally were withdrawn from throughout the South in 1877, marking the conclusion of Reconstruction. Although many prewar secessionists bitterly resented federal intervention in state and local affairs, conditions in North Carolina were not always as bad as they depicted them nor as bad as in some of the other Southern states. Former Whigs and men of unionist sympathies before the war accepted the innovations passively at times and at others with something almost approaching enthusiasm. Many of the changes wrought in the state were long overdue, but the suddenness of their implementation disturbed many people. The nearly paranoid fear of many whites that there would be black uprisings such as the slave rebellions they had heard about or experienced before the war was a controlling factor. This fear was not understood in the North nor was there any general realization of how unprepared most ex-slaves were to manage their own affairs as freedmen, much less to participate in government. The debilitating experiences of slavery left them unprepared for the responsibilities of citizenship. Federal laws designed to regulate the treatment of blacks applied equally to all regions of the United States, of course, and in many places outside the South people came to a new understanding and an appreciation of how blacks had been treated. Racial injustice was recognized as a national question, but it was not one that North or South seriously attempted to solve for many years.

10

A Change of Pace

*R*EMARKABLE changes, particularly in the direction of industrialization, took place in many parts of the South between 1865 and the beginning of the twentieth century. It has been said that the sectional struggle was the great moving force that created a modern America. It ended the Old South and released the energy and the urge that created a dynamic New South. The industrialized postwar South is often contrasted with the staple-crop agriculture of the antebellum South. By implication at least, the Civil War was responsible for the industrial development of the present South. Yet in North Carolina a closer look at the thread of economic growth and business leadership from the years before the war suggests that this theory is not entirely correct.

In the depressing days of Reconstruction many people saw only a dismal economic future for the South. Northern men and their bags of money, many believed, were all that could change this. This was not entirely correct, however, as it was often the gentle prodding of a remarkable group of native businessmen that set the South—and North Carolina in particular—on the road to industrial advancement. With relatively little outside planning or financing, North Carolina contributed significantly to the industrialization of the South. In textiles, tobacco, and furniture, now the state's leading industries, and in the essential auxiliary fields of banking, finance, trade, and transportation, the outstanding figures with few exceptions have been natives of the state. Notable among the exceptions were R. J. Reynolds and George W. Watts in tobacco; Moses and Ceasar Cone, Daniel C. Tompkins, and Simpson B. Tanner in textiles; and they were born in other Southern states. Most of the leaders came from families that had been in the state for several generations or that had come from a neighboring state a generation or so before: the Dukes, Carrs, and Haneses in tobacco; the Battles, Cannons, Frieses, Holts, and Moreheads in textiles; the Lambeths and Wrenns in furniture; and A. B. Andrews, William J. Hawkins, Robert R. Bridgers and the Pages in transportation.

The "rags to riches" tradition that has long prevailed in America is applicable to the industrial development of North Carolina in only a few instances. Historian J. Carlyle Sitterson has demonstrated that 49.2 percent of the business leaders of North Carolina between 1865 and 1900 were born into the upper economic class and had the advantages associated with that class. He found that 37.5 percent were born into the midde economic and social class. These men were sons of planters or farmers, a fact not surprising in view of the prewar occupation of most North Carolinians, but more than one-fourth were sons of men whose livelihood came from their business operations. Leaders in tobacco and textiles generally came from families that had worked in those fields before the war. Of the three most important industries, only in furniture was anything really new undertaken.

Owners of prewar textile mills generally managed to operate during the war and to continue afterwards. It was they who took the lead in establishing new factories after the war. Fifteen of the twenty-nine new mills in operation in 1880 were built by men who had been associated with cotton mills before the war, and several more were built by men who had married into mill-owning families. A grandson of Michael Schenck, the man who built the state's first cotton mill in 1813, opened a new factory in 1873, while his son-in-law became associated with other mills in an adjoining county. Three of his sons also entered the business. Joel Battle's mill, built on the Tar River at Rocky Mount in 1817, was purchased by his cousin in 1848 and is still operated by the family. In Forsyth County in 1836 Francis Fries established a textile mill, and three of his seven sons followed him into the business; it was through marriage that men of the Patterson, Morehead, and Bahnson families entered the business. Edwin Michael Holt in 1837 established a cotton mill in Alamance County where the first colored cotton cloth in the South was woven on power looms; the mills he established continue to be operated by the family. His daughters and nieces brought the Williamson and Erwin families into textiles, and by 1900 at least thirty-five mills had been established by Holts and their relatives.

Sitterson points out that these men and many others in similar circumstances continued to operate numerous small mills even after such limited production was outmoded economically. Executives and managers were reluctant to change the family business or to lose the personal association that they had with their employees. The paternal and personal interest that management had in the workers was of considerable importance in determining the size and the policy of the mill.[1]

About 1880 a Cotton Mill Campaign began, during which the people of the state were convinced that their economic salvation lay in converting their raw cotton into cloth. Local campaigns in many communities scattered across the state raised capital to begin small textile mills. Northern foundries often provided machinery in return for stock in the company. In contrast to those in other states, North Carolina's mills were scattered throughout the piedmont section in many small towns rather than in cities. People seldom had to move to find regular employment, and the population of the state remained dispersed. This is a feature that

---

1. J. Carlyle Sitterson, "Business Leaders in Post-Civil War North Carolina, 1865–1900," in J. Carlyle Sitterson, ed., *Studies in Southern History* (Chapel Hill: University of North Carolina Press, 1957), pp. 111–121.

still marks North Carolina, a state with few large industrial centers.

In addition to the community-sponsored mills, owners of older mills began to expand their operations. With experience to guide them, community confidence to support them, a growing population in need of employment, and an expanding market, mill owners soon opened new types of mills. Hosiery mills appeared before the end of the century, and early in the twentieth century knitting mills were established to make men's and boys' knit underwear. Burlington Industries, now the nation's largest textile concern, began in 1923 and grew rapidly as it experimented with synthetic fibers. Members of the Cannon family in the western piedmont began a yarn mill in 1877, but they sent their yarn to the North to be manufactured. In 1898, however, they began to produce cotton towels and in time the Cannon Mills grew into one of the largest manufacturers of towels in the world.

Tobacco manufacturing was developed largely by men with prewar experience in growing and selling tobacco or who at least lived on farms where it was produced. Many small tobacco factories producing chewing tobacco flourished in the state since before 1840 and considerable quantities of smoking tobacco were manufactured during the war. Union soldiers discovered North Carolina tobacco when they passed through the state in 1865, and from that experience a demand grew for the fine quality tobacco produced in the state.

There are few more impressive examples of the working of private enterprise than that of the success of James Buchanan ("Buck") Duke. In 1865 young Duke and his father began to peddle tobacco that they had manufactured in small quantities on their farm near Durham. Within thirty years Buck Duke was a multimillionaire and head of one of the nation's most powerful trusts, the American Tobacco Company. It was Duke's success in popularizing cigarettes and mechanizing their production that placed his company in a strong position of leadership. Duke's company wiped out or absorbed numerous small competing companies, and by 1904 he controlled three-fourths of the nation's tobacco industry.[2] The monopoly was dissolved by the United States Supreme Court seven years later, but North Carolina retained her leading role in the manufacturing of tobacco. Other large companies, notably those of the Hanes and Reynolds families in the town of Winston, flourished. All were established by men who had grown up in the state or, as in the case of R. J. Reynolds, came from just across the border in Virginia. Another interesting figure was Julian S. Carr, twenty years old when he was released from the Confederate army as a private in 1865. Five years later his father, a Chapel Hill merchant, purchased for him a third interest in a Durham tobacco factory for $4,000. By his skill and industry young Carr was immensely successful not only in the tobacco business but also in textiles, banking, and a variety of other economic enterprises.

It was in establishing the furniture industry, however, that North Carolinians were truly pioneers. There had been skilled cabinetmakers in the state for many years, of course. The Swicegood family in the Lexington and Winston-Salem area produced furniture for three generations, for example, and Thomas Day, a free Negro in Milton, in a shop employing both white and black workers, made furniture of high quality and popular design that was in demand both in North Carolina and in Virginia. These were shops with limited capacity, however, where pieces were individually made. The factory system of furniture production was concentrated in the northeastern part of the United States during most of the nineteenth century, but after about 1870 Michigan and Illinois also became significant centers. The appearance of midwestern furniture in the showrooms and markets in Boston and New York in 1897 and 1898 marked the beginning of the decline of New York's domi-

2. The well known philanthropy of the Dukes which made possible the conversion of Trinity College into Duke University in 1924 and the family's gifts to other schools, hospitals, and institutions was regarded as an effort to "buy off" or silence a disgruntled public. For a fuller and objective account of the Dukes' public benefactions, see Robert F. Durden, *The Dukes of Durham, 1865–1929* (Durham: Duke University Press, 1975), pp. 82–96.

nation of the nation's furniture market. Skilled employees, managers, and even owners of plants in the northeastern states began to move to the South, particularly to North Carolina in the 1890s when some factories began to flourish. Virginia, Tennessee, Texas, and Georgia, in that order, ranked ahead of North Carolina in furniture production in 1880, but with forty-two shops North Carolina was very near the last two. The state's first furniture factory to use power machinery and to begin mass production was organized in the piedmont town of Mebane in 1881 by two brothers, David and William White. The firm they established is still in operation. During that decade half a dozen other factories opened, organized by local men with local capital but often with the advice and assistance of experienced superintendents and workers from outside the state.

Near the end of the century there was nothing to suggest that North Carolina's future in the industry was particularly bright. Georgia had forged ahead with both investment and output six times greater than North Carolina's. During the next ten years, however, the picture totally changed, due almost entirely to developments in and around the town of High Point. Its location along the state's first east-west railroad and in the midst of large hardwood forests certainly gave it two advantages. A number of competitive sawmills stood ready to supply oak lumber at several dollars less per thousand board feet than it cost in Georgia.

Other advantages also favored North Carolina. Just before 1900 a new market for inexpensive furniture developed in the South. The *Southern Lumberman* reported in 1901: "There are thousands of families in the Southern States that have not had a new bedstead, bureau, or set of chairs since the close of the War between the States." [3] This was certainly true in North Carolina, and a demand soon arose for such things. Still another favorable factor was the availability of adequate labor in the region. The old heavy type tobacco formerly grown in the vicin-

3. David N. Thomas, "Getting Started in High Point," *Forest History*, 11 (July 1967): 24.

ity was no longer in demand as tastes developed for the lighter bright leaf tobacco produced farther east. Displaced tobacco farmers in the High Point area were eager for work and they were easily trained to operate the simple machinery of furniture factories.

Labor, transportation, raw materials, and a market, all valuable assets, were by no means unique to High Point. The presence there of business and civic leaders and others willing to invest money made the town different. Industrialization began in 1871 when a Vermont native, William Henry Snow, moved to High Point from nearby Greensboro. Snow passed through the area when he was a captain in the Federal army and liked what he saw. He soon returned because his wife needed a milder climate and also because of economic opportunities that he saw. At one time he was involved with Tourgée in a woodturning operation in a plant with the largest capacity of any in the United States for making handles for axes, picks, and other tools. Nearly all of the plant's output was sold in the North. Snow was well received in the community and highly respected and soon enjoyed success in a variety of business ventures. Speaking of High Point shortly before his death in 1902, Snow said that "in the space of twenty-five years the little idle hamlet has been transformed to a populous city of 6,000 inhabitants and nearly 50 different factories, separate companies and chartered corporations employing over 3,000 men and women who are paid $17,000 for their labor every two weeks." [4] From local sources alone, he noted, over two million dollars had been invested in the town's industry. A dozen furniture plants were supported by 22 business and professional leaders, among whom were merchants, physicians, lumbermen, textile manufacturers, insurance agents, and others. These men transformed their town into the leading furniture center of the South.

The earliest products of these factories were cheap both in construction and in price, often poorly finished and of inferior materials. Bedroom suites consisting of a bed, a dresser, and a

---

4. Thomas, "Getting Started in High Point," pp. 24–25.

washstand sometimes sold for as little as $7.50. For seventy-five cents each, retailers could purchase simple beds. In spite of such prices, one new company reported sales amounting to $75,000 the first year, and it doubled that figure the second. Success almost seemed contagious and investors were eager to make their savings available for enlarging existing factories and opening new ones. Factories also began to spring up in other towns and by 1910 two or more had been built in a dozen towns in the state. In time the industry spread into over forty of the state's one hundred counties and in 1975 there were 595 furniture factories.

When the initial local demand was met and competition began to affect the industry, it turned to national marketing, and North Carolina furniture appeared at wholesale furniture markets in the North. Competition with furniture made elsewhere inspired great improvements in design and quality. Labels, slogans, and trademarks were adopted, some of which have been in use since the first decade of the twentieth century. National advertising also enlarged the market, as did the practice of selling the entire output of a particular factory to a single source as when the Statesville Furniture Company began disposing of everything it made through a Chicago mail order house. Another marketing technique pioneered the sale of furniture parts to be assembled by the purchaser; this reduced the cost of freight and eased the problem of distribution.[5]

Furniture was marketed by being shown in semiannual exhibitions visited by buyers and dealers. Frequently display facilities were inadequate and rivalry developed between the management of different showrooms. In 1912 High Point had five different exhibition companies, so that it became difficult to attract buyers to scattered locations. A group of manufacturers met in the city in 1913 and organized the Southern Furniture Exposition Company, which opened its own building in 1921. The exhibition building has been enlarged and rebuilt a number of times. Manufacturers now maintain displays the year round

5. Thomas, "Getting Started in High Point," pp. 23–32.

while special exhibitions of new lines are held several times each year.

Much of the industrial development in the state occurred during the period of Democratic control of government. Conservative leaders were sometimes referred to as Bourbons because they were believed to have been fond of relaxing and looking back on the ''good old days.'' Their actions between the end of Reconstruction and 1894, when they were rejected at the polls, resulted, nevertheless, in the establishment of many worthwhile programs. Federal taxes helped provide pensions and other assistance to disabled and destitute soldiers in the North, but such aid was denied those who had been Confederate soldiers. In 1885 North Carolina began to provide assistance to needy Confederate veterans and widows in the state, and about the same time the state also took over the operation of an orphan asylum at Oxford that had been established by the Freemasons a few years earlier. A state-supported orphanage for black children was established near Oxford, and hospitals for the insane were opened in Morganton in the west and in Goldsboro in the east to supplement the older one in Raleigh. The State Board of Health worked to control epidemics and infectious diseases and to improve the quality of drinking water throughout the state. The legislature made significant appropriations for the state agricultural department, the state penitentiary, education and assistance of the deaf and blind, and the university.

An especially significant step was taken by the General Assembly in 1877, when it appropriated funds for the operation of two summer normal schools in the state—one for young white men and another for young black men who would become teachers. Governor Vance saw this as the dawn of a new day and an opportunity to ''electrify the State from Cherokee to Currituck,'' as he expressed it.[6] The portion of this program conducted at the University of North Carolina in Chapel Hill that year was the first summer-school session of a university

6. Kemp P. Battle, *History of the University of North Carolina,* 2 vols. (Raleigh: Edwards & Broughton Printing Company, 1907, 1912), 2:142.

conducted in the United States, and it is of further significance because women were admitted to the heretofore all-male institution. The legislature intended that only men should attend the summer normal school, so state funds were used only for them, but young women were invited by the university administration, which found other funds for them. To superintend the program the university employed Professor John J. Ladd of Vermont, a graduate of Brown University who had worked with the public schools of New England as well as with schools in Virginia. The quite successful program was the means of introducing young women to careers in public education.

As a state with extensive agricultural interests North Carolina has a long history of concern for the welfare of the farmer. National policy following the Civil War, particularly the tariff, so clearly favored industry that it caused great concern among the agricultural interests throughout the country. Farmers accustomed to operating on credit were hard hit by such adverse factors as bad weather, surpluses, and economic depression. They frequently pointed out that they were obliged to accept for their produce whatever the purchaser wanted to pay, yet in purchasing seed, fertilizer, food, and clothing, they were obliged to pay whatever merchants asked. This situation they blamed on the great combinations of business that flourished, on the tariff that protected industry, and on discriminatory freight rates that favored long-distance bulk shipments.

Several spokesmen appeared determined to alert hardworking and concerned farmers to the cause of their predicament and to suggest some remedies. Two North Carolinians received national recognition for their efforts. Leonidas LaFayette Polk, relative of President Polk and an experienced farmer from youth, had been a Confederate soldier, had served in the legislature, and was a member of the ill-fated constitutional convention of 1865–1866 the proposals of which were rejected. As early as 1870 he advocated the creation of a state department of agriculture and when that was accomplished in 1877, he became the first commissioner, holding office for four years. In the piedmont town of Winston in 1886 he established a newspaper,

The *Progressive Farmer,* as a means of teaching farmers improved methods of agriculture; within a few years his paper also became concerned with politics and the formation of "farmers' clubs" that might bring pressure on the legislature. Just as he was attempting to unite the farmers, organizers appeared in North Carolina representing the Farmers' Alliance, a farm-oriented organization originating in Texas. Polk cast his lot with this group and in 1887 was its national vice-president, becoming president two years later. Typical of Polk's expression and his reasoning were these words from a speech at Sandy Springs, S.C. in August 1887:

> The siren voice that led the Southern farmer astray after the war was, "Twenty-five cents cotton." In the face of the devastation, destruction and despair brought about by the war, King Cotton promised to shower his blessings on our country, and our farmers listened to his seductive utterances. We told the North we would forget the past, just go ahead and make our cloths, our hats, our shoes, our plows, our axehandles, our fertilizers, raise our mules and our hogs, even grind our flour and meal, and we would raise one crop to pay for all, and the North could put its price on that one crop. We forsook the good old and only safe rule of making a living at home, and went to buy everything—bread, meat, clothing, tools, horses, mules, corn, hay—think of it—hay! *hay!* HAY!
>
> A Southern farmer buying hay to feed a mule to work all summer killing better grass than the North ever knew! Our farmers buy everything to raise cotton, and raise cotton to buy everything, and after going through this treadmill business for years, they lie down and die, and leave their families penniless.[7]

As president of the National Farmers' Alliance with millions of members, Polk was very influential; nevertheless he was unable to get the agricultural reforms he wanted by working through regular political parties. He turned instead to the People's Party and, in February 1892 at St. Louis, presided over a meeting of a great many diverse organizations at an "industrial

7. Stuart Noblin, *Leonidas LaFayette Polk, Agrarian Crusader* (Chapel Hill: University of North Carolina Press, 1949), p. 194, quoting from the Anderson, S. C., *Journal* of August 25, 1887.

conference'' organized to approve the party. In an address at the
opening of the conference he called upon concerned people to
''march to the ballot box and take possession of the government, restore it to the principles of our fathers, and run it in the
interest of the people.'' Neither sympathy nor charity would
help, only justice. ''We want relief from these unjust oppres-
sions,'' he shouted, ''and as I have said from New York to California, in my speeches, we intend to have it if we have to wipe
the two old parties from the face of the earth!'' [8] The speech
was hailed with wild enthusiasm, and Polk's clear willingness to
lead the new party into battle gave him an even stronger position with the alliance. Polk soon became the obvious choice of
the People's party as its candidate for president. A nominating
convention scheduled for Omaha in July, it appeared, would
surely select him. Polk's unexpected death in June, however,
terminated all such speculation.

In North Carolina the desires of the People's Party, or the
Populists as they were commonly called, were ignored by the
Democrats. Populists began to make common cause with the
Republicans, who still had the support of most of the black population. The Panic of 1893 further depressed agriculture in the
state and resulted in a Republican-Populist fusion against the
Democrats the next year. A campaign marked by partisan bitterness and prejudice was conducted in 1894 resulting in a sweep-
ing Republican victory for nearly all of the state and congressional offices. Both houses of the legislature had large
majorities of Republicans, and in 1896 at the next gubernatorial
election a Republican, Daniel L. Russell of Brunswick County,
was elected. A number of black legislators were also elected,
the last to serve until late in the twentieth century. Between
1868 and 1900 there were 26 Negro senators and 101 representatives who served in the North Carolina General Assembly.
Under the administration of Russell a program that required
local tax support for schools was implemented and local self-

8. Noblin, *Polk,* pp. 273–274, quoting from the *Progressive Farmer* of March 15,
1892.

government was restored. The powers of the railroad commission were also enlarged. It was during this period that the Spanish-American War occurred. North Carolina's quota of troops was two regiments of infantry and a battery of artillery, but for the latter, three companies of Negro troops were substituted and organized into the Third Regiment of North Carolina Volunteers. Although none of the state's troops saw action, several North Carolinians in regular service lost their lives. Ensign Worth Bagley of Raleigh became the first American naval officer killed in the war.

Although Polk and his farmer-associates in North Carolina were not entirely successful in accomplishing their goals, they left a number of marks on the state. The *Progressive Farmer* continues as a monthly magazine and is widely read throughout the South. Their efforts brought into existence in 1889 an agricultural and technical college in Raleigh that is now North Carolina State University, serving North Carolina and the nation and providing extension programs in India, Afghanistan, Peru and other Latin American countries, and elsewhere. Farmers' concern over excessive freight rates resulted in the creation of the Board of Railroad Commissioners in 1891, modeled on a similar commission in Georgia. North Carolina's commissioners expected to work closely with the Interstate Commerce Commission. The areas of concern to members of the commission in North Carolina were gradually enlarged to include telegraph rates, telephone companies, street railways, and other public utilities. The legislature of 1899 revised the law and created the North Carolina Corporation Commission with broader powers than the old railroad commission had had, thereby establishing the first corporation commission in the United States.

During this time of deep concern with agricultural problems Priestly H. Mangum, an alumnus of Wake Forest College and a large farmer of Wake County, developed an erosion-checking terrace which he laid out in many of his fields. Soil in plowed fields washed away in almost every rain over the hilly terrain of North Carolina, but about 1885 Mangum abandoned the custom of ditching his land to carry off excessive rain. Instead he laid out broad sloping terraces following the natural contour of the land. These stopped the water that once rushed downhill and channeled it slowly and gently around the hill. Most of it was absorbed by the soil of the terrace. Because they were broad and gentle, these terraces could be plowed over and crops planted in them, thereby eliminating the weeds and grass that formerly grew along the ditch banks. Mangum's terrace was widely copied throughout the state and the South.

Harry Skinner, a Greenville attorney, was also concerned during this period over the welfare of the struggling farmers throughout the nation. His first thoughts on the subject found expression in an article entitled ''A Landed Basis for our National Bank Issue,'' in which some ideas were expounded that later appeared in the Federal Reserve Act of 1913. Skinner's recommendation of a solution to the farmers' problem was further expanded in his article, ''The Hope of the South'' which appeared in *Frank Leslie's Illustrated Newspaper* for November 30, 1889. Read on the floor of the St. Louis convention, it formed the nucleus of the subtreasury plan that was bandied about for a time as offering the ultimate solution to the agricultural problems of the nation. It suggested a means by which producers might hold cotton off the market until manufacturers offered a suitable price. Planters would then cease to be at the mercy of brokers and manufacturers.

The surplus in the United States treasury, Skinner's plan recommended, should be used to build warehouses throughout the South in which farmers might store their surplus cotton. A ''cotton certificate'' would be issued to the grower stating the value of his cotton at a fixed price, while a very modest handling charge would be made for this transaction. Such certificates would be negotiable. It was assumed that manufacturers in dire need of cotton would soon be willing to purchase it at the fixed price. Whether they did or not, however, the purchasing power of the grower would certainly be increased by this scheme. If the grower's cotton was not redeemed at the end of a specified period by which time it was anticipated the market would be better, it might be sold.

Such a plan in 1890 was considered extremely radical. Senator Vance was unwilling to sponsor a bill embodying these provisions on his own initiative as he believed it to be unconstitutional, but he did consent to introduce it "by request." Although grain, tobacco, and other nonperishable crops were also considered to be eligible under this plan, it was generally denounced by all except the members of the Farmers' Alliance. Skinner is remembered in the annals of agricultural history, however, as one of the first to suggest government control of the cotton crop, and his basic idea of government warehouses for the storage of crops as a means of raising or maintaining prices came to be acceptable in the vast planning programs that manipulated the economy in the next century.[9]

Although the state had a tradition of poverty, at one time or another before the Civil War there were twenty-eight colleges of varying quality in North Carolina, and all but two were open at the beginning of the war. Fifteen of them still operate. After the war various welfare agencies, religious organizations, the state legislature, and private citizens established forty new institutions of higher education in the state for the improvement of youth of both races. Twenty-seven of them continue to serve the state and the nation. Farm organizations and individual farmers lent their support to the creation and operation of a number of these which they envisioned as being of particular help to rural people.

Fifteen of the prewar and eight of the postwar colleges were exclusively for women. Salem College, established in 1772 as a seminary, and Wesleyan Methodist College in Macon, Georgia, founded in 1836, are among the oldest colleges for women in the United States.[10]

Schools for Negroes were established promptly after the war although basic education had been available to a few of that race earlier. John Chavis in Raleigh, for example, a black man who

---

9. Henderson, *North Carolina, Old North State,* 2:386–387.

10. Clement Eaton, *A History of the Old South* (New York: The Macmillan Company, 1966), p. 397.

may have been educated privately at Princeton, taught a school for white children during the day and for blacks in the evening. Quakers as well as some Anglican missionaries taught black children in their schools, and as late as 1854 there were day schools for blacks in New Bern.[11] Shaw University in Raleigh grew out of a theological class formed late in 1865 by Dr. Henry Martin Tupper, a recently discharged Union army chaplain. The present Fayetteville State University came under state sponsorship in 1877, when a modest school established in 1867 by the Freedmen's Bureau was taken over. It was the first normal school established in the South for any race.

Denominational schools also flourished during the postwar period. The early precedent set by the Moravians with their school at Salem, was followed by Wake Forest (Baptist), Davidson (Presbyterian), Guilford (Quaker), Greensboro (Methodist), St. Mary's (Episcopal), and Catawba (German Reformed), all in active service for a decade or more before the war. After 1867 additonal colleges were established by nearly all of these denominations, and they were joined by the Roman Catholics, Lutherans, Congregational Christians, and others.

North Carolinians with little or no assistance from outside the state had totally repaired the damage that their state had suffered during the Civil War in the destruction of both public and private property and institutions. They had forged ahead in building railroads and industrial plants of various kinds, in maintaining many old and establishing some new colleges, and in adapting themselves to new social and political conditions. Her people were much more progressive than they had ever been before and were poised on the threshold of a totally different world as the nineteenth century came to an end.

11. John Hope Franklin, *The Free Negro in North Carolina, 1790–1860* (Chapel Hill: University of North Carolina Press, 1943), pp. 164–174.

11

A State Transformed

$\mathcal{N}$ORTH CAROLINA, after the beginning of the twentieth century, underwent an almost total metamorphosis; the attitudes, ideas, and character of her people took a different direction. During the early 1900s she was considered, in some ways, more progressive than most other former Confederate states. She early planned for, supported, and worked toward objectives once referred to by the southern historian Francis B. Simkins as the "trinity of Southern progress"—industrial growth, good roads, and schools.[1] In some other areas, however—race relations, cultural opportunities, concern for her workers—North Carolina's early record was far from impressive.

Professor R. D. W. Connor of the University of North Carolina told the American Historical Association at its meeting in Durham in 1929 that the South had "shaken itself free from its heritage of war and Reconstruction. Its self-confidence restored, its political stability assured, its prosperity regained, its social problems on the way to solution. . . ."[2] Unfortunately the

1. George B. Tindall, *The Ethnic Southerners* (Baton Rouge: Louisiana State University Press, 1976), p. 31.

2. Tindall, *Ethnic Southerners,* p. 31.

Great Depression had just begun, and although some of Connor's predictions of progress seemed about to be realized near the end of the 1930s, they were further delayed by the war of the 1940s.

For most southern states the twentieth century is as clearly divided into two periods by World War II as the nineteenth century was divided by the Civil War. Although World War II did not bring physical destruction to the South, it brought many changes that were equally significant. It was this war that produced unbelievable changes in North Carolina, triggering even greater progress.

Actually, change began after World War I, when 15,000 men and women in uniform returned home from distant places bringing new ideas. A generation later the same thing occurred on a much larger scale, when 264,000 veterans returned after World War II. Approximately 101,000 North Carolinians later saw service in Korea and 168,000 in Vietnam. Many of the men brought home "war brides" who added a cosmopolitan flavor to communities. Veterans who were no longer content to farm or to work in cotton mills set about to improve themselves by taking advantage of the G. I. Bill of Rights and securing technical or college training. Some, of course, left the state for what appeared to be better opportunities elsewhere. Military service gave many of these people new skills and broadened their perspectives, and numbers of them lost old prejudices. Their return contributed significantly to the blunting of class lines in the state and their broader outlook undoubtedly eased the path of desegregation.

Before World War II a single political party was in firm control in North Carolina. The state during that period has been described as "a 'progressive plutocracy' run by an 'enlightened oligarchy.' " [3] Factional rivalries existed within the powerful Democratic party, however, and primary elections often gave

3. Charles P. Roland, *The Improbable Era, The South since World War II* (Lexington: University Press of Kentucky, 1975), p. 5.

the people a choice among candidates with different views. This made considerable progress possible under what might otherwise have been an oppressive political machine.

Simultaneously with the beginning of the twentieth century North Carolina inaugurated a new governor who, although he advocated white supremacy, was a man with a worthwhile goal for his state. Charles B. Aycock during his campaign and again in his inaugural address spoke convincingly of "the equal right of every child born on earth to have the opportunity 'to burgeon out all that there is within him.' " [4] It was his earnest desire to provide educational opportunities for all the children of the state so that everyone could lead a more meaningful life and contribute to the betterment of the state. He wanted every young man to be able to read and write by the time he was twenty-one so that he might vote intelligently. He hoped to establish a just political climate that would enable citizens to get the maximum benefit from their government. His program met with considerable success, and he laid the foundations on which the state built as the century advanced.

Aycock, the son of a small but successful planter in eastern North Carolina who lost much of his property at the end of the Civil War, was born in 1859, and he knew from bitter experience the privations suffered by many people in the decades of his own youth. He walked miles to attend an academy, inspired to secure an education by the knowledge that his mother could not write her name. Graduated from the University of North Carolina in 1880, he also studied law. As a successful attorney he attracted statewide attention, and during a brief period as superintendent of schools in his native Wayne County he became concerned about the quality of education available to young people.

He campaigned for governor as a Democrat on a platform that proposed educational improvements, and he succeeded a Republican who had been elected on the Fusionist ticket of Republicans and Populists, the combination that brought many blacks

4. Tindall, *Ethnic Southerners,* p. 79.

into public offices. Democrats, of course, were pleased to be back in office again, but as sociology professor Rupert B. Vance later observed, "advocates of white supremacy, without at all intending to, in plain truth turned up an idealist." He further characterized Aycock as having risen "as far above prejudice as it has proved possible for any native-born Southerner to do." [5] The Democratic party's goal was disfranchisement of the Negro, while Aycock's goal was education for both blacks and whites to enable them to make wise political decisions and to participate fully in all elections. Separate schools for the races were then acceptable to the courts and to Congress, and the new governor wanted the state to provide adequate schools for both races. It was his belief in education for *all* the people that marked him as different from previous advocates of improved schools in the state. Aycock also differed from his predecessors in advocating a uniform school system throughout the state with the use of both state and local funds for its support. Tax money spent for education, he convincingly argued, was a splendid investment. Educated North Carolinians would attract better industry, the people would be more productive workers, prosperity would abound, and Tar Heels would all benefit.

In many respects Aycock envisioned schools much like those of the pre-Civil War system—schools located by districts and within walking distance for every child, taught for four months each year, and under proper supervision of local and state educators. He also called for generous support of the state's colleges and the university so that opportunities for higher education might be available to all who qualified. A state appropriation in 1901 provided money to equalize local schools of the state and to bring those in the poorer counties up to the same standard as those in the more prosperous ones. A similar program, never fully implemented, existed before the Civil War but was abandoned during or immediately afterwards. [6]

5. Rupert B. Vance, "Aycock of North Carolina," *Southwest Review,* 18 (Spring 1933): 288–289.

6. Oliver H. Orr, Jr., *Charles Brantley Aycock* (Chapel Hill: University of North Carolina Press, 1961), pp. 295–312.

The foundations laid during this administration were sound and the policy of public support firmly established. In 1907, two years after Aycock left office, high-school grades through eleven were added to the state system and a few years later the term was extended to six months. At the same time steps were taken that led to the consolidation of many small rural school districts. The transportation of pupils at public expense also began, but not until 1917 did motorized school buses supplant horse-drawn vehicles. North Carolina in the 1920s led the nation in building rural consolidated schools, and before long more children in North Carolina were riding to and from school each day than in any other state.[7] During the Depression of the 1930s additional state funds were made available to maintain the schools in the counties where local revenues were inadequate, and the system weathered the hard times, although the length of a term was sometimes reduced, and library and laboratory resources frequently suffered.

The state's first twentieth-century governor set a precedent, perhaps unwittingly, in his successful educational program. He acquired the title of Educational Governor soon after taking office. Subsequent governors have laid great stress on a particular program and thereby acquired similar titles. Perhaps it was because North Carolina governors could not succeed themselves that they sometimes chose a program which could be implemented and pushed to a successful conclusion in a four-year period. Cameron Morrison was known as the Good Roads Governor, and W. Kerr Scott made a name for himself with his farm-to-market roads. A. W. McLean is remembered for his implementation of sound fiscal policies, including a budget bureau, and Luther Hodges for the development of business and industry.

During the years on either side of World War I the state flourished, and her leadership in many programs caused her to be called "the Wisconsin of the South." Tax revenues in-

7. D. J. Whitener, "Education for the People," *North Carolina Historical Review*, 36 (April 1959): 193.

creased 554 percent from 1913 to 1930. State expenditures in the ten years after 1915 increased 847 percent—a rate greater than in any other state and more than double the national average. A reorganized tax system, extension of the income tax, and revaluation of property made this possible. A state public welfare system was formed in 1917, and the budgets of state institutions were increased in 1919.

During the decades following World War II further improvements came in the state's public schools with the addition of a twelfth grade and the lengthening of the term to nine months, advancements that a few city systems had implemented in the 1940s. Curriculum revisions broadened opportunities for young people by offering practical courses leading to employment in business and industry. Black schools in most of the South received about three-fourths as much from tax revenues as white schools, but in North Carolina in the early 1950s black pupils received slightly more than whites.[8]

The contrast of schools in this century before and after World War II is striking indeed. Some rural schools in the late 1920s and early 1930s were still one- or two-teacher schools conducted in identical and inadequate wooden buildings. By the late 1930s most of these had been abandoned in favor of brick consolidated schools, many of which were constructed under the various federal work programs of the Depression years.

In the 1950s the problem of racial integration became critical. The May 1954 decision of the U.S. Supreme Court outlawed racial segregation in the public schools, and efforts to delay or circumvent this decision were made for several years. The governor appointed a biracial committee, headed by Thomas J. Pearsall, a Rocky Mount attorney, to study the legal aspects of the question and to recommend "a policy and a program which will preserve the State public school system by having the support of the people."[9] In 1955 the General Assembly eliminated from the school laws any reference to race, transferred authority

8. Roland, *The Improbable Era*, p. 34.
9. Lefler and Newsome, *North Carolina*, p. 687.

over enrollment and pupil assignment from the state to county and city boards of education, turned over ownership, operation, and control of the state's 7,200 school buses to local units, and substituted annual contracts with teachers for the continuing contracts of the immediate past.

At the recommendation of Governor Luther Hodges the schools in 1955 were operated as they always had been. He called upon children of all races to "voluntarily attend separate public schools." [10] Although some newspapers and some individuals in the state praised this move, the National Association for the Advancement of Colored People and other individuals and groups within the state denounced the suggestion.

Three Negro graduates of a Durham high school applied for admission to the University of North Carolina in the spring of 1955, but the trustees directed that they be denied admission. The NAACP threatened to take the cases to federal court, and applicants were admitted after three federal judges ruled that the university must process their applications without regard to race or color.

In 1956 a special session of the General Assembly acted upon the report of Governor Hodges's committee. Two days of televised hearings were held, out of which grew a constitutional amendment that was approved by a vote of the people in September. This amendment, reportedly designed as a "safety valve," provided tuition grants from the state for children whose parents did not want them to attend school with members of another race. Such children then might attend private academies. A few such schools were opened, but comparatively few pupils attended them, and little use was made of the "Pearsall Plan," as it was called. By giving parents an alternative, however, it prevented what might have been serious confrontations when schools opened later that year. North Carolina's reaction was much more moderate than that of her neighbor to the north. Virginia took the lead in resisting school integration and in 1956 began "massive resistance" by repealing compulsory education

10. Lefler and Newsome, *North Carolina*, p. 688.

laws and withholding funds from previously white schools to which a black pupil was admitted.

School boards in Charlotte, Greensboro, and Winston-Salem admitted blacks in 1957. Craven and Wayne counties followed in 1959, while Chapel Hill, Durham, and other city schools followed in 1960. In 1961 Indians were also admitted to Dunn High School, and Davidson College and Duke University began to accept blacks. Most of the state's school districts were integrated by the end of 1965.

In North Carolina, as in other states, white families began to move from cities and towns into rural areas where there were fewer blacks. This often left only a few white children in previously all-black schools. In a landmark case, a federal district court in 1970 ordered busing in the Charlotte-Mecklenburg County schools to establish a desired racial balance. This decision was upheld by the U.S. Supreme Court the next year as being necessary to break up the former pattern of segregated schools. From this beginning the busing of pupils spread throughout the South in 1971 and 1972 and eventually to other parts of the nation.

During the years of educational uncertainty the state gave no serious thought to abandoning the system of public schools. In fact, considerable attention was paid to advancing the cause of education, and several innovative plans were carried out. In Winston-Salem in 1964 the North Carolina Advancement School opened. Designed for "high-potential low achievers" it offered three months of special training for eighth graders under the supervision of the Learning Institute of North Carolina. To give blacks and other disadvantaged boys and girls an introduction to a broad range of subjects and to cultivate new interests, special summer programs were inaugurated at state-supported colleges. Living in dormitories for several weeks, these children attended special classes and enjoyed sports and other events planned for them by faculty, staff, and students of the host institution. In 1965 also in Winston-Salem the North Carolina School of the Arts opened as the first state-established and state-supported school in the nation for the performing arts. Pupils from high school through college age attend this degree-granting school, which is a part of the University of North Carolina system.

Although North Carolina devoted 30.9 percent of the state budget to public schools, it ranked forty-fourth among the states in 1971–1972 in per-pupil expenditure. The sum spent on education was consistently increased beginning in 1966, and North Carolina was generally ahead of the other states in the Southeast. A public kindergarten program was implemented in 1969, and with better preparation of children at this impressionable age, educators anticipated a higher percentage of high-school graduates among the youth of the state.[11]

Several relatively insignificant but sometimes irritating by-products of the school-integration furor appeared. In 1955 the Patriots of North Carolina, Inc., an all-white association formed to try to maintain "the purity of the white race and of Anglo-Saxon institutions," was chartered, but it made no lasting impression on the state. The Ku Klux Klan was also revived but quickly faded into obscurity after 1958, when about a hundred robed Klansmen attempted to intimidate some Indians in Robeson County. About 350 Indians raided the Klan meeting, and both groups were dispersed by the state highway patrol. Signs appeared in scattered communities in Eastern North Carolina declaring "This Is Klan Country," but Klan meetings, if they were held at all, convened in greatest secrecy. Signs also sometimes appeared in cow pastures and broom-sedge fields urging "Impeach Earl Warren," but no petitions to that effect seem to have circulated. As Chief Justice of the United States Supreme Court, Warren was counted responsible for recent Court decisions. Such devices as these were means of venting pent-up frustration over a situation which some people disliked but could not alter. What they did was sometimes embarrassing, but it was ineffective and relatively harmless.

A movement that was to have nationwide significance began

---

11. James W. Clay, and others, eds., *North Carolina Atlas* (Chapel Hill: University of North Carolina Press, 1975), pp. 250–253.

in Greensboro on the first day of February 1960 when a group of black students from the North Carolina Agricultural and Technical College entered a local store, sat down at a lunch counter for whites, and refused to leave. Similar demonstrations soon occurred throughout the South. In North Carolina, except for a few arrests under the trespass laws, such actions were peaceful and effective. Although a few lunch counters closed and some removed the seats so that everyone had to stand, most were opened to all, and the policy spread in due time to restaurants, hotels, and theaters. The Civil Rights Act of 1964, of course, played a role in the extension of the goals of the Greensboro students. Subsequent acts of Congress guaranteed the rights of minorities still further, and in North Carolina as elsewhere they had the desired effect.

In the years after the 1920s much of the forward-looking leadership of North Carolina originated in Chapel Hill. Harry W. Chase, a native of Massachusetts, was elected president of the University of North Carolina in 1920. He had been a member of the faculty for nine years, and it was largely he who transformed the university from a good college into an effective university. Old departments were expanded and new ones added. Chase made the university a serviceable tool for the state by enlarging physical facilities, bringing young, enthusiastic faculty members to Chapel Hill, and enlisting the support of students, alumni, and the General Assembly. The new president's sound judgment, his good sense, and his fearlessness in the face of opposition that he deemed unjustified won him friends both on campus and around the state. His unflinching support of his faculty—when members faced occasional attacks because of the nature of some of their scholarly publications and interests—was the marvel of friend and foe alike. When a bill outlawing the teaching of evolution was introduced in the General Assembly of 1925, his opposition to it contributed significantly to its defeat. At the risk of jeopardizing the university appropriations from the General Assembly, he spoke in support of academic freedom and won on that point without losing the legislative financial support so badly needed.

During Chase's administration, the General Assembly appropriated nearly $5.5 million for a building program. Under his direction the Graduate School, which had been established in 1903, was reorganized; schools of law, medicine, pharmacy, engineering, and education began to offer professional training, and a large new library was opened with an enlarged professional staff. The Department of Music was reorganized, while the Carolina Playmakers, formed under the direction of Professor Frederick A. Koch, were acclaimed throughout the South for the training offered in dramatic art largely through the use of folk plays. Following the establishment of the University of North Carolina Press in 1922, Chapel Hill became a center for the publication of books and periodicals dealing with the state and the region. There were only three other state university presses then in existence—at the universities of Illinois, Washington, and California—and of these only the one in California published more than an occasional book. Studies dealing with race relations and other sociological and political topics were among the most notable products of the Chapel Hill press. Sociologist Howard W. Odum was the author, coauthor, or editor of nine widely read and influential regional books.

Chase was succeeded as president of the university in 1930 by Frank P. Graham, who continued to lead the institution into new and worthwhile fields of service to the state, the region, and the nation. Graham also became a leader of national and international importance, serving as a public member of the National War Labor Board and as Administrator, Defense Manpower, United States Department of Labor. He was the first president of the Oak Ridge Institute of Nuclear Studies, a member of the Committee on Civil Rights, chairman of the National Advisory Council on Social Security, and United Nations mediator in the disputes between the Dutch and Indonesia and between India and Pakistan. He also filled the unexpired term of J. Melville Broughton in the United States Senate, 1949–1951.

In 1977 there were 116 colleges and universities in the state; only slightly more than 58 percent of the high-school graduates in 1972, however, sought higher education of any kind. Degree-granting colleges attracted 54.6 percent of them, a figure considerably below the national average of 62 percent. There were forty-eight senior institutions, including sixteen maintained by the state, eleven private junior colleges, seventeen community colleges, and forty technical institutes. The creation by the General Assembly in 1955 of the Board of Higher Education with responsibility to plan and "promote the development and operation of a sound, vigorous, progressive, and co-ordinated system of higher education in the State of North Carolina," [12] resulted in a balanced system of institutions well spread throughout the state. Evening classes, special-interest courses, and training for the handicapped were offered at most of these schools.

Changes equally as significant as those in education occurred in other areas. Some new industry was established in the state before the end of the nineteenth century, but it was after 1900 that impressive growth occurred. Textile factories scattered across the state were the primary industry in numerous small towns. The value of denim, damask, yarns, towels, underwear, hosiery, and blankets grew from a mere $30 million in 1900 to $450 million thirty years later. Tobacco manufacturing was the leading source of income in a handful of towns, but it was a significant industry, nevertheless. The value of tobacco products grew from $16 million in 1900 to over $400 million in three decades. The value of furniture grew from $1 million to $54 million in the same time span.

During World War II industrial plants were built in North Carolina and elsewhere in the South to produce war materials. After the war, when industry began to replace obsolete techniques and worn-out machinery and to build new plants, many companies elected to relocate in the South. So great were the changes in the industrial patterns in the state that in 1973 textile products were valued in excess of $3 billion, tobacco in excess of $1 billion, and furniture in excess of $686 billion.

Diversification in industry began about 1929 when the Enka Corporation began producing man-made fibers at its plant near

12. State of North Carolina, *1955 Session Laws and Resolutions,* Chapter 1186.

Asheville. Nylon hosiery mills soon followed, and in the succeeding years fabrics of various kinds came to be produced. The
Burlington Industries in 1934, just ten years after being established, had become the largest weaver of rayon yarns in the
nation; in the late 1970s it had plants across the continent and in
many foreign countries, with an annual output valued at around
$2 billion. Manufacturing spread from the piedmont, where it
originated and flourished in the nineteenth century, until it transformed the economic base of nearly every part of the state. Certain cities and towns are known as centers of a particular kind of
industry, but new industry since 1945 has generally located in
rural or suburban settings where carefully planned buildings
blend with the surroundings. Most cotton-mill villages that once
flourished around mills in many eastern and piedmont towns
soon disappeared. In some cases the houses were sold to their
occupants, while in others they were simply removed when
workers chose other housing.

A great many industrial workers in North Carolina moved to
farms and commuted to work. In many parts of the state at road
junctions and country stores workers parked their cars each
morning, joined a car pool, and rode to work. In the evening
they picked up their cars and returned home to tend livestock
and work the land, both as a form of recreation and for the
added income.

One of the most striking developments in the state began in
1957 with plans for the development of the Research Triangle
Park under the leadership of Governor Luther Hodges. Lying
approximately equidistant from Raleigh, Durham, and Chapel
Hill, the locations respectively of North Carolina State University, Duke University, and the University of North Carolina, the
park occupies 5,000 acres. In a campuslike setting many buildings of interesting and unique design were erected for research
facilities and technically oriented manufacturing organizations.
Agencies were formed to provide contract research in a variety
of fields. The park soon became the home of a number of state
and federal agencies dealing with such matters as environmental
protection, forestry research, and national health. Private con-

cerns there began research related to medicine, chemistry, fibers, education, communications, and other fields. The data-processing laboratory of the National Center for Health Statistics was located in the park as was the Triangle Universities Computation Center, operated by the three adjacent universities. Not all of the activity in the park was science-oriented; the American Academy of Arts and Sciences established the National Humanities Center there. The center was planned to promote humanistic studies in America, and each year fifty scholars became Fellows to study broad cultural, social, and intellectual issues. Organized as an autonomous agency, the National Humanities Center was administratively structured along the lines of the Center for Advanced Study in the Behavioral Sciences at Palo Alto, California. The existence of the Triangle Universities Center for Advanced Studies, Inc., at the Research Triangle Park played a significant role in the decision to locate the National Humanities Center there.

The construction of good roads was one of the three primary goals of Southern progress, and North Carolina's Governor Cameron Morrison in his inaugural address in 1921 called upon the forces of "progressive democracy" to wage "war for righteousness with the reactionary and unprogressive forces of our State." [13] He was victorious in his campaign for good roads, and before the end of his administration, more than $65 million were provided for that purpose. Largely through the effective work of Miss Harriet Morehead Berry, Secretary of the North Carolina Good Roads Association, a bond issue was approved. A well-planned program to construct asphalt, concrete, sand-clay, and gravel roads connecting all county-seat towns, other leading towns, and all state institutions quickly brought recognition to North Carolina as the Good Roads State. Before the Great Depression curtailed such work, the state's highway sys-

13. D. L. Corbitt, ed., *Public Papers and Letters of Cameron Morrison, Governor of North Carolina, 1921–1925* (Raleigh: Edwards & Broughton Company, State Printers, 1927), p. 14.

tem included over 7,500 miles of road, nearly 4,000 miles hard-surfaced. The state thereby reclaimed areas that had come to be considered "lost provinces" in the western mountains and beyond the coastal swamps. The state's faith in this plan was well placed, as increased revenue from gasoline and automobile taxes was sufficient to cover the costs. At the end of the decade only Texas of the other Southern states had more surfaced roads than North Carolina, while in the nation North Carolina ranked eleventh.

Because of reduced local resources during the Depression, the state took over the maintenance and construction of county roads in 1931. This resulted in better overall planning and the development of standards of quality and safety. New construction was virtually halted after Pearl Harbor, but between 1949 and 1953 under the leadership of Governor W. Kerr Scott a new program of road building was begun to improve rural roads and to help farmers get their produce to market. In the following years not only did the state build many new roads and bridges, but the network of interstate highways also provided easier passage through the state. The state's highways, roads, and streets increased in miles from almost 68,000 in 1955 to over 86,000 in 1973.

In the area of organized labor North Carolina has made little or no progress during the twentieth century. By the early 1970s 27.9 percent of all labor in the United States was organized. In some states outside the South as much as 43 percent was organized, but in North Carolina the figure was 7.8 percent, the lowest in the nation. North Carolina was also one of seventeen states with a right-to-work law.

In the period immediately after the Civil War farm laborers found that working in new mills in town was preferable to farm work because mills offered employment the year around and paid regular wages. Long hours, night work, child labor, exploitation by the company store, and other aspects of their employment did not appear to be serious. A second generation of laborers was tied to the work by ignorance, fear of the employer, and dependence upon the company for both home and job. Before the end of the nineteenth century there was no organized labor in North Carolina textile, tobacco, or furniture factories. Nevertheless, a few skilled workers such as printers, locomotive engineers, bookbinders, and bricklayers had been unionized. With the turn of the century the American Federation of Labor, having failed earlier to make any significant headway, directed its attention again to the South. In the textile industry sixteen unions were organized, but the failure of strikes in four towns shortly afterwards led to a decline of interest in the labor movement for more than a dozen years. When, between 1913 and 1918, the United Textile Workers' union was active in the South, it made no effort to organize in North Carolina because of the known strong antiunion sentiment there. In 1919, however, the UTW did become active in the state, but a strike in Charlotte was only partially successful. It was settled on an open-shop basis, but the work week was reduced from 60 to 55 hours at the same pay. In the next decade several other strikes failed, and union activity in the state ceased. Because of lagging wages and unsatisfactory working conditions, laborers struck several times between 1929 and 1934, incurring some bloodshed and, in a few cases, moderate success.

After World War II laborers were kept content by the prosperity of the state and the attractive surroundings of the new industries that moved into the region. Federal regulation of working hours and conditions as well as a state minimum-wage law eliminated many of the conditions that might have made union membership attractive. Antiunion propaganda, of course, had its effect, and a traditional loyalty to employer was difficult to break. An observer of the period of the 1970s commented that Southern workers had "always been fickle in their affections for unions, embracing them in lean years and shunning them in fat times." [14]

If North Carolinians had a closed mind where organized labor

14. Roland, *The Improbable Era*, p. 18.

was concerned, they had open minds in other respects. By 1930, in fact, North Carolina was considered to be a very liberal state in many respects as states in the South were viewed. An internationally noted instance of support for intellectual freedom grew out of attacks on a member of the faculty at Trinity College (now Duke University) in Durham. Professor John Spencer Bassett, native of Tarboro and a doctor of philosophy from Johns Hopkins University, published an article in 1903 in the *South Atlantic Quarterly* that brought down upon him the wrath of many Southerners. Bassett spoke of Booker T. Washington as "a great and good man, a Christian statesman, and take him all in all the greatest man, save General Lee, born in the South in a hundred years. . . ." [15] Newspapers, religious publications, and individuals in North Carolina and elsewhere in the region denounced Bassett for his "advanced views" and demanded that President John D. Kilgo dismiss him. A boycott of Trinity College was recommended, and parents were urged to remove their children. Bassett submitted his resignation, and when the trustees met to consider it, President Kilgo, other members of the faculty, and the student body urged that the resignation be rejected. The principle of academic freedom, they maintained, must be upheld. The entire faculty notified the president that it would resign if Bassett left. The trustees, few of whom actually agreed with the professor's appraisal of Washington, voted 18 to 11 not to accept the resignation. Trinity's enrollment increased the next year, and its prestige and influence grew.

Yet North Carolina was not entirely free of those who would stifle intellectual freedom, and other battles were yet to be fought. Following the conviction in July 1925 of John Thomas Scopes, teacher in Tennessee, for violating the law against teaching the theory of evolution there, religious fundamentalists turned to North Carolina. Governor Cameron Morrison the previous year banned two "evolution textbooks," so North Caro-

15. John Spencer Bassett, "Stirring Up the Fires of Race Antipathy," *South Atlantic Quarterly,* 2 (October 1903): 299.

lina seemed to promise another victory. An antievolution bill was defeated in the 1925 General Assembly by a vote of 67 to 46, but its advocates warned of a renewed attempt to come in 1927. Some local school boards and several religious denominations that opposed the teaching of the theory of evolution were supported by many people in the state who believed that only a statewide antievolution law would bring about a return to godliness. A legislator willing to introduce such a bill was not difficult to find.

Fundamentalists converged on the state and began to organize. A Committee of One Hundred, composed largely of Baptists and Presbyterians, was formed in Charlotte to direct activity in each of the one hundred counties and to do everything possible to combat "all influences in the schools that tend to destroy the faith of the people in the Bible as the Inspired Word of God." [16] Early in May 1926 over three hundred antievolutionists met in a Presbyterian church in Charlotte to adopt a plan that they agreed to protest the teaching of evolution in state-supported colleges as well as in the public schools. Delegates at the meeting proved to be so intemperate and disorderly and profane that they had to be reminded that they were "in a house of God." The meeting was also attended by a group of young men who described themselves as friends of the University of North Carolina, and when the floor was opened for general discussion, they spoke out boldly against the purposes of the gathering. Various civic leaders and UNC alumni asked embarrassing questions that generated heated exchanges with some of the leaders among the antievolutionists. Assorted delegates soon began arguing among themselves, and a fight was narrowly averted. Unfavorable publicity immeasurably damaged the reputation of the Committee of One Hundred.

From outside North Carolina prominent opponents of the teaching of evolution arrived. Friends of William Jennings

16. Willard B. Gatewood, Jr., "Politics and Piety in North Carolina: The Fundamentalist Crusade at High Tide, 1925–1927," *North Carolina Historical Review,* 42 (July 1965): 279.

Bryan held public meetings and preached the doctrine of such organizations as the Bible Crusaders and the Anti-Evolution League of America. The "God or gorilla" theme was widely discussed, and a tract, *Hell and the High Schools,* attracted attention. T. T. Martin, an official of the Bible Crusaders, announced a public debate on the question of evolution with some noted atheist supported by the American Association for the Advancement of Atheism. H. L. Mencken was Martin's choice, but Mencken ignored the call. When Martin learned that Charlotte officials would not allow such a debate in the city, he ironically complained of the lack of respect there for freedom of speech.

North Carolinians were shocked at the actions of many of the delegates and even some antievolutionists became disillusioned. Few people were willing to see anything like the notorious Scopes trial take place in their state. Evolution, nevertheless, was an issue in the fall campaign. North Carolina was a state of fundamentalists, and the outcome of the campaign was far from certain. Many antievolutionists were elected, particularly in the piedmont counties. On the other hand, attempts to unseat some avowed opponents of such legislation, who were running for reelection, were unsuccessful.

When the General Assembly convened in January 1927, petitions containing over 10,000 names were submitted in support of an antievolution bill. The bill was referred to the House Committee on Education, to which a number of new members had recently been appointed, and the new membership left the fundamentalists greatly outnumbered. The committee rejected the bill by a vote of 25 to 11, and against such odds floor leaders recognized their cause as lost.

Since most North Carolinians held fundamentalist beliefs, they totally rejected the idea of evolution. The same people, however, refused to follow those who called for a law against teaching evolution as a remedy for the "modern infidelity" [17]

17. Willard B. Gatewood, Jr., *Preachers, Pedagogues, & Politicians* (Chapel Hill: University of North Carolina Press, 1966), p. 230.

of the day, which they saw in persons of more liberal views. They were passively fundamentalist and disturbed by the secularism around them, but susceptible, nevertheless, to the moderating influence of such men as William Louis Poteat, prominent Baptist and president of Wake Forest College, and of Harry W. Chase of the university. They listened to reason and were willing to grant freedom of thought and teaching to those who held different views. A militant minority was not, however, and the tactics of this minority offended the majority. To the majority, tampering with the principles of religious liberty and the separation of church and state seemed more dangerous than infidelity. Infidelity might be a challenge to the church, but the assistance of the state in combating it was not necessary. By their extremism the antievolutionists lost the support of large numbers of moderate people who might have joined them. North Carolinians had rejected such people before, notably among the rabid antislavery men in the nineteenth century, yet even then they permitted such moderates as William Gaston to speak freely. They were to do the same again when they rejected the die-hard segregationists of the 1950s and listened instead to such moderates as Thomas J. Pearsall and Luther H. Hodges.

Another blow against freedom of thought in the state occurred as the 1963 General Assembly was preparing to adjourn. A bill was rushed through to deny the use of the facilities of any state-supported college or university to known members of the Communist party, to any known advocate of the overthrow of state or federal government, or to anyone who had pleaded the Fifth Amendment to the Constitution in refusing to answer questions concerning certain activities. This act was widely believed to be aimed at the university in Chapel Hill where controversial speakers frequently appeared. When the effect of this law was recognized, widespread opposition developed. There were, to be sure, some people in the state who thought it was not a bad idea to place such restrictions on speakers who might sway the youth of the state in the wrong direction. Nevertheless, the fear was strong that the state's institutions of higher education might lose their accreditation because of this infringement on free speech. In the meantime, speakers who were denied the use of campus facilities appeared in Chapel Hill anyway and spoke from boxes and other makeshift platforms along the town streets. At a special session of the General Assembly in 1965 the Speaker Ban Law was repealed, and in 1968 a federal court declared the original law unconstitutional.

Although North Carolina was isolated from most of the rest of the world before the building of improved roads, several events of national and even international significance occurred on the coast of the state. Reginald A. Fessenden, Canadian-born physicist and inventor who at times worked with Thomas A. Edison and for the Westinghouse Company, conducted pioneer radio-transmission experiments from Roanoke Island in 1901 and 1902. The United States Weather Bureau was seeking a way to transmit weather forecasts, particularly to ships at sea, and Fessenden selected a site that offered proper conditions as well as security from possible competitors. From an experimental wireless station, using a liquid barretter that he invented, he succeeded in transmitting sound waves over water between three stations, including a ship at sea. On Christmas Eve 1906, from an experimental station at Brant Rock, Massachusetts, Fessenden made the first known radio broadcast in the United States.

The isolation of the site and suitable weather and wind led Orville and Wilbur Wright of Dayton, Ohio, to North Carolina's Outer Banks opposite Roanoke Island for experiments with kites, gliders, and finally a motor-driven airplane. Arriving in the fall of 1900 the Wright brothers found the wind currents at Kitty Hawk ideal for experiments with gliders. They returned several times, and finally on December 17, 1903, made man's first powered flight in a craft heavier than air. For twelve seconds their plane stayed aloft and under its own power covered 120 feet. On the fourth flight it flew 852 feet in 59 seconds.

Later another experiment, not entirely unlike that of the Wright brothers in significance, also took place in North Carolina. Camp Davis, an antiaircraft training base on the coast near Wilmington, opened in April 1941, just before the United States entered World War II. It was staffed by military personnel with specialized interests and there, beginning about the middle of 1941, the United States Navy began a program of research, study, and testing of rockets and guided missiles. Late in the year the federal government leased Topsail Island on the Atlantic Ocean not far from Camp Davis for further experiments.

After the war the Navy retained control of the installations in the area including the Topsail Island facility. Located in Pender and Onslow counties between the Intracoastal Waterway and the Atlantic Ocean, the island extends from New River Inlet to Topsail Inlet, a distance of approximately 25 miles, and it seemed to be a suitable place to develop rockets. A firing pad was built near Topsail Inlet, and along the beach at intervals were erected seven tall, thick concrete towers housing cameras to record the flight of rockets. The firing of a rocket activated cameras in the towers connected by wires to the firing pad. Scientists were thus able to study photographs of rockets in flight and to correct problems that appeared. These rockets were designed for a second-stage firing while in flight to accelerate their speed. The second-stage firing overshot the 25-mile range, necessitating the removal of the operation to New Mexico, where a longer range was under construction. Topsail Island was returned to its owners in 1948, but the concrete observation towers still stand along the beach.

Topsail Island and Camp Davis were significant during the infancy of United States rocketry experiments that eventually took man to the moon and brought to Earth pictures of Mars taken on its surface. North Carolinians like to think that since the first airplane flew on North Carolina's coast, it was fitting that experiments leading to the nation's interplanetary flights also were conducted there.

Perhaps the greatest change to occur in North Carolina during the twentieth century was at the cultural level. In view of the other changes that began with the new century it is not surprising that this one began then also. In 1900 a group of Raleigh citizens called a public meeting that resulted in the organization that fall of the State Literary and Historical Association. Membership was open to anyone interested in stimulating literary and historical activity in North Carolina, and newspapers throughout the state lent enthusiastic support to the idea. An annual address came to be one of the highlights of the association's program, and some of the nation's most distinguished leaders have appeared for that purpose. Among them have been Henry Cabot Lodge, William Howard Taft, Harry S. Truman, John Spencer Bassett, William E. Dodd, U. B. Phillips, Carl Sandburg, Charles Kuralt, and an assortment of ambassadors, cabinet members, generals, authors, and philosophers.

One of the earliest and most significant undertakings of the association led to the passage of legislation to establish the North Carolina Historical Commission, now the Division of Archives and History, an agency of state government. The commission soon was recognized as one of the best-planned and most efficiently operated state historical agencies in the nation, and its first head, R. D. W. Connor, became the first Archivist of the United States in 1934. In succession, Connor planned the program and directed the organization of both North Carolina's and the nation's records depositories.

The State Literary and Historical Association in 1901 sponsored the first of a long series of North Carolina Day programs for the boys and girls of the state. For more than a quarter of a century the association collaborated annually with the Department of Public Instruction in planning public exercises that appealed to young people and stimulated their interest in the history of the state. Each year a pamphlet on a special topic was published furnishing information for that year's observance. Within a short time the youth of North Carolina had opportunities to study and appreciate their heritage. The association was also interested in stimulating literary and historical interests among adults, and in addition to programs of its own it assisted in forming other and more specialized groups. Members played leading roles in organizing the North Carolina Folklore Society, the State Art Society, the Historic Preservation Society of North Carolina, and the North Carolina Society of County and Local Historians.

During a week in the early winter of each year the parent society is joined by the newer organizations for a series of meetings to which all contribute. Scholarly addresses are made, business and progress reports are read, plans are drawn for the succeeding year, art exhibitions are mounted, music and dance programs are presented, and prizes are awarded for excellence in history, literature, art, and other areas. Many years ago when Jonathan Daniels was editor of the *Raleigh News and Observer,* he jokingly dubbed this period Culture Week in North Carolina, and the societies embraced the term with enthusiasm. It came to be used with considerable pride throughout the state.

The Literary and Historical Association successfully participated in a statewide movement to improve and broaden library resources, to establish a state museum of history, to establish county and local historical societies, and to mark historic sites. One of its most significant accomplishments got under way in 1924 following a suggestion that a state art society be formed. Shortly afterwards such an organization was formed and charged with promoting interest in art throughout the state and providing an art museum in Raleigh. Through gifts and purchases the North Carolina State Art Society began to grow, and for its gallery in a state office building it borrowed paintings and objects of art for exhibition. Traveling exhibitions were sent around the state and sometimes speakers or lecturers accompanied them.

The precedent set by the General Assembly in 1815, when it appropriated $10,000 for a full-length statue of George Washington by Antonio Canova, was followed after many years. In 1929, when a private collector presented paintings worth almost $1.5 million to the State Art Society, the General Assembly became a patron of the Society by making a modest appropriation. During the depression federal assistance made possible the renovation of enlarged quarters in a state building for an art museum, and during World War II plans were laid for extensive improvements as soon as conditions permitted. Members of the society initiated a campaign that culminated in the appropriation of $1 million by the General Assembly in 1947 for the purchase of works of art—an unprecedented act by any state legislature. The appropriation was made contingent upon the receipt of a matching gift, and in 1951 the S. H. Kress Foundation exceeded that condition when it gave the state art valued at around $3 million. Two years later the General Assembly provided funds to convert a former state office building into a museum, and the North Carolina Museum of Art rapidly became one of the country's outstanding art museums. Works which it owns have been lent for exhibition in the United States as well as abroad. It pioneered in the creation of a gallery for the blind featuring three-dimensional art. Sculpture, ceramics, fabrics, and other forms aid the blind in understanding things they read about, such as wild animals, athletes, and plants. This idea has been widely copied by other galleries.

These accomplishments at the state level spawned regional and local museums. The Mint Museum of Art in Charlotte, housed in the restored United States Mint building, the Ackland Museum in Chapel Hill, and the Duke University Art Museum are excellent, while good ones also exist in Asheville, Hickory, Statesville, Rocky Mount, Fayetteville, and elsewhere. This interest in art has also created a market for the work of state artists, while studios, galleries, and shows of individual and associated artists have become popular.

Music developed hand in hand with art, and the North Carolina Symphony followed a course not unlike that of the Museum of Art. At a more or less spontaneous meeting in the office of University President Frank P. Graham, in 1932, a symphony society was formed. Lamar Stringfield, Pulitzer-prize-winning composer and flutist, was eager to start an orchestra in his native state, and in 1932 at the age of 35 he became the founding conductor. With 48 volunteer musicians from sixteen communities around the state and after only five rehearsals, a concert of Wagner, Tchaikovsky, and Beethoven was presented in Chapel Hill in the spring of 1932. Funds raised by the society and Federal Emergency Relief Administration loans supported the orchestra for several years until Stringfield left the state. He was succeeded by Benjamin Swalin of the university music department, who reorganized the orchestra. Enthusiastic supporters appeared to assist in financing this work, and the General Assembly appropriated $4,000 for the 1943–1945 biennium. This was historic legislation, as North Carolina was one of the first states, if not the first, to appropriate tax funds for an orchestra. Support grew, musicians were employed on a full-time basis, and in 1945 the first of a continuing series of tours around the state and outside was made. Each season the tours become more extensive; free concerts are given for schoolchildren with evening concerts for adults. In recent years the orchestra has operated on a budget in excess of $1 million, sixty percent of which is provided by the General Assembly.

A variety of other cultural activities exists in the state with something for almost everyone. Paul Green's outdoor "symphonic drama," *The Lost Colony,* has been presented every summer since 1937 (with the exception of World War II years) in an amphitheater on Roanoke Island. This was the first development of a dramatic form that has since been widely imitated. Several outdoor dramas in the mountains of the state have very long histories, while others sometimes flourish for a season or two to mark special occasions and then disappear. Summer theater has also become popular, and many communities have regular seasons.

North Carolina has been a trailblazer in the field of historic preservation, with the Division of Archives and History as a state agency providing guidance, advice, and frequently funds as well, for a great deal of the work. Public buildings and private homes of various styles and times are now open to the public along with schools, churches, shops, and other structures. One of the most noted restorations is Tryon Palace at New Bern, work on which was made possible by a magnificent gift to the state. Old Salem at Winston-Salem is an outstanding example of a village preserved and restored as a whole through private efforts, while Historic Halifax is a state-supported undertaking.

State and national parks and forests dot the state, and there are several nature preserves. Weymouth Woods in Moore County has a large stand of virgin longleaf pine. Recreation facilities exist at many such places as well as at a number of private amusement parks and sites. The damming of many rivers and streams in the state for flood control or for the generation of hydroelectric power since World War II has created large lakes, which provide sailing, boating, fishing, swimming, and other water sports. But this kind of development has not been permitted to continue unchecked. A public outcry in 1976 resulted in the preservation of the wild gorge of New River in the northwestern corner of the state from being flooded by a hydroelectric company.

Clean air and water have posed relatively little trouble for the state in the past. The nature of her industries and the absence of large cities mean that smog and pollution have been rare, but with the recent widespread national concern over these problems, North Carolina has taken steps to ensure that her record continues. A law of 1911 provided for the acquisition of land for public forests, and in the 1920s, largely through efforts within the state, the Great Smoky Mountains National Park was created. Also during the 1920s the state legislature placed responsibility for zoning with the counties. Since few counties took advantage of the opportunity to control and regulate planning and growth, the state stepped in. A state land-use policy was envisioned in a statewide development policy promulgated in 1972, and multicounty planning regions were designated. Many North Carolinians were determined that their land should continue to be the "goodliest land under the cope of heaven," as it was described in the sixteenth century. To demonstrate their earnestness, in 1972 they approved a $150 million bond issue for clean-water projects and for pollution control.

North Carolina in the last quarter of the twentieth century would scarcely be recognized by one who knew it in 1900 and had not seen it since. Abandoned fields were no longer eroded and few streams carried topsoil to the ocean. Extensive reforestation and other conservation measures made the face of the land green again. Pastures supporting herds of beef cattle replaced many of the fields of stubby cotton. Although countless family farms still existed, extensive commercial farming on thousands of acres was common in many places. Four-lane highways crossed the state in every direction, and paved local and rural roads removed the feeling of isolation between the regions. Regional and municipal airports offered regular service to all parts of the nation. An impressive number of motor freight companies chartered in the state delivered tobacco, furniture, and textiles everywhere, from Canada to Mexico. Rail service and bus service, of course, were also available.

A feeling of confidence in the future pervaded the state. The sectionalism that once broke the people into eastern and western factions all but disappeared. Although the state remained largely rural in character, its growing urban centers, particularly those in the Piedmont Crescent stretching through a dozen counties, suggested pending changes under the watchful eyes of local and regional planning councils. Although there was no single newspaper read through the state, there were many, such as those in Asheville, Charlotte, Greensboro, and Raleigh, that served large and overlapping areas. These tended to foster a feeling of community in their readers, and, as objective conveyors of the news of the state, they enlarged the horizon of many.

The 1970s found North Carolina with many assets—a pleasant natural setting, an honest and respected government, a school system that was aware of its shortcomings and was striving to overcome them, a balance between agriculture and industry, good means of communication, impressive cultural opportunities and recreational facilities. Problems remained, but the people of North Carolina could look forward with optimism to the future.

Suggestions for Further Reading

The most helpful guide to almost every aspect of North Carolina history is Hugh T. Lefler, *A Guide to the Study and Reading of North Carolina History* (Chapel Hill: University of North Carolina Press, 1969). Regularly since 1934 in the April issue of the *North Carolina Historical Review* there has appeared a classified bibliography of North Caroliniana published during the previous year. Material concerning the state is also to be found in Mary L. Thornton, *A Bibliography of North Carolina, 1589–1956* (Chapel Hill: University of North Carolina Press, 1958). A readable narrative account of the historical literature and source material of the state will be found in H. G. Jones, *For History's Sake, The Preservation and Publication of North Carolina History, 1663–1903* (Chapel Hill: University of North Carolina Press, 1966). A general source book is Hugh T. Lefler, *North Carolina History Told by Contemporaries* (Chapel Hill: University of North Carolina Press, 1965) containing extracts from more than two hundred documents arranged chronologically and topically.

The state has been blessed with a progression of good narrative accounts. The current favorite is Hugh T. Lefler and Albert R. Newsome, *North Carolina, The History of a Southern State* (Chapel Hill: University of North Carolina Press, 1973). The nineteenth century saw the publication of half a dozen or so histories, but Samuel A. Ashe's two-volume *History of North Carolina,* volume 1 (Greensboro: Charles L. Van Noppen, Publisher, 1908) and volume 2 (Raleigh: Edwards & Broughton Printing Company, 1925) was the first general history to rest soundly on primary sources. R. D. W. Connor, William K. Boyd, and J. G. de Roulhac Hamilton collaborated, each producing a volume in the three-volume *History of North Carolina* (Chicago: Lewis Publishing Company, 1919). The work, in large measure, is one on which many subsequent historians have relied. Connor's *North Carolina, Rebuilding an Ancient Commonwealth* (Chicago: American

Historical Society, 1929) in two volumes incorporated some new material as well as much that had already appeared. Archibald Henderson, *North Carolina, the Old North State and the New* (Chicago: Lewis Publishing Company, 1941) in two volumes was another trailblazing work, containing for the first time much new social and cultural history. The two geographic extremes are covered in two books by David Stick, *The Outer Banks of North Carolina, 1584–1958* (Chapel Hill: University of North Carolina Press, 1958), and *Graveyard of the Atlantic, Shipwrecks of the North Carolina Coast* (Chapel Hill: University of North Carolina Press, 1952), and by Maurice Brooks, *The Appalachians* (Boston: Houghton Mifflin Company, 1965).

An account of the native inhabitants will be found in Douglas L. Rights, *The American Indian in North Carolina* (Winston-Salem: John F. Blair, Publisher, 1957), Ruth Y. Wetmore, *The North Carolina Indians* (Winston-Salem: John F. Blair, Publisher, 1975), and E. Lawrence Lee, *Indian Wars in North Carolina, 1663–1763* (Raleigh: Carolina Charter Tercentenary Commission, 1963). Much of the present knowledge of Indians in North Carolina is drawn from John Lawson's *A New Voyage to Carolina,* published in London in 1709 and reprinted a number of times. The most useful edition was prepared by Hugh T. Lefler and published in 1967 by the University of North Carolina Press with an introduction, annotations, and an index.

Works dealing with various aspects of the colonial period are numerous, but the only recent volume covering the whole period is Hugh T. Lefler and William S. Powell, *Colonial North Carolina, A History* (New York: Charles Scribner's Sons, 1973). A source book that contains all of the known documents relating to the sixteenth-century attempts by England to establish a colony in the New World is David B. Quinn, editor, *The Roanoke Voyages* (London: The Hakluyt Society, 1955) in two volumes. The proprietary period is discussed in William S. Powell, *The Proprietors of Carolina* (Raleigh: Carolina Charter Tercentenary Commission, 1963), and in Hugh F. Rankin, *Upheaval in Albemarle, The Story of Culpeper's Rebellion, 1675–1689* (Raleigh: Carolina Charter Tercentenary Commission, 1962). Harry R. Merrens, *Colonial North Carolina in the Eighteenth Century* (Chapel Hill: University of North Carolina Press, 1964) is a study in historical geography, dealing in large measure with the economy of the colony. Robert

W. Ramsey, in *Carolina Cradle, Settlement of the Northwest Carolina Frontier, 1747–1762* (Chapel Hill: University of North Carolina Press, 1964), examines afresh the origins and contributions of the pioneer settlers of a region in North Carolina in which many of the settlers of the midwestern American frontier originated. Blackwell P. Robinson, *The Five Royal Governors of North Carolina, 1729–1775* (Raleigh: Carolina Charter Tercentenary Commission, 1963), Lawrence Lee, *The Lower Cape Fear in Colonial Days* (Chapel Hill: University of North Carolina Press, 1965), Duane Meyer, *The Highland Scots of North Carolina, 1732–1776* (Chapel Hill: University of North Carolina Press, 1961), and Carl Hammer, Jr., *Rhinelanders on the Yadkin* (Salisbury: Rowan Printing Company, 1965) are useful studies of special topics of the royal period.

The earlier years of the American Revolution are dealt with in Lindley S. Butler, *North Carolina and the Coming of the Revolution* (Raleigh: North Carolina American Revolution Bicentennial Committee, 1976). A detailed but very readable specialized study is Hugh F. Rankin, *The North Carolina Continentals* (Chapel Hill: University of North Carolina Press, 1971). M. F. Treacy, *Prelude to Yorktown, The Southern Campaign of Nathanael Greene, 1780–1781* (Chapel Hill: University of North Carolina Press, 1963) recounts the events of a very significant aspect of the Revolution in the South. A work dealing with dissidents of the period is Carole W. Troxler, *The Loyalist Experience in North Carolina* (Raleigh: North Carolina American Revolution Bicentennial Committee, 1976).

Although there are many studies of North Carolina during the pre-Civil War period dealing with such aspects as agriculture, politics, transportation, education, and other subjects, Guion Johnson's *Ante-Bellum North Carolina, A Social History* (Chapel Hill: University of North Carolina Press, 1937) is a truly magnificent work. Drawing on contemporary sources, Mrs. Johnson presents a fascinating and well-rounded account of the period.

The relatively brief period of Civil War and Reconstruction has attracted a great deal of attention from both professional and amateur historians, but insofar as North Carolina is concerned the subject is adequately covered in a few works. John G. Barrett's *The Civil War in North Carolina* (Chapel Hill: University of North Carolina Press,

1963) is basic, while his *Sherman's March Through the Carolinas* (Chapel Hill: University of North Carolina Press, 1956) supplements it. Otto H. Olsen, *Carpetbagger's Crusade: The Life of Albion Winegar Tourgée* (Baltimore: The Johns Hopkins Press, 1965), Allen W. Trelease, *White Terror, The Ku Klux Klan Conspiracy and Southern Reconstruction* (New York: Harper & Row, Publishers, 1971), and William McKee Evans, *Ballots and Fence Rails, Reconstruction on the Lower Cape Fear* (Chapel Hill: University of North Carolina Press, 1967) deal with special aspects of the postwar period, while Richard L. Zuber, *North Carolina During Reconstruction* (Raleigh: State Department of Archives and History, 1969) is a concise survey of the whole period.

The State Department of Archives and History published a series of pamphlets on the various wars in which the state has been involved. In addition to those on the Revolution and the Civil War, the following provide broad views of general interest: Sarah M. Lemmon, *North Carolina and the War of 1812* (1971), William S. Hoffmann, *North Carolina in the Mexican War, 1846–1848* (1959), and both by Prof. Lemmon, *North Carolina's Role in the First World War* (1966) and *North Carolina's Role in World War II* (1964). A more detailed study is Sarah M. Lemmon, *Frustrated Patriots, North Carolina and the War of 1812* (Chapel Hill: University of North Carolina Press, 1973).

The twentieth century, particularly the current scene, is best revealed in James W. Clay, and others, editors, *North Carolina Atlas, Portrait of a Changing Southern State* (Chapel Hill: University of North Carolina Press, 1975), while Luther H. Hodges, *Businessman in the State House* (Chapel Hill: University of North Carolina Press, 1962) deals with the significant years between 1954 and 1961 when school integration, industrialization, planning, the ecology, and other problems arose. Much of the history of the recent years can best be understood through the biographies of leaders of the time. Among these are: Oliver H. Orr, Jr., *Charles Brantley Aycock* (Chapel Hill: University of North Carolina Press, 1961), and three books by Joseph L. Morrison: *Governor O. Max Gardner, A Power in North Carolina and New Deal Washington* (Chapel Hill: University of North Carolina Press, 1971), *W. J. Cash: Southern Prophet* (New York: Alfred A.

Knopf, 1967), and *Josephus Daniels: The Small-d Democrat* (Chapel Hill: University of North Carolina Press, 1966).

Black history is by no means new to North Carolina. Since 1924 the *North Carolina Historical Review* has published twenty scholarly articles dealing wholly with this subject, while countless others have at least touched upon it. Lengthier studies are John Hope Franklin, *The Free Negro in North Carolina, 1790–1860* (Chapel Hill: University of North Carolina Press, 1943), Frenise A. Logan, *The Negro in North Carolina, 1878–1894* (Chapel Hill: University of North Carolina Press, 1964), Margaret Elaine Burgess, *Negro Leadership in a Southern City* (Chapel Hill: University of North Carolina Press, 1962), and Walter B. Weare, *Black Business in the New South, A Social History of the North Carolina Mutual Life Insurance Company* (Urbana: University of Illinois Press, 1973).

Index